Ancient
WORLD

First published in 2007 by Miles Kelly Publishing Ltd
Harding's Barn, Bardfield End Green, Thaxted, Essex, CM6 3PX, UK

Copyright © Miles Kelly Publishing Ltd 2007

This edition published 2010

2 4 6 8 10 9 7 5 3 1

Editorial Director Belinda Gallagher
Art Director Jo Brewer
Editor Rosalind McGuire
Cover Designer Simon Lee
Page Layout Ian Paulyn
Production Manager Elizabeth Collins
Reprographics Anthony Cambray, Rick Caylor, Ian Paulyn
Assets Manager Bethan Ellish

British Library Cataloguing-in-Publication Data
A catalogue record for this book is available from the British Library

ISBN 978-1-84810-349-8

Printed in China

Every effort has been made to acknowledge the source and copyright holder of each picture.
Miles Kelly Publishing apologises for any unintentional errors or omissions.

Made with paper from a sustainable forest

www.mileskelly.net
info@mileskelly.net

www.factsforprojects.com
The one-stop homework helper — pictures, facts, videos, projects and more

Ancient WORLD

Rupert Matthews

ANCIENT EGYPT

ANCIENT MESOPOTAMIA

ANCIENT GREECE

ANCIENT ASIA

ANCIENT ROME

ANCIENT ROME

ANCIENT AMERICA

Rescue and salvage archaeology

- **Rescue archaeology** involves carrying out urgent excavations against the clock. These usually occur in areas where developers are waiting to move in, or if environmental changes are threatening an important site.

- **The most famous example** of rescue archaeology in action began on 6 April 1959, when the Egyptian government issued an appeal to UNESCO because the temples of Abu Simbel were in danger of being flooded as a dam was built.

- **Each temple was rebuilt** in exactly the same state as they had been in – broken statues were not repaired. As the temples were originally carved out of a sandstone cliff, an artificial mountain was created.

- **A museum was built** at Abu Simbel to house all the finds unearthed during the building work. Over 3000 artefacts were found, including four mummies of Egyptian nobles.

- **In the modern city** of Alexandria the rescue archaeologist Jean-Yves Empereur has started to look for traces of the Tower of Pharos. He has already salvaged some pieces of the Tower at the foot of Qaitbay Fort and hopes to find more.

...FASCINATING FACT...
When the temples of Abu Simbel were threatened by the Nile waters, they were cut out of the rock, lifted above the floodplain, and rebuilt in a safe location.

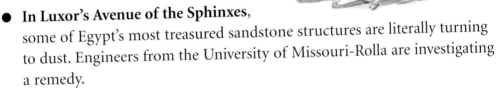

▶ *The Tower of Pharos was built in the Ptolemaic period, and it is likely that it was the first lighthouse ever built. Archaeologists have found the foundations, but are searching for remnants of the structure today.*

- **The remains** of the city of Pharaoh Akhenaten are little more than rubble at present. A British company called Akhenaten City PLC, is trying to reconstruct the central area of the city. The city is situated on Luxor's west bank and it is hoped that it will be a major tourist attraction.

- **In Luxor's Avenue of the Sphinxes**, some of Egypt's most treasured sandstone structures are literally turning to dust. Engineers from the University of Missouri-Rolla are investigating a remedy.

- **In November 2002**, UNESCO began assessing water damage at Luxor Temple and monuments at Abu Mena.

- **Plans to construct** a massive canal across Egypt's northern Sinai Desert would affect several valuable archaeological sites. In 1991 the North Sinai Salvage Project was launched to survey the canal's path and suggest a possible alternative route.

- **In 2000**, government officials in Egypt called for a major salvage operation to protect the ancient monuments of the northern agricultural region known as the Nile Delta. Antiquities ministers revealed that many treasures were under threat from building works and rising ground water levels.

Advanced techniques

- **In the past,** mummies have been badly damaged by archaeologists doing research. Today, scientists use endoscopy instead of conducting an autopsy.

- **Bone X-rays** have enabled scientists to calculate height, age at death and if the person suffered any fractures during their lifetime.

- **In 1977,** an international team began fieldwork at Giza, Saqqara, and Luxor using geographical techniques such as acoustic sounding and magnetometry.

- **Aerial photography** and thermal infrared imagery techniques have yielded results at Giza, Saqqara and Luxor.

- **A hieroglyphic text** processing programme has been developed in Holland and is now relied upon by Egyptologists around the world.

- **Radar technology** has been used to confirm the existence of a secret chamber in the Great Pyramid of Khufu at Giza.

- **Medical science** is being used to help solve the mystery of who killed Tutankhamun. An X-ray has been carried out on the pharaoh's mummy.

- **On 5 January 2005,** the pharaoh's mummy was given a CAT scan to build up a three-dimensional picture of the bones.

- **The Theban Mapping Project** has created a detailed map and database of every part of Thebes.

- **The project is** also making 3-D computer models of every tomb in Thebes.

▶ *The mummy of Tutankhamun is prepared for a scan that will reveal its internal structure and show up any signs of injury or disease.*

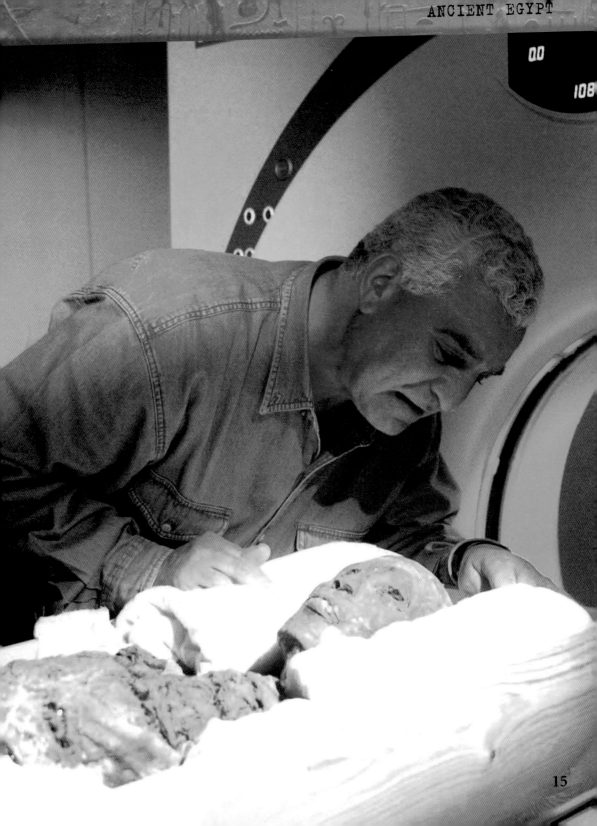

On the banks of the Nile

- **Over 90 percent of Egypt** is scorching desert, so it is sometimes called the 'red land'. Yet it also contains the greatest river on Earth – the Nile.

- **The Nile is the longest river** in the world – over 6400 km in length. It flows from the highlands of Central Africa to the Mediterranean Sea. This mighty river provided the basis for the great civilization of ancient Egypt.

- **The Nile results** from three great rivers coming together – the White Nile, the Atbara and the Blue Nile. The White and Blue Niles merge in the Sudan, near Khartoum.

▲ *Water was lifted from the Nile using a device called a shaduf.*

- **Flood season** in Egypt lasts from mid July to the end of September. When the floodwater retreats (between November and March) farmers begin to sow their crops, ready to harvest between April and June.

- **The first Egyptian farmers** waited for the Nile to flood to nourish their crops, but by 5000 BC they had started to devise ways to control the great river. They dug canals to channel the floodwater to distant fields.

- **The first reservoir** was built at Fayum, about 60 km southwest of Cairo. The Egyptians surrounded the plot with about 30 km of dykes and reduced a huge saltwater lake into the freshwater Lake Moeris.

- **The Egyptians** lived on the banks of the river Nile or by canals springing out from it. This land was the best and most fertile in the country, and was called 'Kemet' – the 'black land'.

- **The farming year** began when the Nile flooded, washing mineral-rich silt deposits onto the land. This usually led to a bountiful summer harvest.

- **The height of the Nile flood** was crucial to the survival of crops. The amount of water was monitered using 'nilometers' – stone staircases that led down into the river. The speed at which the water covered the steps told the Egyptians how fast and intense the flood was likely to be.

- **Even when the floods receded**, the Nile provided the people of Egypt with a life-saving source of water in the otherwise hot and arid landscape, without which the Egyptians' empire would have crumbled.

▲ *Nilometers were invented to keep track of the height of the river, which was crucial for the success of farming in ancient Egypt.*

Uniting the kingdoms

- **The union of Upper and Lower Egypt** was very important to the ancient Egyptians. The capital of the new kingdom, Memphis, was close to where the Nile Valley meets the Delta.

- **The ancient Egyptians** divided their kings into families that are now known as dynasties. The 1st Dynasty began when the first king ruled over the united kingdom.

- **Records from** the 1st and 2nd Dynasties are confused. Historians are unable to give names or dates accurately to these rulers.

- **Archaeologists have discovered** a piece of slate called the Narmer Palette showing the king vanquishing his enemies. On one side the king is wearing the white crown of Upper Egypt, and on the other he wears the red crown of Lower Egypt.

▲ *The Narmer Palette was found in the Pre-Dynastic capital of Hierakonpolis by the British archaeologist J E Quibell in 1898.*

- **King Narmer was succeeded** by Menes in *c*.3100 BC, who founded the 1st Dynasty. Most historians believe 'Menes' was actually a title taken by the king, whose name was Horus Aha.

- **King Menes was the founder** of the city of Memphis. He also built a great temple there.

- **This period in Egyptian history** saw the beginning of two dynasties. The first lasted from 2925–2715 BC, and the second lasted from 2715–2658 BC.

- **The kings of the first two dynasties** of the united Egypt all came from a place called This. The site has not been located by archaeologists yet, but it is likely to have been near Abydos in Upper Egypt, as the tombs of these kings lie in the cemetery of Abydos.

- **The king of the united kingdoms** was usually depicted wearing a double crown, which was made up of the Red Crown of the Delta and the White Crown of the Valley.

. . . FASCINATING FACT . . .
King Menes lost his life in an accident that occurred while he was on a hippopotamus hunt!

The Old Kingdom

- **The Old Kingdom** lasted from 2686–2181 BC and is viewed as one of the more stable times in ancient Egyptian history. This period covered a line of kings from the 3rd to the 6th Dynasties.

- **During this period**, Egypt made great use of the vast mineral wealth that lay beneath its deserts, and gained wealth trading with other nations. The wealth was used to glorify the nation's rulers.

- **Few written records** of the Old Kingdom survive. What the rulers of this period did leave behind was a building programme unprecedented in its scope and imagination.

- **A series of mud-brick temples** were built in the Old Kingdom. Statues of gods adorned these temples, alongside statues of the kings of Egypt, who were regarded as living gods.

- **This era of Egyptian history** was one of great pyramid building. Under the orders of King Djoser, a vast step pyramid was built during the 3rd Dynasty, while during the 4th Dynasty straight-sided pyramids appeared at Meidum, Dashur and Giza.

- **At the end of the 4th Dynasty**, a new line of kings took to the throne. They called themselves 'Sa Ra' ('Sons of Ra'), and built stone temples for the sun god, Ra. This period was the height of the cult of this god.

> ...FASCINATING FACT...
> The cost of building the pyramids was staggering both in terms of the taxes needed and the labour involved. Much of the government budget was spent on them.

- **Pyramids continued to be built** during the 5th Dynasty, but they were not as large as previous structures. At Saqqara, they were inscribed with pyramid texts to help the dead king reach heaven.

- **Old Kingdom officials** also built grand tombs and statues to mark their deaths. These were decorated with paintings depicting their lives and careers. Towards the end of the Old Kingdom they rivalled those of the pharaohs in terms of grandeur.

- **The 6th Dynasty ended** with the death of Queen Nitiqret and a period of great stability came to an end. The unified kingdom of Egypt broke up into several small states as local governors became independent of the pharaoh.

▶ *The only step pyramid ever completed is situated at Saqqara. It was built by King Djoser.*

The First Intermediate Period

- **After the stability** and growth of the Old Kingdom, the First Intermediate Period (7th–11th Dynasties) saw the power of the central government in ancient Egypt decline. It began with the death of Queen Nitiqret and lasted until the rule of Mentuhotep II.

- **During this period**, the 7th and 8th Dynasties (2150–2130 BC) were still based at the capital of the united Egypt, Memphis. However, their leaders had great trouble controlling their unruly subjects.

- **The weakness of these rulers** and the decline of the kingdom is illustrated by their tombs. They are tiny when compared with the gigantic royal pyramids of the Old Kingdom.

- **Archaeological evidence** suggests that there were few skilled craftsmen during this period. Pots, bowls and other artefacts are not of the quality of those unearthed in earlier sites.

- **The weakness of the ruling kings** at Memphis meant that much of the power was held not by the king but by governors of the different nomes.

- **The rulers of the 9th and 10th Dynasties** established themselves at Herakleopolis, to the south of Memphis. They included Neferkare VII, Kheti and Merikave.

- **After the disintegration** of the Old Kingdom, the governors of Thebes became independent local rulers. Their power soon rivalled that of the 9th and 10th Dynasties at Herakleopolis.

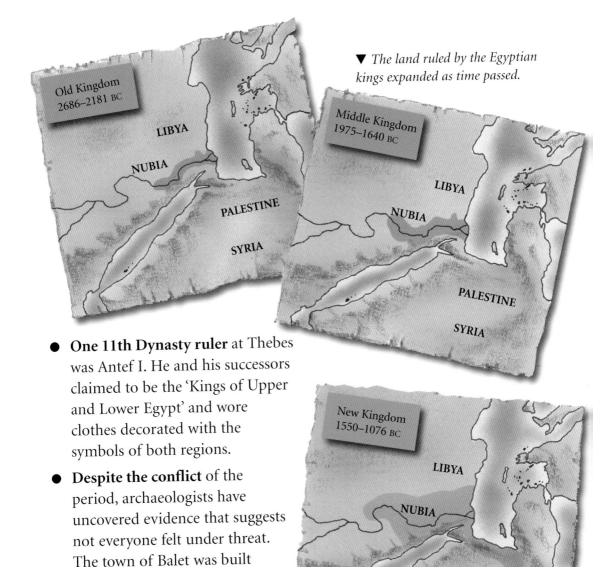

▼ *The land ruled by the Egyptian kings expanded as time passed.*

Old Kingdom
2686–2181 BC

LIBYA

NUBIA

PALESTINE

SYRIA

Middle Kingdom
1975–1640 BC

LIBYA

NUBIA

PALESTINE

SYRIA

New Kingdom
1550–1076 BC

LIBYA

NUBIA

PALESTINE

SYRIA

- **One 11th Dynasty ruler** at Thebes was Antef I. He and his successors claimed to be the 'Kings of Upper and Lower Egypt' and wore clothes decorated with the symbols of both regions.

- **Despite the conflict** of the period, archaeologists have uncovered evidence that suggests not everyone felt under threat. The town of Balet was built without a fortified wall, suggesting a sense of security among the residents.

- **Art during this period** showed signs of decline. Artwork was often of a lower quality than that of the Old Kingdom.

23

The Middle Kingdom

- **Conflict and division** in the First Intermediate Period was ended by a Theban called Nebhepetra Mentuhotep. He reunited the country by conquest, heralding the start of the Middle Kingdom.

- **The Middle Kingdom** (1975–1640 BC) was a high point for art and literature. Jewellery and paintings from the period are of an exceptional quality, while many poems and books of wisdom were written.

- **Mentuhotep asked for shrines** to be built all over Egypt to local gods and goddesses. He also built a great memorial temple at Deir el-Bahri.

◀ Scarab amulets were very popular during the Middle Kingdom, and were worn for good fortune. They were carved from gems, stones and semi-precious stones.

...FASCINATING FACT...

Queen Sobekneferu was the last ruler of the 12th Dynasty. It was very unusual at the time for a woman to rule Egypt. Her death marked the end of the golden period of the Middle Kingdom.

- **Mentuhotep was succeeded** by a number of sons, but when the last of these died, his vizier Amenemhet became the founder of the 12th Dynasty.

- **The most popular king** of the 12th Dynasty was Senusret I (1965–1920 BC), who helped to make Egypt a great power once more. Under his reign Egypt conquered part of Nubia and defeated the Libyans.

- **The reign of Senusret III** (1818–1859 BC) saw the establishment of a number of fortresses in Nubia. A canal was also constructed that allowed boats to travel around the Nile's first waterfall, an otherwise impossible series of rapids.

- **During the 12th Dynasty,** two pyramids were built at Dahshur, and others at Fayum. The funerary temple of Amenemhet III was one of the most impressive sights of the ancient world. A new royal residence was also established during this period at el-Lisht.

- **There are few** of the great buildings of the Middle Kingdom left in good condition. The pyramids have been severely damaged by the weather, while many buildings were pulled down during the New Kingdom.

- **The Middle Kingdom ended** when a succession of weak rulers saw their control over Egypt undermined, until eventually the Delta region was conquered by foreigners. Nubia was lost and became an independent state.

The Second Intermediate Period

▲ *The chariot provided the Hyksos people with an incredibly mobile army, which quickly overpowered the Egyptian forces.*

> ...FASCINATING FACT...
> Archaeologists have found three golden flies, awarded for
> valour in battle, in Queen Ahhotep's tomb.

- **The Second Intermediate Period** (1750–1550 BC) was a difficult time for Egypt. Invaders called the Hyksos settled in the Delta. They were to reign as the 13th–17th Dynasties of pharaohs.

- **The Hyksos** had better weapons than the Egyptians. They overran local forces, and began to call themselves kings.

  - **The Hyksos** built a new, heavily fortified, capital city called Avaris in 1720 BC. It was built on the ruins of the Middle Kingdom.

  - **During this time**, the Theban kings of the 17th Dynasty maintained control of southern Egypt.

  - **The division of Egypt** was not peaceful. The Theban king Sequenenra Taa was killed. His mummy shows axe and knife wounds.

  - **The Theban king Kamose** erected a memorial in the temple of Karnak to record his victories in battle.

  - **During one battle** against the Hyksos, the Theban army was led by Queen Ahhotep.

  - **King Ahmose** finally expelled the Hyksos from Egypt. He also destroyed their strongholds in Palestine to ensure they could not be a danger again.

  - **Under Ahmose**, the Nubian territories that were lost at the end of the Middle Kingdom were reclaimed. A new period of strength for Egypt was about to begin.

The New Kingdom

- **The expulsion of the Hyksos** marked the beginning of the New Kingdom, which lasted from 1550–1076 BC, (18–20th Dynasties). During this time, ancient Egypt enjoyed unprecedented power, peace and prosperity. Territory was greatly expanded, which brought wealth flooding in.

- **Much is known** about this period of Egyptian history because of what has been left behind – letters from kings, ruins of great towns, and artefacts that shed light on daily life.

- **With the founding** of the 18th Dynasty, the city of Waset (Thebes) became the capital of Egypt. This was to be the site of the temples of Luxor and Karnak, the Valley of the Kings and the Valley of the Queens.

- **The first ruler** of the new dynasty, Ahmose, followed up his victory over the Hyksos by pursuing them into Palestine and Syria, and taking territory there, before consolidating the northern borders of Egypt.

- **Ahmose's successors**, Amenhotep I and Thutmose I built on his great military victories. The Egyptian empire grew to include parts of Palestine, Syria and most of Nubia.

- **Egypt's most successful warrior king** was Thutmose II. He led his army on 17 campaigns, conquering cities and forcing them to pay tribute (taxes) to Egypt in return for mercy.

- **The tribute** that flowed into Egypt made the empire the wealthiest on Earth, and allowed the pharaohs to build even more temples. Mud-brick buildings were torn down and replaced with great stone structures.

- **The pharaohs of the 19th Dynasty** were descended from a vizier called Ramesses. Sety 1 protected the empire from a neighbouring race called the Hittites. His son, Ramesses II, became one of Egypt's most famous pharaohs.

- **Towards the end of the dynasty**, central power began to weaken again. Such was the religious hold of the high priest Herihor that he even claimed royal powers!

- **The kings of the 20th Dynasty** faced an onslaught from many directions, including the Libyans and Sea Peoples. Although Ramesses III repelled these invaders, much of the empire was lost and Egypt was greatly weakened.

◀ *Also called Ramesses the Great, Ramesses II lived to the age of 96, and was said to have had 200 wives, 60 daughters and 96 sons.*

The Third Intermediate Period

- **After the fall** of the 20th Dynasty, the kings of Egypt retreated to the Delta. They had little control over the south of the country. Smendes (1069–1043 BC) became the first king of the 21st Dynasty after the death of Ramesses XI in 1070 BC.

- **Power in Egypt** was divided between the high priests of the god Amun at Thebes in the south, and the kings of the 21st Dynasty (1070–945 BC) at Tanis in the north in Lower Egypt.

- **In the 10th century** BC, the 22nd Dynasty began in the north. Instigated by Sheshonq I (945–924 BC) of Libyan descent, these kings established a powerbase to the east of the Delta, so Thebes became less important.

- **The new rulers** brought statues and obelisks (tall tapering stone pillars) from other sites in Egypt. Archaeologists have also uncovered many gold and silver treasures in their tombs.

- **Under the rule of Takelot II** (850–825 BC), the 23rd Dynasty began. The two dynasties governed simultaneously for around 90 years.

- **By the 8th century** BC, the power in Egypt was no longer central. By this time, the 24th Dynasty, ruling from the city of Sais, had also appeared, in the form of a man called Tefnakht (724–717 BC).

- **During this period**, Nubia was ruled from the city of Napata. Although the country had a strong culture of its own, the people worshipped Egyptian gods. An independent native dynasty had begun to rule at around 760 BC.

- **The new Nubian government** extended its influence into southern Egypt. In 729 BC, Egyptian rulers Namhet and Tefnakht united to try to force out the Nubians, but their attack provoked a full-scale invasion.

- **In the 8th century** BC, King Piy of Napata, Nubia, invaded Egypt and captured all the main cities.

- **Piy was successful** in uniting Egypt. The various Egyptian leaders submitted to his rule at Memphis in 728 BC. The rule of the Nubian kings is known as the 25th Dynasty and the Late Period of Egyptian history began.

GOD	DUTY	REPRESENTATION
Ra	God of the Sun	Falcon-headed man wearing a sun disk on his head
Osiris	Chief judge in the underworld	Mummified king
Horus	God of the sky Protector of the king	Falcon
Sekhmet	Goddess of fire	Lion-headed woman
Hathor	Goddess of motherhood Protecter of pregnant women	Cow
Anubis	Prepared bodies for mummification	Jackal
Thoth	Moon god scribe	Ibis-headed man

The Late Period

- **Egypt's new Nubian rulers** showed great respect for the country's religion. They began a programme of repairs to the major temples and built new structures and statues to celebrate the Egyptian gods.

- **In the 7th century** BC, a new threat to Egypt emerged from the Near East – Assyria. The Assyrians were warlike people who had tried to invade Egypt in 674 and 671 BC. The next attempt was successful, and the Nubian kings were thrown out.

- **When the Assyrians had conquered Egypt**, they sent most of their troops home. An Egyptian collaborator called Nekau was left to run the country.

- **In the absence of Assyrians to protect him**, Nekau was murdered by Tanutamani, the last king of the 25th Dynasty. However, his victory was short-lived – he was forced to flee when the Assyrians returned.

◄ *The Assyrians left behind a rich legacy of sculptures and wall carvings throughout ancient Egypt.*

- **When the Assyrians** were attacked by other enemies, Egypt again had an opportunity to fight for its independence.

- **The leader of the 26th Dynasty** was Psamtek I (Psammetichus) – son of the murdered Nekau. He led the Egyptians to victory against the Assyrians around 653 BC.

- **This period of ancient Egyptian history** was one of great creativity. Arts and crafts blossomed, with exquisite items made out of ceramics and bronze.

- **Peace was short-lived**, and the country was soon invaded again. King Psammetichus III was defeated by the king of Persia, and Egypt became a province of Persia. Persian kings counted as the 27th Dynasty of Egypt but they were not popular and there were a number of rebellions.

- **The 28th–30th Dynasties** saw a series of Egyptian leaders struggle for power. King Nectanebo II was the last native Egyptian to rule ancient Egypt.

...FASCINATING FACT...
The 26th Dynasty included some rather unusual rulers.
One of these was King Amasis, who insisted that his subjects
worship a statue forged out of his footbath.

Greek-Roman Period

- **The young Macedonian king,** Alexander the Great, defeated Egypt's Persian rulers in the 4th century BC, and became Egypt's new leader.

- **Alexander incorporated** Egypt into his own empire. He founded the city of Alexandria in 332 BC, and then left Egypt to the control of two Greek officials. He died in 323 BC.

- **In 305 BC,** Alexandra's general, Ptolemy, proclaimed himself pharaoh. He founded the Ptolemaic dynasty, which lasted until 30 BC.

- **During this dynasty**, the temple of Edfu was completed and work started on the temples of Dendera, Komo Ombo and Philae.

- **During the Ptolemaic dynasty**, most important posts were held by Greeks. However, Egyptian laws and religion were largely left untouched.

- **During the Greek Period**, Ptolemy I introduced the cult of the god of Serapis in an attempt to unify Greeks and Egyptians.

- **In the later Greek Period**, civil wars once again became a part of Egyptian life. Egyptians in the south tried to rebel against their foreign rulers, and there were sporadic outbreaks of violence in Alexandria.

- **In 48 BC, Roman general** Julius Caesar went to Egypt to aid Queen Cleopatra VII, who had been deposed by her brother Ptolemy XIII Philopator.

- **Cleopatra was later defeated** by the Roman leader Octavian in 30 BC. Octavian appointed himself pharaoh and Egypt became a Roman province.

- **Many Roman emperors** commissioned temple wall paintings with themselves depicted as Egyptian pharaohs.

▼ *The Battle of Actium (31 BC) was a turning point in the history of Egypt. The Roman leader Octavian's forces repelled those of Mark Antony and Queen Cleopatra of Egypt, and forced them to flee.*

What was a pharaoh?

- **The term 'pharaoh'** was originally used to describe the royal court, but from the time of the New Kingdom onwards it was used to refer to the king himself.

- **It was unusual for a woman to rule Egypt** in her own right. A queen was referred to as 'Great Royal Wife'. Hatshepsut and Nefertiti were exceptions to this rule.

- **The ancient Egyptians believed** that the pharaoh was the god Horus in human form. He could not be addressed directly by name. The pharaoh was the representative of the gods, and looked after the harmony of the universe.

- **No one else** in the ancient Egyptian government had more power than the pharaoh. He was in charge of law and order, trade and industry, and the taxation of the temple lands and private estates.

- **There was a long period of training** to become a pharaoh. A prince had to work on his military and sporting skills and then hope to persuade a pharaoh to take him on as his 'co-regent'. When a pharaoh died, control went to his co-regent.

...FASCINATING FACT...
Artists always had to portray pharaohs as youthful
and handsome in Egyptian art, regardless of whether
or not this was actually the case!

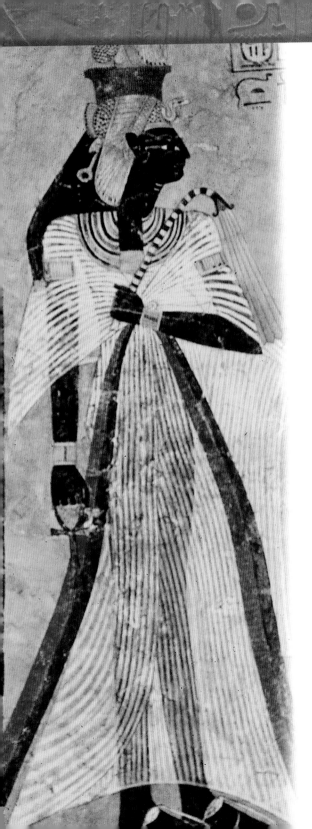

- **The pharaoh was the religious head of state.** He performed lots of religious ceremonies and was the honourary high priest of every temple.

- **It was believed** that pharaohs were the only people who were allowed to approach and touch the gods. Pharaohs are the only people shown making offerings to the gods in temple wall paintings.

- **The pharaoh** was also the head of Egypt's legal system. If an Egyptian felt he had been wronged, he could appeal directly to the pharaoh for justice.

- **One of the duties of a pharaoh** was to protect Egypt from its enemies. Some pharaohs, such as Thutmose III, actually led the Egyptian army into battle.

◀ *Queen Nefertiti was the wife of the Egyptian pharaoh Amenhotep IV. It is thought she may have ruled in her own right, as pharaoh, following the death of her husband.*

37

The royal court and palace

- **The pharaoh and his advisers** gathered together for special state occasions. Many types of buildings were used for these gatherings.

- **Royal courts** were decorated in gilded metals and jewels. Fragments of tiles from the court of Pharaoh Akhenaten offer a glimpse of the splendours of life at court.

- **Courtiers chosen by the pharaoh** populated the court, either relatives or talented scribes. Ceremonies were frequently held to dispense rewards to these loyal servants.

- **There were strict rules to obey** at court. If the pharaoh approached anyone they had to fall before him and kiss the ground beneath his feet.

- **Life at the royal court** could be dull, so dancers, jesters, magicians and musicians kept the pharaoh entertained.

...FASCINATING FACT...
Wild birds were a menace in some royal courts. Courtiers
dealt with them by hurling wooden throwsticks shaped
like boomerangs at the creatures.

- **The court throne** was made of wood overlaid with gold leaf. Archaeologists have reconstructed Queen Hetepheres' throne.

- **There were unofficial 'guilds'** of women made up of the wives of important officials. They reported to the goddess Hathor.

- **Some jewellery** was only allowed at court at certain times. A figurine of the royal crown could only be worn when the king was riding his chariot.

- **Only the finest materials** were used at court. Vases and plates were forged from gold, which was considered to be the most precious metal of all.

▼ *People were employed in royal courts and temples as singers, musicians and dancers (shown in the wall painting below). These positions were esteemed.*

Divine symbols

▲ *The ankh symbol was based on a representation of a sandal strap.*

- **Some symbols** were only carried by the king or queen. The ankh – the sign of life – indicated the power to give or take away life, and could not be carried by ordinary Egyptians.

- **The sphinx** was one of the most important symbols in Egypt. It was depicted with the body of a lion and the head of a pharaoh. The sphinx was a beast of the sun god, stressing the king's role as the son of Ra.

- **The lotus flower** flourishes on the banks of the Nile. It opens its large petals with the rising of the sun. To the ancient Egyptians it represented the rebirth of the sun and the banishing of darkness.

- **The crook and flail** were carried by every Egyptian pharaoh. The crook was shaped like a shepherd's staff, and symbolized government, while the flail was shaped like a shepherd's fly-whisk, and symbolized the power of the pharaoh to punish his enemies.

- **The falcon was an important symbol**. Ra, the sun god, was most commonly represented as a falcon.

- **Bees had great religious significance** in Egypt. In one myth they were the tears of the sun god, Ra. Bees were also linked with the goddess Neith, and her temple was called 'The house of the bee'.

- **Obelisks were needle-like stone monuments**. They were based on the shape of the benben stone, upon which it was said the first rays of sunlight fell.

◀ *A scarab charm (amulet) made of green jasper that was buried with the pharaoh Sobekemsat.*

● **Beards were considered** to be divine attributes of the gods. Both male and female pharaohs often wore false beards secured under the chin by a cord.

● **The apis was a sacred bull**, which was chosen to live in the temple of Ptah in Memphis. Its birth was considered divine and its death provoked national mourning.

● **The large, black-green scarab dung beetle** rolls up animal droppings into a ball, which it pushes along with its head and front legs. The Egyptians associated the scarab with the god Khepri, who they believed rolled the sun across the sky every day.

▶ *Jewelled falcons represented the sun god and were worn by the pharaohs.*

41

Menes

- **The Egyptian historian Manetho** (305–285 BC) states that it was King Menes who was responsible for uniting Upper and Lower Egypt and founding the First Dynasty.

- **There is a lot of uncertainty** however, as to whether King Menes actually founded the Egyptian state.

- **Some think** that Manetho is referring to a king called Horus Aha, who succeeded King Narmer. Narmer was the last king of the Pre-Dynastic Period in Egypt.

▲ A scene from the tombstone of King Djet of the 1st Dynasty shows the falcon god Horus perched on top of the royal palace.

- **Other historians** believe that Narmer and Menes were actually the same person, because the two names have been found linked together on jar-sealings from Abydos. This mystery has not yet been solved.

- **What is certain**, is that a figure who has become known in history as King Menes was responsible for founding the city of Memphis. He dammed off part of the river to create dry land for his capital.

- **King Menes was regarded** by the ancient Egyptians as the first human ruler. Before his ascension, the country was run by a succession of mythical rulers. According to Egyptian legend, when the throne was passed to Menes by the god Horus it stayed in human hands until the 5th Dynasty.

- **During his reign**, Menes waged wars against the Nubians and Libyans in neighbouring territories. Scholars of ancient history believed he was a warrior king who defeated all his enemies.

- **During his rule**, Egyptian trade thrived. Trading with nearby countries in the Middle East appear to have been well established.

- **When Menes died**, he was succeeded by Djer. This ruler became known as 'the serpent king' because when his name was written in Egyptian script the symbols resembled a snake.

...FASCINATING FACT...
The king before Narmer is known only by the symbol that
he had carved on his possessions – a scorpion.

Khufu

- **Pharaoh Khufu reigned** from 2560–2537 BC. He was the son of the great pyramid builder Sneferu, and was called Cheops by the Greeks. Khufu is short for 'Khnum-kuefui', which means 'Khnum protects me'.

- **Khufu's greatest achievement** was the Great Pyramid at Giza, one of the Seven Wonders of the ancient world. It was the tallest structure on Earth for nearly 4500 years.

- **Khufu's burial treasure** was stolen long ago by grave robbers. Only an empty coffin (sarcophagus) was found by archaeologists. Two cedarwood boats were found buried next to the Great Pyramid.

- **Archaeologists have found** part of the funerary equipment of Khufu's mother, Hetepheres, in a tomb near the Great Pyramid of Giza.

- **The untouched tomb of Khufu's son,** Hardjedef, has also been discovered at Giza to the east of the Great Pyramid.

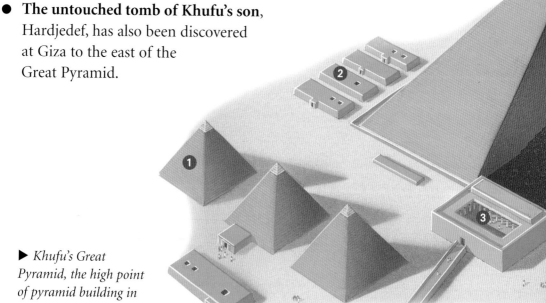

▶ *Khufu's Great Pyramid, the high point of pyramid building in ancient Egypt.*

- **A giant trading expedition** set off to secure resources for the pharaoh's building programmes. Khufu's name is inscribed at the turquoise and copper mines of Wadi Maghara in the Sinai Peninsula.

- **There were also mining expeditions** into the Nubian Western desert. The pharaoh's name has been scratched into gneiss quarries there, 65 km to the north-west of Abu Simbel.

- **Egyptian legend** suggests that Khufu was a wicked tyrant, using money and manpower for building the Great Pyramid rather than for bettering the country.

- **Only one complete likeness of the pharaoh** has survived. It is a tiny ivory statuette of a king wearing the red crown of Lower Egypt, seated on a throne.

- **The statuette was recovered** from the temple of Khentimentiu at Abydos by the English explorer Flinders Petrie in 1903.

KEY

1. The queen's pyramids
2. Mastaba tombs
3. Funeral temple
4. King's chamber
5. Grand gallery
6. Queen's chamber

Thutmose III and Hatshepsut

- **King Thutmose III** was king during the 18th Dynasty. He took the throne as a child, so his aunt and stepmother Hatshepsut was made queen regent.

- **After a few years as regent**, Hatshepsut had herself crowned 'King of Egypt'. This meant Thutmose did not come to power for a further 20 years. Hatshepsut wore the pharaoh's crown and royal ceremonial beard.

- **When Thutmose finally became king** following Hatshepsut's death, he built up the army and led a series of daring campaigns in Palestine and Syria.

- **Thutmose III's most famous victory** is recorded on an inscription at the Temple at Karnak. It describes a surprise attack on Megiddo, Israel, where his army of 10,000 soldiers captured the city.

- **Thutmose's military victories** resulted in even more wealth for Egypt, and many more elaborate temples were built.

- **In the later years of Thutmose's reign** he removed many of the images of his stepmother from Egypt's monuments. At Deir el-Bahari, he ordered a number of her statues to be destroyed.

...FASCINATING FACT...
At Karnak, the walls record the many plants and animals
Thutmose imported. Historians think he might be responsible for
introducing chickens to Egypt.

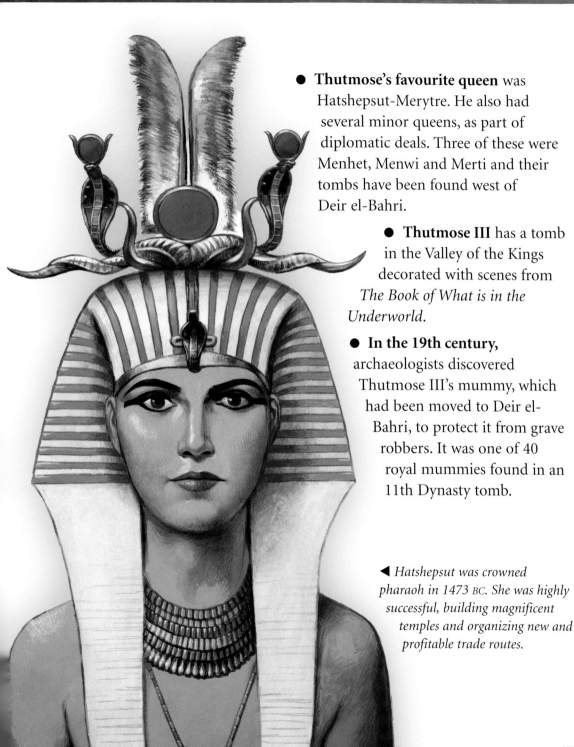

- **Thutmose's favourite queen** was Hatshepsut-Merytre. He also had several minor queens, as part of diplomatic deals. Three of these were Menhet, Menwi and Merti and their tombs have been found west of Deir el-Bahri.

- **Thutmose III** has a tomb in the Valley of the Kings decorated with scenes from *The Book of What is in the Underworld.*

- **In the 19th century,** archaeologists discovered Thutmose III's mummy, which had been moved to Deir el-Bahri, to protect it from grave robbers. It was one of 40 royal mummies found in an 11th Dynasty tomb.

◀ *Hatshepsut was crowned pharaoh in 1473 BC. She was highly successful, building magnificent temples and organizing new and profitable trade routes.*

Akhenaten and Nefertiti

● **Pharaoh Akhenaten** was originally called Amenhotep, and was born in the 14th century BC. He was a younger son of Amenhotep III, and came to the throne because his older brother died.

● **Akhenaten ruled ancient Egypt** from about 1352 BC. At first he probably ruled jointly with his father, then later shared power with his wife, Nefertiti.

● **One of Akhenaten's first major projects** was the great temple at Thebes, which was dedicated to a new god named Aten. Many paintings of the king and his wife decorated the temple walls.

◀ *Nefertiti was the main wife of Akhenaten. Her name translates as 'A Beautiful One has Come'.*

- **Akhenaten wanted to go beyond** constructing temples. A new capital, called Akhetaten, was built at a place we now call Tell el-Amarna. The best-preserved example of a New Kingdom settlement, it includes temples, palaces and mud-brick houses.

- **Akhenaten and Nefertiti were so devoted** to the god Aten that they prohibited the worshipping of the old gods, including Amun-Ra. The king was no longer known by his original name of Amenhotep but by Akhenaten – which means 'Effective Spirit of the Aten'.

- **People were made to worship** images of the pharaoh and his family being blessed by Aten – even in their own homes.

- **Archaeologists know a lot** about ancient Egyptian life during Akhenaten's reign from the Amarna letters, which were discovered in 1888. These were sent to Akhenaten from different rulers of the Middle East.

- **Some of the letters** tell how parts of the Egyptian empire felt neglected. Others speak of plots to assassinate the king.

- **Nobody knows what happened** to Akhenaten's body. It is likely that it was destroyed. His name was left out of the official list of kings and he was not prayed for in temples.

...FASCINATING FACT...
Legal documents reveal just how the status of Akhenaten plummeted after his death. He became known as 'The Great Criminal'.

Tutankhamun

- **Pharaoh Tutankhamun was born** around 1330 BC and lived in the palace of Queen Nefertiti at Amarna. Historians do not even know who his parents were.

- **Tutankhamun became king** when he was just eight or nine years old, and he married one of Akhenaten's teenage daughters.

- **Tutankhamun was responsible** for restoring the old gods that Akhenaten and Nefertiti had banned. This made him popular with the people of Egypt.

- **The capital was moved** away from Akhetaten and back to Memphis. High officials began to be buried at Saqqara once more, rather than at Thebes.

- **Historians know little** of the personal life of Tutankhamun. It is thought that he had two stillborn children and that he did not survive beyond the age of 18.

- **Forensic examinations** of the king's mummy show that he was probably killed by a blow to the head. Whether this was an accident or murder is impossible to tell.

- **He was probably intended** to be buried close to the tomb of Amenhotep III who may have been either his father or grandfather. This spot was taken by the vizier Ay, and Tutankhamun was buried in the smallest tomb in the Valley of Kings.

- **Thousands of wonderful objects** were crammed around Tutankhamun's tomb. His resting place was a fantastic solid gold coffin with a beautiful golden funeral mask.

- **The treasures** of Tutankhamun survived. The entrance to his tomb lay hidden under building debris and was missed by bandits searching for loot.

● **The tomb lay undisturbed** for thousands of years until it was found by Howard Carter's archaeological team in 1922. They were about to make the discovery of the century.

▶ *Tutankhamun's beautiful gold coffin features a royal cobra and a vulture's head, representing the unification of Lower and Upper Egypt.*

51

Ramesses II

- **Ramesses was the most popular name** among ancient Egyptian royalty – eleven pharaohs were named this in all. The most famous was Ramesses II, who lived between 1279–1213 BC.

- **Pharaoh Ramesses was determined** to immortalize himself by reviving the earlier colossal style of building. He ordered the building of numerous great statues of himself throughout Egypt.

- **An impressive temple** stood at Abu Simbel, on the Upper Nile. It was built to honour Ramesses and the gods Amun, Re-Harakhty and Ptah.

▲ *Ramesses II led Egypt into a period of peace and prosperity.*

- **Another great construction** stands at Karnak. This huge temple complex covers hundreds of acres in modern day Luxor, and was dedicated to the gods Amun-ra, Mut and Montu. It was surrounded by the thriving city of Thebes.

- **Faced by a growing military threat** from the Hittites, Ramesses II took personal charge of the Egyptian army. Ramesses claimed it was his bravery that saved his men from destruction.

...FASCINATING FACT...

Ramesses II had several wives, including Queen Nefertari, to whom the smaller temple of Abu Simbel was dedicated. He is rumoured to have fathered up to 120 children!

- **Both the Hittites and the Egyptians** claimed victory at Qadesh, but Ramesses later decided to make peace. He married a Hittite princess as part of a peace treaty.

- **As well as his temple-building programme** across Egypt, Ramesses II built a new capital city called Piramesse in the Egyptian Delta.

- **The mortuary complex** on the west bank at Thebes is known as the Ramesseum. A giant statue of the pharaoh stands there today.

- **After his death,** the mummy of Ramesses II was moved to a secret place to prevent possible tomb robbers stealing it.

▶ *Ramesses II built his Ramesseum on the site of Seti I's ruined temple. The temple took 20 years to complete.*

Cleopatra VII

- **Cleopatra was the name of seven Ptolemic queens**. The most famous was Cleopatra VII. She and her half-brother Ptolemy XIII ruled Egypt from 51 BC.

- **Ptolemy forced his sister** out of power, but Cleopatra called on her close ally, the Roman general Julius Caesar. Ptolemy XIII was killed in a civil war.

- **Julius Caesar rode into Egypt** and made Cleopatra queen, although she had to share the throne with another brother, Ptolemy XIV.

- **After Caesar returned to Rome**, Cleopatra gave birth to a son. She called him Caesarion, claiming that Caesar was his father. When her half-brother died, Cleopatra made Caesarion her co-ruler.

- **Cleopatra's subjects** greatly admired her, and the way she ruled the country, comparing her to the goddess Isis, also a single mother.

- **Cleopatra is famous** for her disastrous love affair with the Roman general Mark Antony. He had promised to marry the Roman emperor Octavian's sister, and his affair with Cleopatra was to end in tragedy.

▶ *The goddess Isis was held in high esteem by the Egyptians, so to be compared to her was considered a great honour.*

▶ *The marriage of Cleopatra and Mark Antony hastened the end of Egypt's independence and led to it becoming part of the kingdom of Rome.*

- **Cleopatra and Mark Antony** had three children. She used her great wealth to pay for his armies. In return, Mark Antony made Alexandria the capital of a new independent Egyptian Empire to be ruled by Cleopatra and her children, in an act called the Donations of Alexandria.

- **Antony had acted** without permission from the Roman government, so bitter fighting soon erupted. Antony and Cleopatra were defeated at the battle of Actium by the Roman Emperor Octavian.

- **Antony killed himself** when Octavian closed in upon Alexandria. Cleopatra committed suicide soon afterwards. Caesarion was murdered and Egypt was incorporated into the Roman Empire.

- **Cleopatra's palace** has been found underwater at Alexandria. There is hope that her tomb will be found, and may contain the remains of the queen.

Food and drink

- **Most of what we know** about the diet of the ancient Egyptians comes from scenes painted in private tombs, and from the remains of food found in burial complexes.

- **It is likely that most Egyptians** enjoyed a good diet. Although their crops were sometimes struck by plagues of locusts and other pests, the average table would have boasted food including meats, fish, vegetables and fruits.

▲ *Wall art in temples and tombs depicts rich Egyptians enjoying delicacies such as butter, cheese, fowl, and beef.*

- **Meat that was eaten includes** sheep, poultry, oxen and wild animals such as antelope. It was expensive, and the poor often ate fish instead. Some also went hunting or fowling.

- **Spice was an important feature** of an Egyptian feast. The world's major trading routes passed through the country, bringing exotic eastern spices.

- **The Egyptians grew grapes** that they both ate and made into wine. Wine could also be made from dates. Beer made from barley was more widely available, and was thick and gloopy.

- **Dates and honey** were used as sweeteners. Bees were kept in pottery hives, and the Egyptians thought of them as tiny birds rather than as insects.

- **Bread formed the staple diet** of most Egyptians. Wall paintings show workers placing loaves into flat round moulds to bake them. Cakes were also made using fruits such as dates and figs.

- **The kitchen was often a corner of the courtyard** or on the flat roof. Ancient Egyptians cooked in clay ovens or charcoal fires. Food was baked, boiled, stewed, fried, grilled or roasted.

- **An ancient papyrus** casts some light on what Egyptians considered to be special foods to eat. *The Story of the Shipwrecked Sailor* reveals that the hero delighted in figs, grapes, cucumbers, fish and birds.

- **Kitchen utensils** included storage jars, bowls, pots, pans, ladles, sieves and whisks. Ordinary Egyptians used dishes made from clay, while the rich used ones made from gold, silver or bronze.

▼ *During banquets, guests were entertained by dancers, musicians and acrobats.*

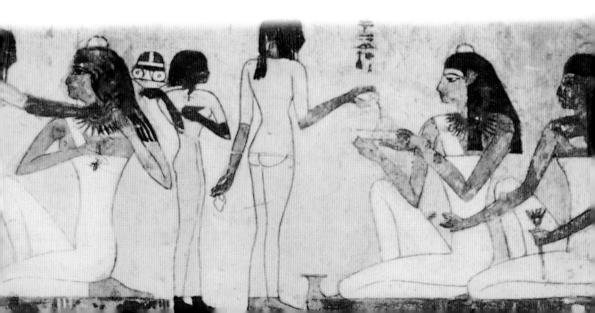

Women in society

- **All the most important posts** in ancient Egypt were filled by men. Women were expected to provide a stable family environment.

- **Women performed many of the agricultural tasks** in ancient Egypt.

▼ A non-royal Egyptian woman was referred to as the 'mistress of the house'. Richer households had servants to help with tasks ranging from getting dressed to cleaning.

- **Egyptian women** were usually free to go about in public without the company of an escort. They were not required by law to wear veils.

- **There were several ways for Egyptian women** to acquire possessions and property. Usually they were given as gifts or were inherited from parents or from a husband.

- **Under Egyptian property law**, a woman had claim to one-third of all the property the couple had built up since they were married.

- **If a woman brought private property** to a marriage it remained hers, although the husband often had free use of it. In the event of divorce her property had to be returned to her, plus any divorce settlement.

- **Women enjoyed a degree of legal protection** after marriage that was almost unrivalled in the ancient world. If a wife was badly treated, she could divorce her husband. She was then free to marry again.

- **Women played many roles in society**. At the highest end of the social scale they could be pharaohs, dowager queens and regents. Most ordinary women were expected to look after the family and the home, but some acted as housekeepers, servants, workers or skilled labourers.

- **Women were not usually taught** how to read and write. Only between one and five percent of women were literate between the Old Kingdom and the Late Period.

. . . .FASCINATING FACT. . . .
Women could be national heroines. Queen Ahhotep of the
18th Dynasty became a legend for saving Egypt from the Hyksos,
receiving Egypt's highest military decoration at least three times.

Family and marriage

- **Family was the centre** of ancient Egyptian life. Tomb paintings show different generations of Egyptians sharing a home together. Servants and slaves were often considered to be part of the family in wealthy homes.

- **The head of the household** was always a man. He was in charge of financial matters and discipline. His wife was called the 'mistress of the house' and was responsible for the daily running of the household.

- **Marriage in ancient Egypt** was quite informal. No legal ceremony was required, and it was not until the Late Period that marriage contracts came into existence. A couple simply moved in together if both families agreed.

- **Marriages usually took place** between people of the same social class. There seem to have been few restrictions with regards to race or nationality. Unions between northern Egyptians and Nubians, or even with people from distant countries are recorded.

- **Children were central** to family life, and married couples were expected to have several children.

- **If a baby died**, the family mourned, and sometimes buried it under the house. Some Egyptian houses were fitted with false doors called *mastabas* to allow the spirits of the dead to come and visit.

> ...FASCINATING FACT...
> The elderly were treated with great respect. Small figures
> of dead ancestors were often kept around the house to keep
> their memory alive.

▶ *On her wedding day, the bride wore a long linen dress or tunic. Gold, silver or gems such as lapis lazuli were also worn by richer women.*

- **It was common practice** for a prospective husband to pay a sum of money to the bride's father. Later this practice was reversed, and the father of the bride paid the future husband for the upkeep of his daughter.

- **Girls from poor families** married as early as 12. Boys were usually working before they married, so rarely wed before the age of 15. In royal marriages, the participants were often much younger. Tutankhamun married when he was around eight or nine years old.

- **Many portraits, statues and wall paintings** suggest that ordinary Egyptians settled down in lifelong marriages to only one partner.

Children

- **Children were considered a blessing** in ancient Egypt. If a couple could not have their own children, they could try to adopt orphans.

- **Children were important** because of belief in the afterlife. Family members needed to ensure their funeral rites would be carried out exactly. Children would also look after aged parents.

- **Life for a child** was precarious. Disease and accidents claimed the lives of one out of every two or three births. To compensate, families had on average four to six children, and some had as many as 15.

▼ *Toys and games have been found by archaeologists, as well as paintings showing children playing.*

- **The ancient Egyptians** had tests for determining a woman's fertility and even for finding out the sex of an unborn child. They believed that a woman should sprinkle her own urine onto emmer wheat and barley. If the barley grew, it was thought that her child would be a boy. If the emmer grew, the child would be a girl. If neither grew, the woman would not have children.

- **Childbirth was dangerous**, and many women died during it. In the tomb of King Horemheb at Saqqara, the remains of his queen, Mutnodjmet, were found to contain the bones of a full term foetus. It is likely that she died as a result of a problem during pregnancy.

- **The chief goddess of pregnancy** and childbirth was the hippopotamus goddess, Taweret. Women would put an ivory wand on their stomachs to ask for her help during childbirth.

- **A child was usually named immediately** and then registered with the Egyptian authorities. Some names were a few letters long, while others represented a phrase. Many children were also named after gods.

- **Babies were nursed by their mothers** for about three years, carried around in a sling around her neck to allow her to carry on working.

- **From the age of five**, children were expected to begin helping their parents to earn a living or run the household – assisting with the harvest or running errands. Young boys' heads were shaved, except for a ponytail worn to one side. When they reached the age of twelve this was shaved off and they were allowed to grow their hair. From this age, boys were considered old enough to do adult work on the family estates. Girls helped around the house.

- **In the very poorest families**, the fate of children was not so pleasant. They might be given away to work in temples or even sold as slaves.

Education

- **Few Egyptians** received any formal education. Most were illiterate, and received vocational training aimed at preparing them for their future employment. Skills such as carpentry were passed on through generations.

- **Schooling was very expensive**, and many families were unable to afford it. The ability to read and write could sometimes lead to being given a position as a scribe, which was one of the most coveted jobs in Egypt.

▼ *Learning how to write was a very laborious process that was restricted to children from only the richest families. Would-be scribes were sent to special schools to learn their trade.*

- **To become a scribe**, you went to a special school at the age of about nine. Training took between 7 and 12 years to complete. Only then were scribes allowed to write on papyrus scrolls.

- **Students made their own brushes** and colours and copied out long lists of words and phrases. They then progressed to copying whole texts.

- **The texts** were usually moral works, packed full of advice about how a young Egyptian should behave.

- **There were many employment options** for scribes. You could seek work in a temple, a law court, within the government, or as a travelling war reporter with the Egyptian army.

- **The ancient Egyptians** believed that writing was sacred – a skill given to them by the god of wisdom, Thoth.

- **Schools were attached to temples** and government offices. Royal children had their own schools inside palaces.

- **Education seems to have been** almost entirely restricted to men. There is evidence of only one girl being taught to read and write – a 20th Dynasty letter from a man to his son says, 'You shall see that daughter of Khonsumose and let her make a letter and send it to me.'

...FASCINATING FACT...

There was no set number of years at school. One man recorded that he started school aged five. At the age of 16 he was appointed a wab priest. After 39 years he was appointed high priest.

Law and order

- **Crime prevention** was the responsibility of local officials and police forces funded by the Egyptian treasury. They investigated incidents following complaints. Police patrols used dogs and, on occasions, trained monkeys!

- **Cases were constructed** against suspects by interrogation, re-enactments, and checking records. In some cases, beatings seem to have been given out to extract information.

- **There do not seem to** have been any written laws or any lawyers. Cases were tried by groups of judges, who would all have had other jobs.

- **The ancient Egyptians** believed that justice lay with the gods, both on Earth and in the afterlife. Pharaohs maintained justice on Earth because they were believed to be the living embodiment of the gods.

- **The head of the Egyptian legal system** was the vizier, second in rank only to the pharaoh. Courts were run by magistrates.

- **The office of a judge** or magistrate was very highly regarded, and became a valued profession.

- **Egyptians brought before court** would probably have represented themselves. Any previous record would have been taken into account by the judge and the defendant would be required to swear by their favourite god that they were telling the truth.

> **...FASCINATING FACT...**
> Some crimes were judged by gods speaking through priests.
> In Deir el-Medina, Amenhotep I was worshipped as a god,
> and was asked to decide many cases from beyond the grave.

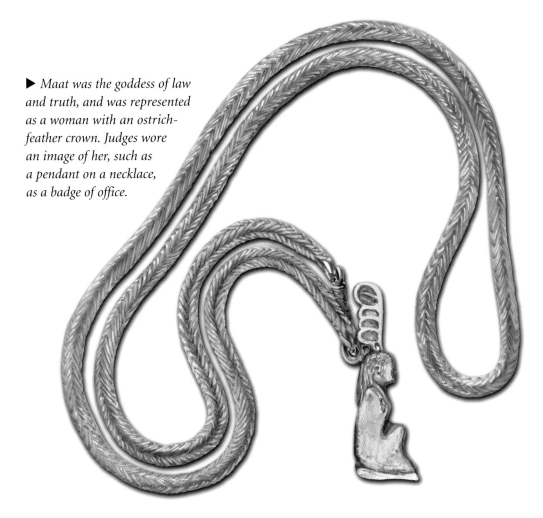

▶ *Maat was the goddess of law and truth, and was represented as a woman with an ostrich-feather crown. Judges wore an image of her, such as a pendant on a necklace, as a badge of office.*

- **Stealing and receiving stolen goods** were common crimes in ancient Egypt. More serious crimes included assault, kidnap and treason.

- **A confession was basis for a conviction** in court. The methods by which this confession was achieved were deemed largely irrelevant, even if they including beatings.

Punishments

- **Punishments were severe** in Egyptian society. For example, forgers had their hands cut off, and disobedient soldiers were asked to make amends by performing heroic deeds.

- **One of the fiercest punishments** was reserved for grave robbers, and particularly for those caught stealing from royal tombs. The official penalty was to be burnt alive or to be impaled on a stake and left to die.

- **Another punishment** was to be banished to a remote oasis of the Western Desert. You were unlikely to ever escape, as there was no practical way to cross the vast expanse of sand.

- **Many Egyptians believed** that there was no such thing as escaping justice, and that even if you escaped punishment on Earth you would be punished during the afterlife.

- **There were no long-term prisons** in Egypt. Criminals were sentenced to time in back-breaking labour camps, where they had to haul massive stone slabs across the desert.

- **When an offender was punished**, their family ofen suffered as well. If a man committed the crime of deserting military service, he could be imprisoned along with his entire family.

- **Offences were rarely forgiven** during the early periods of Egyptian history. In later years, pardons seem to have been used quite frequently.

> **...FASCINATING FACT...**
> A strange quirk of Egyptian life was that a thief could register their profession and declare their earnings. If a victim of theft identified their possessions, they could claim back only 75 percent of them.

▲ *If somebody was caught trying to escape paying tribute to the pharaoh, harsh punishments were given out. This prisoner awaits his fate after sacks of grain given to the government were found to be short of what had been demanded.*

● **Sometimes people were punished** after their death. King Teti's bodyguards were said to have assassinated him, so their names were scratched from their graves, and the statues on their tombs were defaced.

● **The ancient Egyptians believed** that spirits could be punished. A spirit found guilty of being an enemy of Ra, could be boiled in a cauldron or burned in a lake of fire.

69

Politics and government

- **The ancient Egyptians** have left much evidence about the way their country was administered. Written and archaeological sources reveal the supply and demand of items such as grain.

- **Everything was noted down** by scribes. Documents recovered include wills, title deeds, census lists, conscription lists, orders, memos, tax lists and letters.

▶ *Egyptian society was hierarchical, with the pharaoh at the top, and the peasant workers and slaves at the bottom.*

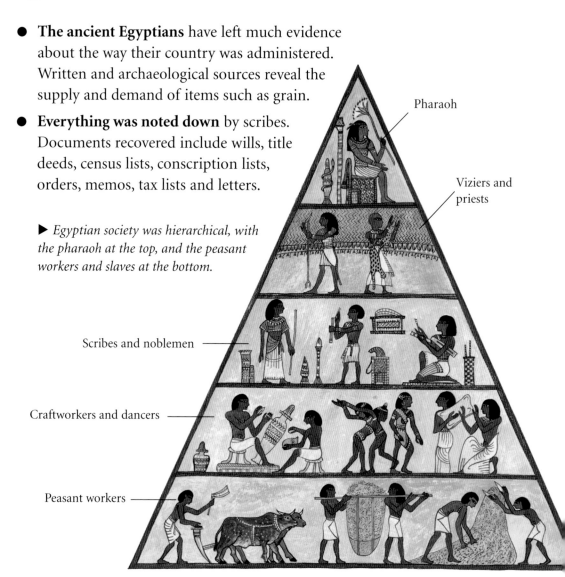

Pharaoh

Viziers and priests

Scribes and noblemen

Craftworkers and dancers

Peasant workers

- **The most important person** in Egypt after the pharaoh was the vizier (prime minister). The earliest-known holder of the post was a man called Menka.

- **The vizier was responsible** for overseeing the development of the royal monuments and for the registration of people and property for tax purposes. His titles were High Priest of Heliopolis and Master of Works.

- **Scribes were crucial** in every aspect of government, from assessing taxes to drawing up building projects and compiling war reports.

- **Egypt was governed locally** by a series of administrative districts called nomes. There were 42 nomes in total – 22 in Upper Egypt and 20 in Lower Egypt. Each nome was governed by a member of the royal family or by a figure appointed by the pharaoh. They were called nomarchs.

- **Foreign affairs were managed** by the governors of foreign provinces. Diplomats travelled between countries.

- **It was possible to overcome class barriers** and reach high office from a humble background, as noted by a scribe called Ptahhoptep: 'Do not be arrogant towards (a worthy man) for knowing his former state; respect him for what he has achieved by his own efforts.'

- **By the time of the New Kingdom** national administration was divided into three parts – the dynasty, internal administration and external affairs.

- **Internal administration** was itself split into four parts – the royal domain, the army and navy, religious hierarchy and civil officials.

Towns and cities

- **Most Egyptian towns** were built on raised land, far enough away from the Nile to minimize flooding, but close enough to allow access to water.

- **Memphis was Egypt's first capital**, probably founded by King Narmer in about 3100 BC after the unification of Upper and Lower Egypt. Little of the city remains.

- **Thebes first became important** during the Middle Kingdom when the 11th Dynasty kings made it their capital. During the New Kingdom, a number of kings were buried in rock-cut tombs in the Valley of the Kings. Queens, princes and princesses were buried in the Valley of the Queens.

- **El-Amarna**, on the east bank of the Nile between Minya and Asyaut, is the most complete city to have survived. It was founded by Akhenaten during the New Kingdom.

- **Alexandria was founded** in the 4th century BC by the Greek general Alexander the Great, who envisaged the city as the centre of his empire. It was laid out on a grid system like a Greek city, and divided into districts.

- **A number of towns** were built around specific trades. A workers' village was built at Giza just outside Cairo. It was constructed to house the men who laboured over Khufu's mighty pyramid.

- **The town of Illahun** (Kahun) was discovered by Flinders Petrie. It once housed the workers that built the pyramid of King Senusret. It was also home to mortuary priests.

- **Fortress towns** were built in Egyptian-controlled Nubia from the Middle Kingdom onwards. Buhen, 250 km south of Aswan, was constructed on an Old Kingdom site with an inner citadel, surrounded by a mud-brick enclosure wall 5 m thick and up to 9 m high.

- **At the height** of the ancient Egyptian civilization there were about 17 cities and 24 towns that were governed by the national capital. Their estimated population was between 100,000 and 200,000. Small towns had up to 3000 inhabitants, while Memphis and Thebes had up to 40,000.

- **Craftworkers, scribes**, priests and shopkeepers lived and worked in cities, while farmers and herdsmen left the towns to travel to the countryside to work each day.

▼ *The town of Deir el-Medina lay in a valley on the west bank across from Luxor. It was built to house the workers who constructed the royal tombs in the Valley of the Kings.*

73

The army

- **There was no permanent army** in the Old Kingdom. Forces were conscripted for specific expeditions, although there is evidence that a royal bodyguard was retained to protect the pharaoh and his family.

- **Until Lower Egypt was conquered** by the Hyksos people in 1674 BC, Egypt had never fought a large-scale war with another country. Most conflicts had been civil wars, or short campaigns in countries such as Nubia.

- **By the time of the 17th and 18th Dynasties** of the New Kingdom, the Egyptian army had become professional. At a time of empire building in the Middle East, it was no longer practical for the army to rely on conscripts. The army gradually became dominated by noblemen, who fought as charioteers and officers.

- **From this period onwards**, many specialized units began to evolve. These ranged from trench diggers to units armed with heavy battering rams and deadly groups of Nubian archers.

- **The pharaoh** or his son was usually in charge of the army. The army itself was split into a northern and a southern corps overseen by chief deputies. Ranks were similar to those in the modern army, including generals, battalion commanders and lieutenants.

> **. . .FASCINATING FACT. . .**
> Army divisions were named after a god such as Amun. Appeals were made to the god of the province to boost the spirits of the soldiers.

- **The armies** of ancient Egypt were tiny in comparison to modern armies. In the New Kingdom, under the leadership of Seti I, the army comprised of just three divisions. Under Ramesses II there were four divisions.

- **A division** would contain several thousand men – around 4000 infantry and 1000 charioteers. These would be divided into battalions of 500 soldiers, and subdivided into 250 platoons of 50 men. Within these platoons, soldiers operated in ten-man squads.

- **An Egyptian army's tactics** were usually to march in divisions of about 50 men towards the enemy lines. It was hoped that sheer weight of numbers would prevail. The pharaoh himself often took part in military campaigns.

- **From the Old Kingdom onwards**, mercenaries (soldiers available for hire) were recruited into the Egyptian army. By the time of the latter part of the New Kingdom, mercenaries formed the majority of the forces. Slaves were also drafted, together with prisoners of war.

▶ *Ancient Egyptian soldiers would have carried stone or bronze weapons such as spears, axes and daggers. Shields, were made first from turtle shells, and then from leather.*

Weapons and warfare

- **During the Old Kingdom**, Egyptian soldiers used a variety of weapons, including spears, cudgels, maces, daggers, bows and arrows and axes.

- **The bow and arrow** was the most important weapon. The earliest metal arrowheads date from around 2000 BC.

- **The first arrowheads** were made of flint or wood, and later, bronze. A horseshoe shape was designed to wound, and a triangular shape was designed to kill.

- **Archery units** were deadlier when used with the chariot, introduced around 3000 BC by the Sumerians. These provided a platform for the soldier to fire from.

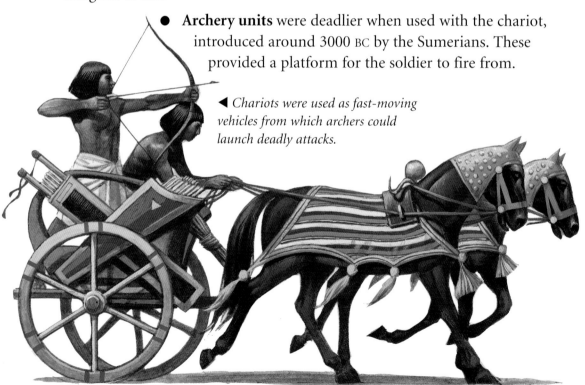

◀ *Chariots were used as fast-moving vehicles from which archers could launch deadly attacks.*

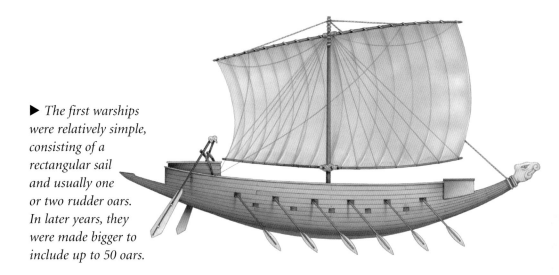

▶ *The first warships were relatively simple, consisting of a rectangular sail and usually one or two rudder oars. In later years, they were made bigger to include up to 50 oars.*

● **Operating a bow and arrow** was difficult, and specialist equipment protected the archer. Archaeologists have found bone finger guards and wrist guards that protected the archer from the whip of the bowstring.

● **The sling required** considerable skill to be effective on the battlefield. Pebbles, and later lead, were used as missiles, but the purpose of this weapon was probably more to distract the enemy.

● **Armour was light** – leather jackets covered with metal scales were usual, and wooden shields protected against spear thrusts. Pharaohs may have worn armour inlaid with semi-precious stones.

● **During the New Kingdom**, soldiers carried spears, battle-axes, scimitars and daggers. Thutmose III was one of the first Egyptians to use a scimitar – a deadly curved eastern sabre (sword).

● **Egyptian war galleys** (boats) were used to ferry men and supplies to battlegrounds. Some were fitted with battering rams to sink enemy ships.

● **During peacetime**, weapons were kept in royal armouries. When Egypt was at war, they were distributed in lavish ceremonies.

A soldier's life

- **Egyptian soldiers lived together** in large compounds based around forts. Donkeys were used to carry army possessions.

- **Camps were rectangular**, protected by a fence of leather shields. The king had a separate tent in the centre and senior officers had their own tents.

- **Scribes organized the logistics** of supplying such a huge number of men. An army of 10,000 soldiers would have probably needed around 20 tonnes of grain and 95,000 l of water every day.

- **Camp life** was run on a system of rationing. Conscripts were registered, then allocated rations, which they could then barter. They were paid in food or tokens according to experience.

- **When the Egyptians began a military campaign**, they prayed to the gods to protect and assist them in striking down their enemies. A mast on the pharaoh's chariot carried a symbol of the sun representing Amun-Ra.

- **There were other awards** granted for valiant service. Land, slaves and other goods were distributed among brave soldiers. Some even won the right to be buried at the pharaoh's expense.

...FASCINATING FACT...
Bravery was rewarded. Necklaces with golden flies or bees were awarded to men who had excelled in combat by persistently 'stinging' Egypt's foes.

● **As the Egyptian army grew reliant** on the services of mercenaries, it became vulnerable to desertion and even rebellions. Herodotus writes of the toppling of King Apries (589–570 BC) by disgruntled foreign mercenaries.

● **The profession of soldier** seems to have been scorned by some other professions. The scribe Wenemdiamun warned students: 'Come, [let me tell] you the woes of the soldier, and how many are his superiors.'

● **Despite this**, it was possible for a talented soldier to increase his position in society through his achievements on the battlefield. There are examples of army commanders who became kings – notably Horemheb and Ramesses I.

◀ *Many Egyptian rulers believed that the king of the gods, Amun-Ra, fought with them in battle and helped them to victory.*

Buildings and technology

- **Buildings in ancient Egypt** were usually constructed from stone or mud-brick. Stone was reserved for temples and tombs.

- **Mud-brick** was ideally suited to the hot Egyptian climate. It baked quickly, kept the inside of buildings cool in the hot weather, and was simple to build with.

- **The Egyptians** were superb bricklayers. They used mud-bricks for everything from simple structures to great forts and city walls stretching for many miles.

- **Building materials** included yellow limestone from Al-Silsila Mount, white limestone from Tura, grey or red granite from Aswan and alabaster from central Egypt.

- **Rock monuments** such as the temple complex at Abu Simbel were carved out of cliffs. First the shape of the monument was cut out of the rock. Then masons smoothed walls and shaped columns.

◀ *The two temples at Abu Simbel were carved into a cliff. Outside the temple sit 20-m-high statues of King Ramesses II.*

▼ *To make bricks, mud from the river was mixed with sand, straw and water, poured into moulds and then removed and left to dry in the sun.*

● **Teams of sculptors**, plasterers and painters were employed in the final building stages to add embellishment.

● **Temples and tombs** were constructed from solid stones using copper or bronze tools. Blocks, columns and crowns, beams and ceilings were hoisted over earth ramps to the top of sand heaps adjacent to walls. Rollers, ropes and levers were used to lift the materials.

● **Teams of workers** were employed to row boats that carried huge stones across the Nile, and then haul these gigantic blocks to their destination.

● **Masons were employed** to smooth walls and shape columns. Smooth stones were used to give an even finish.

● **Copper and bronze tools** were used to chisel out both soft limestone and harder rocks and stone, and to inscribe fine text on them.

● **Major building works** were usually carried out during flood season when labour was most readily available. Farmers with no other work during this period were often enlisted as unskilled labourers by royal officials.

81

Transport

- **Most ancient Egyptians** travelled everywhere on foot. Sandals were the preferred footwear, but for long distances they were taken off and carried to avoid excessive wear and tear. Sticks were used for support and also as weapons against bandits.

- **Chariots were invented** by the Sumerians in about 3000 BC. The Egyptians used these wheeled vehicles for long journeys and in warfare.

- **For short journeys** the pharaoh was carried in a palanquin, or litter. This was a canopied chair hoisted up on two poles by four of the king's servants.

- **Sledges were used for transporting heavy statues**, as they were much stronger than wheeled vehicles.

- **Donkeys were used** for both riding and carrying heavy packs, and they were kept in huge numbers. Excavations of Aha's tomb at Abydos have uncovered ten donkey skeletons.

- **There is little evidence** of the camel being used by the ancient Egyptians. It was not introduced into the country until 500 BC.

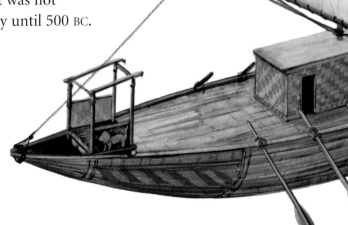

▶ *Sea merchants kept their ships close to shore. They were fitted with a large rectangular sail and only a few oars.*

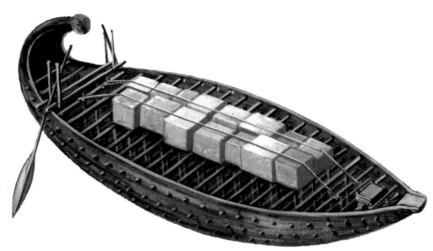

▶ *Simple wooden barges were essential to the Egyptians for the transport of heavy building materials such as blocks of stone.*

● **Archaeologists have uncovered an early hearse** in Egypt. In the tomb of the high priest Petosiris (300 BC) there is a painting of a mummy being transported on this vehicle.

● **The earliest Egyptian boats** were constructed of papyrus stalks bunched tightly together and strapped to a frame. The explorer Thor Heyerdahl successfully sailed a reconstruction of this type of boat from Egypt to America in 1970.

● **The famous Royal Ship** of King Cheops (Khufu) is a perfect example of a wooden boat, discovered around 1954.

● **Models of Egyptian river boats** show that they had small sails, were propelled by oars and were steered with a large oar at the stern (rear), which acted like a rudder.

Farming

- **Farming was very important** in ancient Egypt. Most Egyptians from the working classes worked on the land for at least part of the year. The growing season lasted for 8–9 months.

- **Egyptian farmers** divided the year into three seasons – 'Akhet' (June–September) was the flooding season. 'Peret' (October–February) was the growing season, and 'Shemu' (March–May) was the harvesting season.

- **Land belonged to the king** or to institutions such as temples. Field boundaries were marked out with stones. Officials checked these every two years to make sure no land had been stolen, and also to ensure that the farmer was paying the correct amount of his crop to the king in taxes.

- **The most important crops** were emmer wheat and barley, which were used to make bread and beer. Also important were flax, to make linen, and papyrus, to make paper.

- **Farmers grew vegetables** including onions, garlic, leeks, radishes, lettuce, cucumbers, lentils, beans and many kinds of spices.

...FASCINATING FACT...
Records exist that show that baboons were used to help
with the harvest. They were trained to pick fruit.

- **Fruit included** melons, pomegranates, vines, figs, dates and apples. When the fruit of a date tree was ripe, men climbed the trunk carrying knives between their teeth to cut down the harvest.

- **A good harvest** depended on the height of the Nile flood. If it was too low, the crops would be parched. Too high and they would be washed away.

- **Irrigation** was essential to good farming. The fields were watered by a system of canals, the 'shaduf' (water scoop) or the 'sakkia' (water wheel).

- **Animals were used** to trample seeds into the ground or to plough the fields after flood season.

▼ *Farming not only provided food but was also
a way for the pharaoh to gather taxes.*

Buying and selling

▲ *Egyptian workers carried their oil to market. It would then be exchanged for anything they needed.*

● **Trade took place** through bartering – goods were swapped for items of equivalent value instead of money. The value of goods would be given in terms of their equivalent in weight to a type of copper called a deben.

● **Sales recorded on stone** provide insights to the rates of exchange. This was never constant because the value of something depended on its availability.

● **At market places** in towns, villages and quaysides, people met to swap goods. They were also frequented by travelling salesmen looking to pick up interesting merchandise.

● **Foreign coins** were introduced to Egypt in the 5th century BC. In the 4th century BC the Egyptians began to mint their own coins.

● **Lending money** was fairly common. Sometimes these were informal loans – other times they were official loans with interest rates that could reach rates of up to 200 percent!

- **As early as the Pre-Dynastic Period**, merchants were buying exotic items to bring into Egypt, including leopard skins, giraffe tails, monkeys, ivory and gold.

- **The army organized** international trading expeditions. These were often dangerous. Hatshepsut's expedition to Punt took over three years.

- **Historians** are not exactly sure where the land of Punt was. It is thought to have been in the region of the river Atbara in what is now Ethiopia.

- **The ancient Egyptians** usually traded with the adjacent countries along the Mediterranean Sea and the Nile River to the south. At various times they set up trade routes to Cyprus, Crete, Greece, Syro-Palestine, Punt and Nubia.

- **Greek traders** were such regular visitors to Egypt that they were permitted to set up their own town in the Nile Delta.

▼ *Egyptians bought goods at the marketplace by bartering items such as food or textiles they had made themselves.*

87

Building the pyramids

- **The construction of the pyramids** was an astounding feat. The Great Pyramid at Giza was built using over 2 million stone blocks, each weighing 2.5 tonnes. The work was completed using quite primitive technology.

- **Pyramids required a site** on the west bank of the Nile, close to the river so that it was easy to transport stones, but also above flood level. A pyramid needed a strong foundation to support its massive weight.

- **After the ground was levelled**, the next task was to calculate true north, so that the sides of the pyramid could be lined up with the four compass points, probably by using the stars.

- **A pharaoh** would bless the foundations before work began. He would perform sacred rites including marking out the foundations, cutting the earth, pouring seed and moulding the first brick.

- **Ensuring the stone blocks** were smooth was the job of the masons, or stonecutters. They used tools called boning rods – two handles joined by a sharp cutting cord.

- **The core of the pyramid** and the outer casing were made from limestone. Granite was used for coffins, chambers and passages. Sculptures were made from sandstone, and basalt was used to make coffins (sarcophagi).

- **Egyptologists** have found many tools left by pyramid workers. Most were crude devices including rock drills, mallets, clamps and chisels.

- **A huge army** of workers would have been needed to build the Great Pyramid. It is likely that most of the workers were farmers who left their land during the flood season.

● **Historians believe** teams of builders used wooden sledges to drag the huge stone blocks into position, then pulled them up a ramp made of brick and mud.

● **When moving the stones**, the workers probably laid logs across the ramp to prevent the sledges getting lodged in the mud, and make them easier to move.

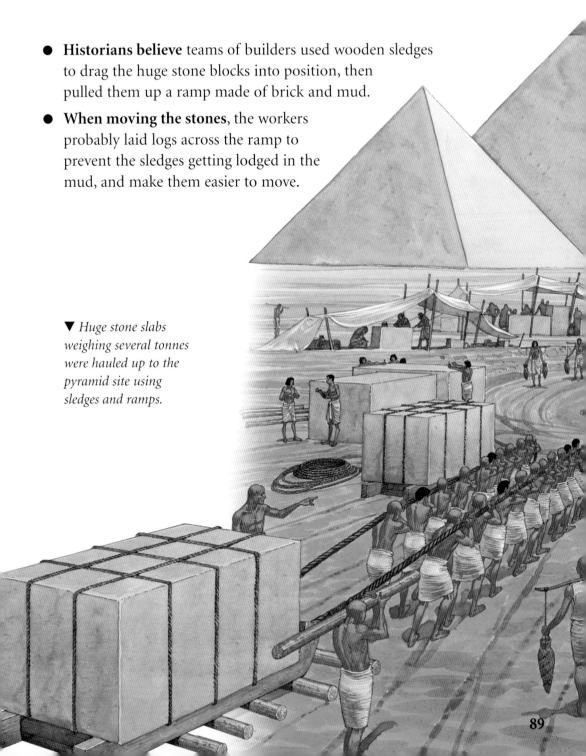

▼ *Huge stone slabs weighing several tonnes were hauled up to the pyramid site using sledges and ramps.*

Servants and slavery

- **Most slaves** in ancient Egypt were prisoners of war or foreigners. On rare occasions, poor Egyptians were forced to sell their children into slavery.

- **A slave had some legal rights.** They were allowed to marry a free person and own property. They could even marry a member of the family they were employed by.

- **A slave could be employed** to perform a number of tasks, ranging from manual labour to government administration. Many thousands were employed in temples.

- **Foreign female slaves** were employed in Egyptian homes to do housework or make clothes. They were often employed by the lady of the house.

- **Egyptian slaves could buy or work** their way to freedom. They could hold important positions in government, and several became high officials in the pharaoh's court.

- **Slaves were often given away as presents**, or could be left in a will to family members who then had to look after the slaves and their families.

- **Sometimes slaves were freed** by their owners. This practice was called manumission. It was not unknown for some slaves to then be adopted by the family of their former owner.

> ...FASCINATING FACT...
> During the Pre-dynastic Period, if the pharaoh died, his slaves would be buried alive with him along with the rest of his possessions.

- **Ownership of slaves** was not restricted to the elite. Some workmen at Deir El-Medina owned personal slaves – one worker owned 12.

- **Films depicting miserable slaves** toiling away at the pyramids are inaccurate. The bulk of the pyramid building was done by peasant farmers during the flood season.

▼ *Servants were responsible for everything from cooking and cleaning to helping their masters and mistresses get dressed in the morning.*

Doctors

- **Egyptian doctors** were famed throughout the ancient world. They relied on magic and medicine to treat their patients, with limited success.

- **Illness was usually regarded** as the result of evil spirits punishing wrongful behaviour. It was rare for a doctor to look purely at the physical symptoms of disease. Doctors would often work with a magician.

- **Prayers to the gods** (especially to Sekhmet, the goddess of healing) were in some cases accompanied by the injection of foul-smelling medicines into the ears or nostrils.

- **It was thought that plants** had both medicinal and magical properties. Some, such as garlic, have been scientifically proven by modern doctors to have great health benefits.

▶ *An Egyptian doctor applies a herbal preparation to a sick patient.*

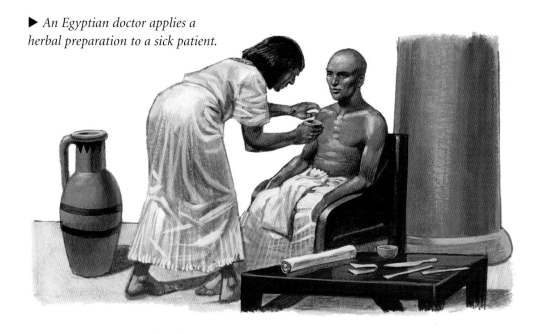

- **The ancient equivalents of doctors** were called 'sinws'. There were also surgeons, called 'priests of Sekhmet', and dental and veterinary practitioners. Doctors were always male.

- **Egyptian doctors** gave out prescriptions. Medical records listing 876 prescriptions for complaints such as stomach problems and skin irritations have been found, along with books that explain how doctors dealt with broken bones and hippo bites.

- **Doctors weighed** out the ingredients of their medicines according to a system known as 'the eye of Horus'.

- **Mummies** show us that people's teeth were usually in poor condition. Dentists prescribed opium to treat severe pain or drilled down into the jawbone.

- **Doctors were also expected** to treat cosmetic problems. They prescribed lotions for skin care, and ointments and remedies to stop hair loss, which included blood and fats from crocodiles, snakes and other wild animals.

▼ *Garlic was a very important healing agent to the ancient Egyptians, just as it still is today to people in many Mediterranean countries.*

Gods

- **The ancient Egyptians** worshipped hundreds of gods. Many were represented by animals. The Egyptian word for 'god' was denoted by a flagpole sign in hieroglyphics (ancient Egyptian script).

- **The sun god Ra** was the most important of all the gods. He could take many forms, including Khepri (a scarab beetle) and Re-Harakhty (a great hawk).

- **The Egyptians believed** that Ra created everything on Earth, as well as the underworld and the other gods that inhabited it. Ra was king of the gods and protector of the pharaoh. He was usually shown as a falcon-headed man wearing a sun disc.

- **The moon god Thoth** was the god of writing, medicine and mathematics, and was the patron of the scribes. He was represented by the ibis because its beak was shaped like the crescent moon.

- **Osiris, god of the dead**, represented the resurrection into eternal life that Egyptians sought by having their corpses embalmed. Mythology states that Osiris was murdered by his brother Seth, but was brought back to life by his wife and sister Isis.

- **The pharaoh** was thought to be the embodiment of the god Horus. This hawk-headed god was the child of Osiris and Isis and the nephew of Seth. He avenged his father's murder by killing Seth.

- **Seth, the red god**, was the Egyptian god of chaos. He was the embodiment of evil, and the murderer of Osiris. The *Book of the Dead* refers to Seth as the 'Lord of the northern sky', responsible for clouds and storms.

- **Ptah was the chief god** of Memphis. The Egyptians believed that he created the Moon, the Sun and the Earth.

- **Bes was a dwarf god** who was believed to guard against evil spirits and bad luck. He became a popular household god throughout Egypt.

- **Khnum was a god of fertility** and creation. With a ram's head and wavy horns, he guarded the source of the Nile.

▼ *Anubis was the canine god of the dead. He was associated with the embalming and mummification process, and was the guardian of burial places.*

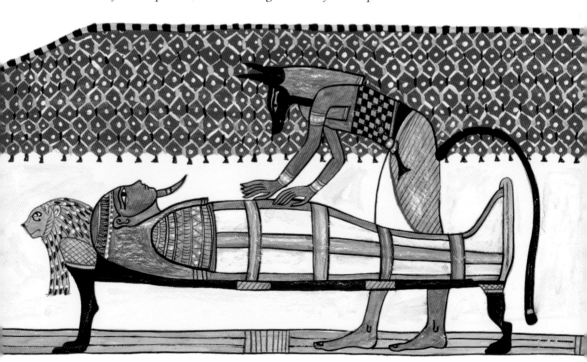

Goddesses

- **Isis was the mother goddess** of fertility and nature. Her worship was combined with that of her brother and husband, Osiris, and her son Horus.

- **Sekhemet was the goddess of love** and protection. Doctors and other healers prayed for her aid. She was depicted as a lioness and was often shown holding a *sistrum* – a musical instrument dedicated to Hathor.

- **Hathor, daughter of the sun god Ra**, was goddess of the sky and of love, mirth and beauty. She was also a goddess of fertility, and of the dead.

- **The Two Ladies** were fierce goddesses called Wadjyt and Nekhbet. They defended the sun god and the pharaohs against their enemies.

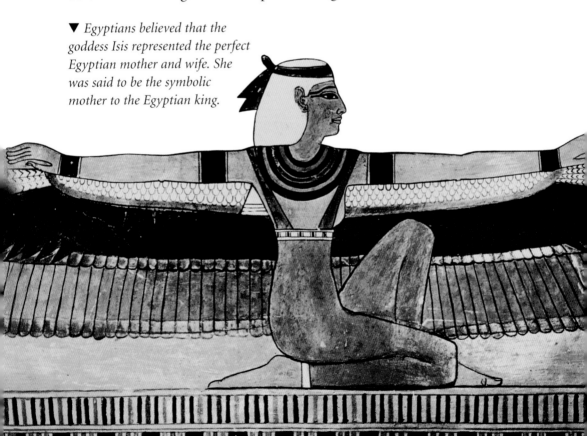

▼ *Egyptians believed that the goddess Isis represented the perfect Egyptian mother and wife. She was said to be the symbolic mother to the Egyptian king.*

▶ *Bastet was a cat goddess who was thought to be the daughter of the sun god. She was often depicted as a woman with the head of a lioness, and later simply as a cat-headed woman.*

- **The cat goddess Bastet** was the daughter of Ra. Her main temple was in the Delta region, where an archaeologists discovered a cemetery stuffed full of mummified cats.

- **Nut was the Egyptian's sky goddess**. She was depicted as a nude or as a giant cow. Legend says she swallowed the sun every evening and gave birth to it again every morning.

- **Nut also protected the dead** and assisted in their rebirth. A spell inside a pyramid reads 'Oh my mother Nut, spread yourself above me so that I can be placed among the unchanging stars and never die.'

- **The goddess Neith** was thought to have made order and chaos, and good and evil. Her blessing often appears on shrouds and mummy bandages.

- **Nephythys was a child** of the earth god Keb and the sky goddess Nut. She was believed to be the goddess of the dead, and appeared as a woman or as a small bird of prey. She was unhappily married to Seth.

- **Taweret was a strange-looking goddess**. She was depicted as part lion, part hippopotamus and part crocodile. She was a kind and generous figure who protected women and children.

Priests

▼ *The mortuary temple of Queen Hatshepsut. Inside, 163 mummies of high-priests have been discovered.*

- **The pharaoh was the high priest** of Egypt, and the only priest allowed to be depicted in the temples. Thousands of lesser priests were employed to look after the temples.

- **A priest's main role** was to care for the temple. Scribes were usually appointed as priests, and in many cases the position became hereditary.

- **The pharaoh was supported** by the chief priest, or 'first prophet'. The 'second prophets' looked after the economy of the temple. The lower orders (wab priests) looked after more menial duties such as cleaning.

- **Documents and art** tell us that there were female priests until the New Kingdom. Many served as priestesses of the goddess Hathor.

- **Ordinary Egyptians were not allowed** inside the inner regions of the temples, and only saw the temple images of the gods during festival processions. They left offerings to the gods in the outer temple courts.

- **Priests were paid** with the offerings in the temple. The essence of these were thought to be consumed by the gods, but the priests ate the physical substance. Most priests worked in a shift system.

- **Some priests had specialist skills** and knowledge. In some parts of Egypt 'hour priests' skilled in astronomy were charged with determining when key festivals took place.

- **Priests had to wash** twice during the day and twice during the night. They also had to be clean-shaven, without body hair, and circumcised. They were not allowed to wear wool or leather.

- **Although religious knowledge** was not a necessary requirement for entering the priesthood, there were strict rules governing the profession, and priests were forbidden to discuss what went on inside a temple.

Temples

- **A temple was a building** or buildings that was considered to be the house of a god. After the pyramids, they were probably the most impressive structures in ancient Egypt.

- **The most important part** of any temple was the shrine, where the statue of the god was kept.

- **Each temple was dedicated** to a particular god, or a family of gods. Every day priests and priestesses would serve the statue with a selection of food and clothing, and play sweet music to it.

- **Few pre-New Kingdom temples** have survived as they were built out of reeds or mud-brick. Later temples were colossal stone buildings.

- **Egyptian temples were not places of worship** for the public. They were normally only visited by priests and kings, except sometimes during religious festivals.

- **Large temples** were funded by the Egyptian state. Some became small towns, with villages for the priests and workers, as well as schools, libraries and other facilities.

- **Temples also served as vast grain banks.** Taxes were collected in the form of this crop, and then later redistributed to workers as wages. Other buildings served as animal slaughterhouses, producing food to feed the temple staff.

- **From the later Middle Kingdom onwards**, massive ceremonial gateways called pylons were added to the temples to make them look more impressive.

- **These pylons were often flanked** by two needle-shaped monuments called obelisks. These were dedicated to the sun god.

- **The Egyptians held many annual festivals** to celebrate their gods and goddesses. People were allowed inside the temples to celebrate.

▼ *Massive pylons often flanked the entrance to great Egyptian temples such as Luxor, followed by a large courtyard.*

Life after death

- **The ancient Egyptians** did not believe that death was the end of life. They believed that if you prayed to the gods and looked after the body through mummification, you could continue to live in another world.

- **The Egyptians believed** that three parts of a person lived on after death – the soul ('Akh'), the life force ('Ka'), and the memory and personality ('Ba'). They also believed that a person's name and their shadow were real entities.

- **After death**, a person's ka would rest while the body was mummified. It then needed to be reactivated for the spiritual transformation of rebirth. A person's ba made this journey through the underworld of Duat.

- **Duat was believed to exist** deep below the Earth. It was a perilous place that the deceased would need every possible help to navigate their way through safely.

- **The Books of the Dead** were exquisitely decorated scrolls of papyrus made as passports through the treacherous world of Duat. They have often been found by archaeologists in the tombs of mummies, sometimes even wrapped in the bandages!

- **Before entering the afterlife**, the deceased was expected to deny all the evil deeds they might have committed in their lifetime. They appeared before the goddess of truth, Maat, to make this proclamation.

- **A dead person's heart** was weighed against Maat. The scales were held by Anubis, while the god Thoth recorded the judgement.

- **If you passed this test**, you were fit to enter paradise – known as the Fields of Iaru or the Field of Reeds. Ancient Egyptians believed this took the form of an agricultural heaven, the domain of Osiris, where the crops were of gigantic proportions.

- **If you failed the test**, your heart would be devoured by a beast called Ammut, who was part crocodile, part lion and part hippopotamus. You would not survive the afterlife.

- **If you failed to enter paradise**, you were sent back as an evil spirit or illness to the land of the living, to be hated and feared by both men and the gods.

▼ *After death and mummification, the Ba left the body and began the journey from the tomb to the underworld.*

Making a mummy

- **A mummy is a dead body** preserved by drying. The term comes from the Egyptian word 'Mum', meaning 'wax', referring to the process of wrapping the corpse in a waxed cloth to stop it rotting away.

- **There had been attempts** at preserving royal corpses during the Old Kingdom, but the practice became common during the Middle Kingdom and reached a peak during the New Kingdom.

- **It was believed** that by preserving the body through mummification the spirit (Ka) of the deceased would be able to live again.

- **We know about the process** of mummy making from tomb illustrations and from the writings of the Greek historian Herodotus.

- **The dead body** was taken to a place called the House of Beauty, where the embalming would be carried out. The body was washed, and the brain was pulled out through the nose with an iron hook.

- **A slit was made** in the left side of the body and the liver, lungs, stomach and intestines were removed and put in special canopic jars. The heart was left in place.

- **The body was packed** with a chemical called natron to dehydrate it. It was left for 40 days and then stuffed with herbs to take away the smell. The skin was rubbed with ointment and coated with resin.

- **The mummy was wrapped** in linen bandages. Amulets and jewellery were wrapped into the bandages to help the deceased in the afterlife.

- **A painted mask** was sometimes put over the mummy's head. In the case of a king this could be spectacularly ornate. The mummy was then placed in the coffin, ready for the funeral.

◄ *The name of the priest in charge of mummification was 'hery seshta' (overseer of the mysteries). He represented the god Anubis.*

105

Funerals and burials

● **The type of burial an ancient Egyptian** was given depended on their wealth. Most peasants were buried in shallow round pits lying on their left side, facing west, with a few of their possessions scattered around.

▼ *In the ritual of the opening of the mouth, the jaw of the coffin was 'opened' using an adze (a tool with a bronze blade). The wall painting below (from Tutankhamun's burial chamber) shows Ay performing the ceremony for the deceased king. Ay became the next pharaoh.*

- **For wealthy Egyptians**, funerals were lengthy occasions. The deceased were taken to their resting place in a funerary cortege with priests, family members and even a group of professional mourners.

- **The family** walked behind the coffin. As a sign of respect, men would be unshaven and women wore blue headbands.

- **Offerings were made** in the name of the pharaoh, as he was the connection between men and the gods. The eldest son was then expected to carry out rituals that were the duties of the heir and successor.

- **The mummy of the deceased** was transported to its final resting place where the 'Opening of the Mouth' ritual was performed, to restore the mummy's senses so that it could see, breathe and hear again in the afterlife.

- **In the Offering Ritual**, the priest recited spells to ensure the spirit of the dead person had everything it needed in the afterlife.

- **By the time of the Old Kingdom**, the rich were buried in grand tombs called *mastabas*. These were thought of as homes for the dead, and they contained rooms for everything the deceased might need for the afterlife.

- **Mastabas contained chapels** fitted with false doors. The Egyptians believed that the spirit of the deceased could go through them to receive offerings and then return to the afterlife. Food and drink were also left for the dead.

- **The soul of the dead** was believed to journey with the sun around the world. A model of the deceased in a boat was often included in tombs from the Middle Kingdom onwards to represent this journey.

- **By the late New Kingdom**, and with the threat of tomb robberies, the lavish tombs with expensive coffins and fittings were replaced with more secretive burials in places that could be more easily protected.

A king's resting place

- **Pyramids have square bases** and four triangular sides sloping up to the top to a pointed tip. Over 80 have been found, most built as royal tombs.

- **Egypt's pyramids** are on the west bank of the Nile. In the Old Kingdom, they were built around Memphis. In the Middle Kingdom, pyramids were built further south.

- **The stepped pyramid** contained a series of burial chambers for the king and his family. It was surrounded by a series of courtyards and ceremonial buildings.

- **Festivals were held** in the courtyards. In the Sed festival, the pharaoh ran round a track to symbolize a renewal of his powers before being re-crowned.

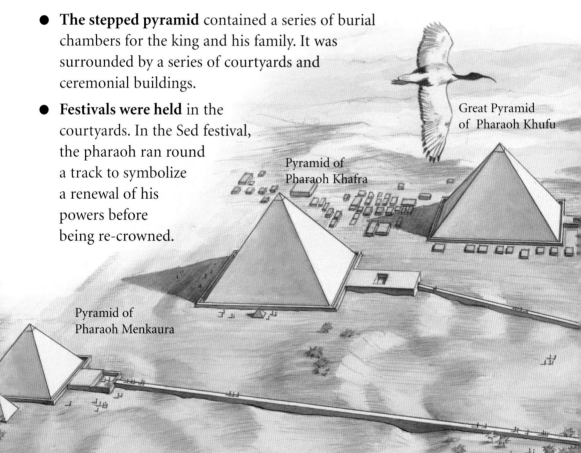

Great Pyramid of Pharaoh Khufu

Pyramid of Pharaoh Khafra

Pyramid of Pharaoh Menkaura

...FASCINATING FACT...

The contents of the stepped pyramid at Saqqara were looted long ago, and when archaeologists finally entered the tomb, only a mummified foot remained!

- **The first smooth pyramid** was developed by Pharaoh Sneferu. It was built out of massive slabs rather than small blocks. The steps were filled in to produce a true pyramid shape.

- **Three great pyramids** were built by Egyptian pharaohs at Giza. These were the pyramids of Menkaura, Khafra and Khufu.

- **The largest pyramid** is the Great Pyramid of Khufu at Giza. It was built for Pharaoh Khufu around 2550 BC. Its sides are almost perfectly aligned with true north, south, east and west.

- **Ten pyramids** stand at Giza. Three pharaohs insisted that smaller pyramids be built alongside their own, for their wives. These are known as Queen's pyramids.

- **The architecture of the pyramids** has influenced architects all over the world. Pyramid tombs have been used in Europe for centuries, and the shape is also used for many innovative building projects today.

◀ *The complex at Giza contains Khufu's great pyramid, and the pyramids of Khafra and Menkaura. The smaller pyramids belonging to queens.*

109

The Great Pyramid

- **The Great Pyramid** of Giza is one of the Seven Wonders of the Ancient World, constructed for Pharaoh Khufu about 4500 years ago. Until the completion of the Eiffel Tower in 1887, it was the tallest structure ever built.

- **The pyramid's ancient name** was 'The Pyramid which is the Place of Sunrise and Sunset'. Its sides were covered with gleaming white limestone, and the tip of the pyramid was capped with gold to reflect the sun's rays.

- **Inside the Great Pyramid** a labyrinth of passages and chambers lead to the king's chamber. The queen's chamber was below this.

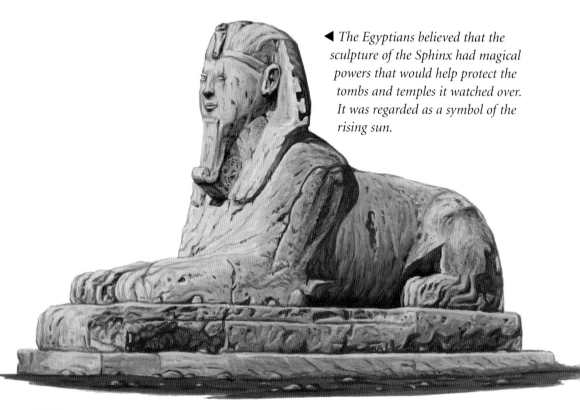

◄ *The Egyptians believed that the sculpture of the Sphinx had magical powers that would help protect the tombs and temples it watched over. It was regarded as a symbol of the rising sun.*

...FASCINATING FACT...

The Great Pyramid contains about 2 million blocks of stone, each weighing over 2 tonnes. Together with the other two pharaoh's pyramids at Giza, there is enough stone to build a 3 m high wall around France.

- **An investigation** into one of the air shafts leading from the queen's chamber in 1993 revealed a blockage half-way along the passage, which might be a fourth chamber or the end of the shaft. Permission for further investigations has not yet been granted.

- **On the east side of the Great Pyramid** stands Khufu's mortuary temple and in front stands the Sphinx.

- **The Great Pyramid was emptied** by grave robbers long ago. Archaeologists did find a stone sarcophagus inside the king's chamber. It was larger than the door, and must have been put there as the pyramid was being built.

- **The Sphinx was a mythical beast**, with the body of a lion and the head of a king. A gigantic stone statue of one has watched over the ancient pyramids for over 4500 years. The sculpture has been submerged in sand for most of its history.

- **In the 19th century**, European tourists paid local people to carry them up to the top of Khufu's pyramid. Many were killed on the treacherous climb, and it is now against the law.

- **Today, the Great Pyramid** is very near to the modern Egyptian capital, Cairo, and the stone is being damaged by pollution from the cars and factories of the busy city.

Valley of
the Queens

- **The Valley of the Queens,** on the west bank of the Nile at Thebes, was the main cemetery for royal wives and children during the New Kingdom. It is called 'Set Neferu', which means 'seat of beauty'.

- **There are about 75 tombs** in the valley. They usually consist of a small antechamber followed by a corridor that leads to the burial chamber.

▼ *The tomb of Nefertari has the best preserved paintings of any Egyptian site yet discovered. They depict the Queen's journey to the afterlife.*

- **When the tombs** of the Valley of the Queens were discovered by the Italian archaeologist Ernesto Schiaparelli at the beginning of the 20th century, they were in a bad condition. Some were in use as donkey stables.

- **The most famous** and the most spectacular tomb belongs to Queen Nefertari, wife of Ramesses II (1279–1213 BC).

- **Nefertari's tomb** contains art depicting the queen worshipping the mummified body of Osiris and offering milk to the goddess Hathor.

- **Despite the Valley's name,** it also contains the tombs of several princes of the New Kingdom, including the sons of Ramesses III – Khaemwaset II and Amenherkhepeshef.

- **Prince Kamuast** had a tomb similar to that of a pharaoh, but much smaller. It is brightly decorated, with scenes of offerings and tributes.

- **Scenes in Prince Khaemweset's tomb** offer a valuable insight into the Egyptian view of the afterlife. He is shown being presented to the guardians of the gates with his father, making an offering and dressed in a robe.

- **Thiti is thought to be the wife** of Ramesses IV. Her tomb has now been restored, and features a beautiful embossed decoration on limestone.

> ....FASCINATING FACT...
> The Valley of the Queens was once known as Ta-Set-Neferu ('the place of the Children of the Pharaoh'), because many princes and princesses were buried there.

Valley of the Kings

- **The Valley of the Kings** also lies on the west bank of the Nile, and is actually made up of an east and a west valley. It contains many of the tombs of pharaohs from the New Kingdom, including Tutankhamun and Ramesses II.

- **The eastern valley** is the burial place of kings of the 18th–20th Dynasties. The western valley (also called the Cemetery of the Monkeys) contains just four tombs, including that of Amenhotep III.

- **At first, tomb entrances** were disguised to prevent anyone locating them. When this practice ended, guards were appointed to watch over the tombs instead, with much less success.

- **Most tombs** were cut into the limestone. They contained three corridors, an antechamber and a sarcophagus chamber. These burial chambers were harder to rob and more skilfully concealed from potential thieves.

- **The corridors ended with the burial chamber** where the pharaoh's body was placed, surrounded by the finest treasures of Egypt. Paintings of gods and goddesses covered the ceiling and walls.

- **The Valley required the skills** of dozens of workmen who lived in the village of Deir-el-Medina. The village thrived for over 500 years and sustained up to 60 families. Its stone foundations still stand.

> **...FASCINATING FACT...**
> Egyptian legend says that the Valley of the Kings was protected by a goddess called Meretseger. She took the form of a cobra and was believed to kill anyone who had evil in mind, or who swore false oaths.

- **The tomb of Seti I** is the longest in the valley – 120 m – and is covered with colourful paintings. The paintings show scenes of the Opening of the Mouth ritual and engraved passages from the *Book of the Dead*.

- **Tutankhamun's tomb** is one of the smallest in the Valley.

- **Despite all the precautions** the Egyptians took, nearly all the tombs in the Valley of the Kings have been looted.

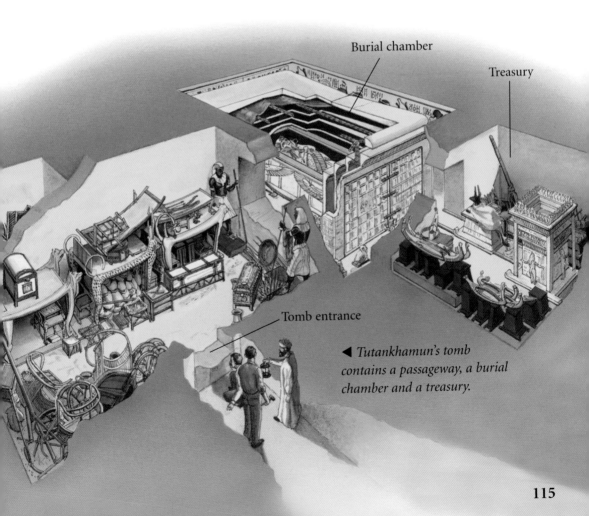

Burial chamber

Treasury

Tomb entrance

◄ *Tutankhamun's tomb contains a passageway, a burial chamber and a treasury.*

Saqqara

- **Saqqara was part of the royal cemetery** of Memphis, and was one of the most important sites in ancient Egypt.

- **It was in use as a burial ground** from the 1st Dynasty to the Christian period. Today it is packed with tombs and galleries.

▲ *Many of the tombs at Saqqara contain spectacular wall paintings, made by mixing mineral pigments with bone, glue and water to create a vibrant and lasting artwork.*

- **The step pyramid of Djoser**, built around 2650 BC, was the world's first monumental stone building. It had an underground burial chamber lined with granite, and a sealed chamber that held a statue of the king.

- **Saqqara became the resting place** for many generations of pharaohs. Kings from the 5th and 6th Dynasties were buried in smaller pyramids. Nobles were housed in tombs called *mastabas*.

- **The Pyramid Texts** were a series of beautiful, elaborate spells carved into the walls of some of the pyramids at Saqqara. They contain many references to the cult of the sun god Ra.

- **During the New Kingdom**, many important officials moved to the city of Memphis. When they died, they were buried at Saqqara.

- **By the Late Period**, vast numbers of sacred animals were being buried at the north end of Saqqara. These included baboons, ibis and hawks.

- **Most of the tombs at Saqqara** were built of very small stone blocks that were often dismantled and used elsewhere. The Christian monastery of Apa Jeremias is built almost entirely from Saqqara tomb blocks.

- **By the time of the Graeco-Roman period**, Saqqara had become a centre for pilgrims, but it remained a burial place for Egyptian leaders until the arrival of Christianity.

. . . .FASCINATING FACT. . . .
The most popular animals to be buried at Saqqara were cats.
Their remains were placed in private funerary monuments rather than in separate burial areas.

Magic and ritual

- **The ancient Egyptians** believed that magical powers came from the gods. The source of these powers was a force called *heka,* used to create the world and protect it from the forces of chaos.

- **They also believed** the gods bestowed magical powers on the pharaohs. Priests and magicians were also thought to possess magical powers.

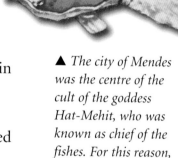

- **Hundreds of books** containing magic spells were kept in temple libraries. Some priests specialized in magic. Some priests were said to be able to turn statues into real objects.

▲ *The city of Mendes was the centre of the cult of the goddess Hat-Mehit, who was known as chief of the fishes. For this reason, fish amulets were commonly worn here.*

- **Many Egyptians thought** that magic could be used to manipulate people's behaviour. It was believed that a magician could use war spells to defend a country from invaders.

- **Some days** were regarded as unlucky in ancient Egypt. Papyrus calendars have some days ringed in red, a colour thought to represent the dry desert, and thus bad fortune.

- **For a magic spell to be successful**, the Egyptians believed that it had to be performed when the conditions were perfect. Dusk and dawn were thought to be good times to cast spells. It was also important that the ingredients for the spell were pure and of good quality.

◀ *The eye of Horus represented the act of healing. Amulets of this symbol were worn for protection and strength.*

▲ *The scarab amulet is made in the form of a scarab beetle. It was the symbol of Khepri, the sun god associated with resurrection. They were one of the most common types of amulets worn in ancient Egypt.*

● **Spells were often accompanied** by a ritual. Some spells required the magician to just wave their hands, while in other spells miniature figurines had to be burned, spat upon or stabbed for the spell to work.

● **Archaeologists have found special bricks** embedded in the side of several New Kingdom tombs. These were sets of four mud-bricks that the Egyptians believed were magical, and would protect the deceased from evil.

● **Each magic brick** held a specific object – an amulet, an Anubis or a shabti figure. Text from the *Book of the Dead* was inscribed on the bricks to defend the deceased from the enemies of Osiris.

. . . FASCINATING FACT . . .
Magic wands were made of bronze or ivory. Sometimes they were shaped like snakes because the goddess of magic, Selket, was depicted as a snake.

Dreams

- **The ancient Egyptians believed** that dreams held great power and called them 'revelations of the truth'. They were seen as a way of communicating the will of the gods and predicting the future.

- **Dream Books** have been found dating back to the Old Kingdom. They list dreams such as breaking stones, losing teeth, having one's face turn into a leopard, drinking warm beer and drowning in the Nile.

- **The library of Scribe Kenherkhopeshef** contained a Dream Book papyrus. It contains the interpretations of over 100 dreams. Most deal with the dreamer's gains and losses, or physical events.

- **The interpretation of a dream** was often based on verbal connections. The Egyptian words for 'donkey' and 'great' were the same, so a dream about a donkey meant good luck.

- **Thutmose IV was told in a dream** that if he cleared away the sand from the feet of the Sphinx at Giza he would become king of Egypt.

- **Revelatory dreams** were thought to be very important. These were dreams that might show the dreamer the location of hidden treasure or a medicine to cure a sick patient. Doctors sometimes asked patients to look for cures in these sorts of dreams.

- **'Teachings for Merikare'**, written by King Kheti between 2070 and 2100 BC, took the opposite approach. It advised that dreams actually meant the opposite of what they appeared to be about.

- **It was also believed** that dreams allowed the living to see the activities of the deceased. People were also afraid of being exposed to malicious spirits while they were sleeping.

- **From the Late Period**, people began to sleep in temple complexes hoping that the intentions of the gods might be communicated to them through divinely inspired dreams.
- **Special priests** were appointed from the Late Period onward to interpret these dreams. These priests were known by the Greek term 'onirocrites'.

DREAM	MEANING
Bed catching fire	Breakdown of a marriage
Cat	Omen of a good crop
Deep well	Time in prison
Mirror	Second marriage
Shining moon	Forgiveness
Plunging into cold waters	Absolution of all ills
Crocodile meat	Good luck
Warm beer	Bad luck

121

Houses and gardens

- **According to the Greek historian** Diodorus Siculus, Egyptian dwellings were constructed of papyrus reeds until the 1st century BC.

- **More sophisticated houses** were built using sun-dried bricks. This technique has been used for nearly 6000 years. Mud from the Nile was mixed with chaff and shaped with frames before being baked in the sun.

▼ *Noblemen usually had large houses in extensive grounds, surrounded by high walls.*

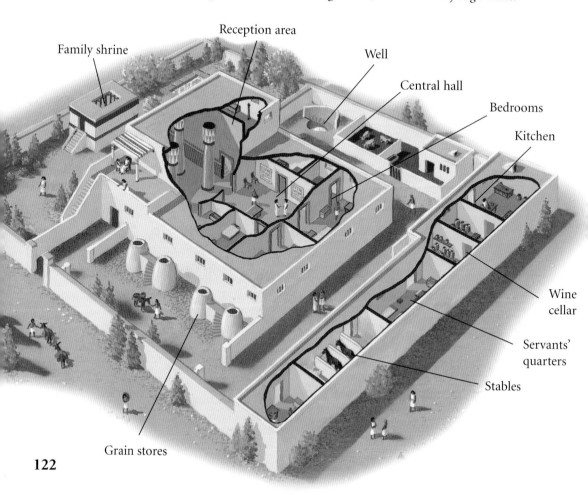

Family shrine

Reception area

Well

Central hall

Bedrooms

Kitchen

Wine cellar

Servants' quarters

Stables

Grain stores

...FASCINATING FACT...

Town houses stood two to three storeys high. The ground floor was usually reserved for businesses, while the upper floors provided family living space. Many people slept on their flat roofs in summer.

- **The rooms of larger houses** would have been arranged around an inner courtyard or on either side of a corridor. Windows would have been covered with shutters or blinds to keep out the dust, insects and constant heat.

- **A worker's house** had between two and four rooms at ground level, and an enclosed courtyard. There were two cellars for storage, and recesses in the walls for items such as household gods.

- **The houses of the rich** had several bedrooms, reception rooms and private quarters. Some may even have had bathrooms, toilets and swimming pools.

- **Water was drawn from wells** from the time of the New Kingdom. The water was raised with a shaduf into a pond.

- **Gardens were very popular**. Egyptian art shows gardens ranging from a few fruit trees to great botanical gardens with exotic trees and ponds, often stocked with fish, caged animals and birds.

- **Tomb paintings, engravings** and other pieces of art suggest that Egyptian gardens may have been very formal.

- **Gardeners were often employed** by wealthy Egyptians and in temples. They watered and weeded plants, and grew certain species from seed, including the date palm.

Hunting

- **The first people** to arrive in Egypt hunted wild animals to survive. These included ostriches, gazelles and giraffes. Scenes of these early chases are depicted in prehistoric cave art in Egypt.

- **Hippos were hunted** by men in papyrus boats armed with harpoons. This was because of the damage they did to crops.

- **Birds provided a rich source of food**, and were hunted and killed by hurling wooden throwsticks. Dogs and cats were trained to collect the birds struck down.

- **Small birds** were caught in nets. Large numbers of migrating species were caught when they landed after crossing the Mediterranean.

...FASCINATING FACT...
On a hunting expedition, the pharaoh rode out in his chariot accompanied by soldiers wearing full military dress. Amenhotep III once boasted of slaying 96 wild bulls during such a hunt.

- **Many examples of Egyptian wall art** depict birds being caught in nets. It was probably to illustrate the preservation of harmony, with the struggling birds in the nets representing the suppression of evil.

- **Fish were usually caught** in baskets made from willow branches, or with nets held between two boats. Bigger fish were tackled with spears. Fishing was also a way to relax and enjoy a day by the river.

- **Angling could be dangerous**. One species of catfish was armed with a poisonous spine. An Egyptian relief shows a man pulling one of these fish out of the catch and extracting the dangerous spine.

- **Wealthy Egyptians** may have been among the first people to have hunted for pleasure. They chased animals such as antelopes, foxes and hares for sport, together with the more dangerous wild bulls, elephants and lions.

- **Egyptian hunting scenes** often show kings tracking wild beasts inside enclosed grounds guarded by soldiers. These scenes have a hidden meaning. Wild creatures were associated with the wicked god Seth, so these pieces of art symbolized the pharaoh's triumph over evil.

▼ *The hippopotamus was viewed as an evil creature, because it often destroyed and ate crops. Hippo hunting was very important – if a king managed to kill a hippo, it was thought to symbolize the slaying of evil.*

Creation myths

- **Like many ancient cultures,** the Egyptians invented creation stories to explain how the world had come into existence.

- **One creation myth** suggested that the world had been made by a god called Ptah by the power of thought. He was depicted as a green-skinned mummy.

▼ *The Sun is linked with many of the Egyptian creation myths. The creator god Atum was a solar god, who was eventually renamed as the sun god Ra.*

- **Another story** puts forward the idea that the universe was originally a sea of chaos inside a god called Nun. One day, a mound of land rose out of this sea, and gradually formed the land of Egypt.

- **Nun was a god of chaos** and infinity, greatly feared by the ancient Egyptians. They believed that he might one day sink the world back into the ocean of chaos.

- **They also believed** that Nun was responsible for darkness, as every night he carried the sun god Ra away through the underworld until the next morning.

- **Ra was the god of the sun** and light. The Egyptians believed that a blue lotus flower appeared on the dark waters of Nun, and unfurled its petals to reveal Ra, who then created the world and everything in it.

- **The Egyptians did not understand** the way the Earth rotates around the sun and why the sun rises and sets every day. They believed the sun was rolled across the sky every day by the god Khepri.

- **Night and day** was explained by the story of the twin gods Nut and Keb. They hugged each other so tightly they blocked out the sun's rays, upsetting the sun god Ra.

- **To create daylight**, Ra ordered that the twins be separated and Nut was raised up to become the sky. Keb became the Earth. As night fell, the twins were reunited, as Nut came down to earth to be with her brother.

- **The Egyptians believed** that the sun god Ra was the first pharaoh. After Ra, they thought that all pharaohs came into the world as humans.

Dance

- **The ancient Egyptians loved to dance**. Pottery vessels dating from before the Pre-dynastic period have been found, decorated with dancers raising their arms above their heads.

- **Professional dancers** were usually women. Scenes suggest they wore skirts or loose tunics with shoulder straps. Sometimes they appeared covered in long shawls.

- **Many ancient wall paintings and carvings** depict scenes of Egyptians singing and dancing. It is difficult to tell exactly what the dance movements of the Egyptians were like, but the scenes show them clapping, hopping and skipping.

- **Dancers also performed acrobatics** including backbends, flips, cartwheels, high-kicks and handstands.

- **Archaeologists have yet to find** any depictions of men and women dancing together. The most common scenes show solo dancers, or groups of female dancers, usually performing in pairs.

- **During the Old Kingdom**, funeral rituals often included dance. Dance was an expression of mourning for the dead and a way of marking the regeneration of the body.

- **Other groups of dancers** followed the funerary procession to the tomb. The *mww*-dancers performed as the procession reached the tomb. Their dance symbolized the dead being led to the underworld.

- **Dance was a way of celebrating** the joy and revelry of feast days.

- **Dancing in temples** marked important festivals such as the jubilee ceremony, known as the Sed. This usually involved a solemn procession carrying a statue of the temple god.

▲ *Dancing was often combined with gymnastics and acrobatics in ancient Egypt.*

● **Dancing dwarfs** were a special attraction. The Egyptians believed that they never grew old because they never grew past the height of a child. Pepy II praised one of his officials for bringing back a dwarf for 'god's dances' from a southern expedition.

Music

- **Egyptian art suggests** that musicians were nearly always men in the Old Kingdom. By the time of the New Kingdom, they were mostly women.

- **There is no evidence** to suggest that the ancient Egyptian used any form of musical notation. Some ancient Egyptian instruments have survived, while many more are depicted on pottery and other artefacts dating back to the Pre-dynastic era.

- **A wide variety** of percussion instruments were played. Rhythms were beaten out on tambourines, ivory clappers, drums, castanets, cymbals and an array of chiming bells.

- **Stringed instruments** included the lyre (a form of lute) and the harp. These resemble versions that were introduced from Asia.

- **Wind instruments** included wooden pipes (similar to modern Egyptian folk clarinets) and early flutes, which were made from reeds and later, bronze. Bugle-like trumpets were used in religious ceremonies and in battle.

- **Festivals and holy days** were marked by music and singing. Groups of musicians would sometimes have to entertain thousands of people.

- **Such festivals were frequent**. One village in the Fayum region dedicated 150 days every year to feasting in the name of the gods.

...FASCINATING FACT...

Both men and women could be musicians in ancient Egypt, but there were some instruments that were played only by men, and some that were played only by women.

- **Music was also** a part of everyday life, providing a natural rhythm to workers' tasks. Farm labourers sang to their livestock, and sticks were clapped together as grapes were crushed at harvest time.

- **In Old and Middle Kingdom tombs**, inscriptions of songs and hymns were sung to the accompaniment of a harp to celebrate the dead.

▼ *Stringed instruments such as harps and lutes were often played during banquets in ancient Egypt.*

Sports

- **It was important** that young men were in good physical condition because it was always possible that they would have to go into the army. Kings, princes and statesmen usually supported sports competitions.

- **Early versions of many modern sports** were played to strict rules. Inscriptions reveal that a wide variety of sports were played, from wrestling and weightlifting, to a host of ball games.

▼ *Scenes of ancient Egyptians boxing for sport were found in the tomb of 'Mery Ra' and the 'Ptah Hotep' tomb in Saqqara.*

- **The ancient Egyptians invented** many aspects of sport that are still in use today. These included neutral referees, uniforms for players and awarding medals to winners.

- **The sport of handball**, depicted on the Saqqara tombs, was played by four women. Each had to throw the ball to the other at the same time. Players could be on their feet or on a teammate's back while exchanging balls.

- **The Saqqara tombs** depict boxing scenes. Two fighters stand fist to fist, dressed only in loincloths. Pharaohs and princes paid to watch.

- **Ball games were popular** among Egyptian boys. Balls made of leather skins filled with tightly-bound papyrus reeds were used in a number of hockey-type games.

- **Swimming was the most popular** competitive sport. The Nile was often used to practise in, but swimming pools were also built in palaces for the use of noblemen.

- **Long-distance running** was a most important sport in ancient Egypt. It had a religious significance when a new pharaoh was being crowned.

- **As part of the coronation**, the king ran a long distance around a temple before spectators, to show his physical strength and ability to rule using his might as well as his brain.

- **Archery was a popular sport**, and the practise of it was also important training for battle. Amenhotep II boasted that he pierced the middle of a thick brass target with four arrows. He offered a prize to anyone who could do the same.

Games and toys

- **Board games** were hugely popular in ancient Egypt. They were enjoyed by both adults and children. Board games and toys are among the oldest items found in Egypt.

- *Senet* **was a game** in which two players competed to be the first reach the kingdom of the gods. Each player had between five and seven pieces at one end of the papyrus board. The object of the game was to move all your pieces to the other end.

- **One of the oldest board games** was *Mehen*, or 'snake'. Players moved pieces around a spiral board until they reached the snake's head in the centre.

- **The game Hounds and Jackals** may be the forerunner of Snakes and Ladders. The oldest board found dates from the First Intermediate Period.

- **Toys were usually simple** and were fashioned out of wood, stone, ivory, ceramics or bone. Surviving examples range from skittles and dolls to whipping-tops and throwsticks.

- **Some of the toys** are fairly elaborate. The British Museum holds a model of a crocodile with a moving jaw. Toys with moving parts that could be made to spin by pulling strings have been found at el Lisht.

- **Children played against each other** for marbles. Their game seems to have been based on a miniature version of skittles.

> ...FASCINATING FACT...
> Archaeologists have discovered mysterious rows of holes bored into the roofs and floors of Egyptian temples. Some think that these were used for a board game called Wari, which is still played in Africa today.

▲ *Board games were a popular family pursuit. Children played with simple toys that were often home-made.*

- **Egyptian children played** games such as leapfrog, tug-of-war, arm-wrestling and juggling. Some of these are shown in paintings and carvings.

- **Many of the games** Egyptian children played may have been early versions of modern games such as Grandmother's Footsteps and Blind-man's Buff.

Ancient storytelling

- **Egyptian stories** were passed on verbally through generations. Some were written down on papyrus and *ostraka* – 'scraps of pottery'.

- **Stories were told for entertainment** but many also contained important, often moral, messages.

- **The earliest written story** dates from the Middle Kingdom and was composed in Middle Egyptian, the classical language of that period.

▼ *The legend of Osiris tells that he was the dead form of an earthly ruler who rose from the dead to become king of the gods.*

- **Ancient autobiographies** have been discovered, including the life story of the official Weni, who served from the reign of King Teti to that of King Merenre. In it, Weni greatly exaggerates his position in court.

- **One of the oldest stories** was the tale of the courtier Sinuhe, preserved in six papyri and two dozen *ostraka*. It tells of his flight from Egypt after the death of King Amenemhat. After many years, Sinuhe writes a letter begging for forgiveness from King Senusret I, who allows Sinuhe to return and be reinstated at the royal court.

- **The story of Sinuhe** was popular with all levels of society. The supervisor of the tomb builders in the Valley of the Kings requested that a copy of the book should be placed in his tomb for him to take to the afterlife.

- **The mythical tale** *The Book of the Cow of Heaven* described how the sun god Ra sent Hathor to quash a rebellion by mankind. She developed a taste for killing and refused to return, so Ra created a beer that looked like human blood. Hathor drank it and became intoxicated.

- **In the story of Setne Khamwas**, a son of Ramesses II encounters the ghost of a long dead magician in his tomb at Saqqara.

- **In the *Tale of the Unlucky Prince***, the Seven Hathors predict that a baby prince will die because he will be attacked by a crocodile, a snake or a dog. A beautiful princess saves him from the snake. Unfortunately, the end of the papyrus is missing, so we do not know how the story ends.

- **Travel stories** that featured magic were popular. *The Tale of the Shipwrecked Sailor* begins with a sailor stranded on a magic island after a storm. A giant serpent rescues him before the island mysteriously sinks beneath the waves.

Festivals

- **Hundreds of festivals** were celebrated by the people of the kingdom. Calendars on temple walls, studded with special markers, reveal that some temples marked dozens of religious holidays a year.

- **In the festival hall** of Thutmose III at Karnak, a list details the 54 feast days that were celebrated every year. Sixty festivals were celebrated every year at the mortuary temple of Ramesses III.

- **Many of these festivals** involved carrying an image of the god from one temple to another. This allowed ordinary Egyptians a glimpse of the image, which would normally be hidden away inside the temple.

- **The Festival of Opet** was celebrated from the early 18th Dynasty onwards in the second month of the season of the *akhet* (flood) season. The main event was the procession that carried divine images from Karnak to Luxor.

- **The Festival of the Valley** took place at Thebes from the 18th Dynasty onwards. The statues of Amun, Mut and Khons were carried from Karnak to Deir El-Bahri on the opposite side of the Nile.

- **The festival of the fertility god** Min was celebrated during the first month of the *shemu* (harvesting) season. The statue of the god was carried out of his temple and placed on a platform in the country. During the reign of Ramesses III the pharaoh himself walked at the front of the procession.

- **A festival was held** to mark the murder of Osiris. His tragic story was performed, and the whole country went into mourning. After several days, priests announced that he had risen from the dead, and only then were people were allowed to celebrate.

- **Divine images** were usually carried by priests in special gilded boats that were fixed to the top of poles.

FESTIVAL	SIGNIFICANCE	CELEBRATION
New Year's Day (Wep-renpet)	Celebrate rejuvenation and re-birth	Feasting
Feast of Wagy	Celebration of the god Thoth	Two feasts
Opet	To honour the God Amun	Procession and ceremony in the temple of Amun
The Beautiful Feast of the Valley	To honour the dead	Offerings are made to the dead
Heb-Sed	To prove that the pharaoh is still fit to rule after 30 years as pharaoh	Ceremony in which the pharaoh must prove himself fit and capable

- **On festival days**, temple altars were piled high with food and drink. For the poor, these events represented a rare opportunity to taste delicacies such as wine and roast beef.

- **The quantity of food consumed** during festivals was staggering. During the Opet festival more than 11,000 loaves and cakes were eaten, and 385 measures of beer were consumed. At the Sokar festival, more than 7400 loaves were eaten and nearly 1500 measures of beer were drunk.

Scribes

▲ *The ancient Egyptians believed that hieroglyphic writing came from Thoth.*

- **The term scribe** is a translation of the Egyptian word *sesh*, meaning the government officials and administrators of the Egyptian kingdom. Scribes were civil servants.

- **Scribes wrote diplomatic letters**, calculated and collected taxes, took notes during court cases, organized building projects, and copied out religious texts.

- **Positions as scribes** were highly coveted and the profession became hereditary. One scribe, Horemheb, became so powerful he went on to become pharaoh.

- **The scribe** was often depicted with legs crossed, and his papyrus across his lap.

- **Evidence of a school for scribes** has been found at Deir el-Medina. Training began with the students copying passages from the *Book of Kemyt*. They then progressed to copying works of literature.

- **A scribe's kit** consisted of a rectangular basalt palette with two holes in it, into which cakes of ink could be inserted. There was also space for reed pens, a water pot, and a knife for trimming papyrus sheets. A stone was carried to smooth the surface of the paper.

- **Thoth was the god of the scribes**. He was depicted as a man with the head of an ibis bird, and carried a pen and scrolls. Scribes prayed to him for success in their work.

- **The profession of scribe** was privileged. Part of a text giving advice to a schoolboy reads: 'Be a scribe! It saves you from labour and protects you from all kinds of work. It spares you from using the hoe and the mattock... the scribe, he directs all the work in this land!'

- **One of Egypt's most famous scribes** was a man called Ahmas (1680–1620 BC). One of his best-known writings was the text 'Accurate reckoning, the entrance into the knowledge of all existing things and all obscure secrets'.

- **The scribe Imhotep** lived 4500 years ago. He was a high priest and also designed the world's first pyramid at Saqqara. After his death, the ancient Egyptians came to see him as a god.

▼ Writing materials used by scribes included papyrus, reed pens, and pots that were used to hold ink.

Hieroglyphics

▲ *Hieroglyphs were painted or carved into walls. Many are still visible in tombs.*

- **Hieroglyphics is a form** of writing using pictures and symbols. There were about 700 symbols in the system, which was first used in the 4th millennium BC.

- **The word 'hieroglyph' is Greek**, meaning 'sacred carving'. The ancient Egyptians called their writing 'the divine words'.

- **Hieroglyphics was often written** on a form of paper called papyrus. It was named after the plant from which it was made, and was first manufactured around 3100 BC.

- **Hieroglyph symbol images** were usually pictures from the natural world of Egypt. The letter 'M', for example, was represented by the barn owl, while other signs included images of quail chicks and loaves of bread.

- **Some hieroglyphs represent sounds**, while others stand for ideas. One symbol showed the sound of a word, followed by another symbol to explain what type of word it was. Vowel sounds were not written down.

- **Hieroglyphics could be written** from left to right, right to left or from top to bottom. If the symbols for animals or people faced left, they were read from left to right. If they faced right, they were read from right to left.

- **Hieratic was a simplified form** of hieroglyphics. This script was used for business transactions and religious documents. It was usually written on papyrus or pieces of stone or pottery called *ostraka*.

- **In the first millennium** BC a script called *demotic* began to replace hieratic. Demotic means 'popular script'. This was followed in the 1st century BC by a form called Coptic Script.

- **Coptic Script** contained the 24 letters of the Greek alphabet and six signs from the demotic script. Vowel sounds were written down for the first time. Knowledge of this script proved crucial in deciphering the Rosetta Stone.

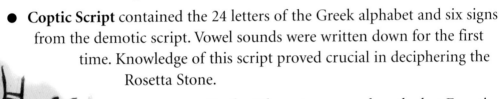

- **By the 6th century** AD, when the last Egyptian temple was closed after the fall of the Roman Empire, the art of reading hieroglyphs was lost until 1799.

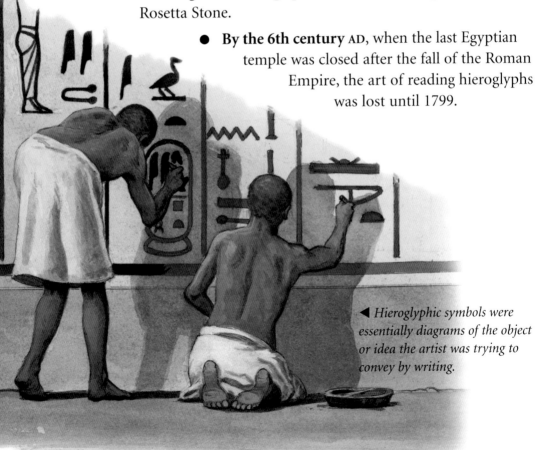

◀ *Hieroglyphic symbols were essentially diagrams of the object or idea the artist was trying to convey by writing.*

Art

- **The first pieces of Egyptian art** were scratched onto cave walls around 5000 BC. They show the type of animals that were hunted for food. It is thought the Egyptians believed that painting these creatures would give the artist the power to capture them.

- **In the age of the pharaohs**, artists were commissioned to paint pictures of important Egyptians after they had died, so that their memory could live on. Many nobles, officials and their families were painted after their deaths.

- **Artists were usually male** and learned their craft when they were young. At the beginning of their training they were given tasks such as mixing colours, fetching water and making brushes, before progressing to making sketches on rocks, stones and scraps of papyrus.

- **The colours** that artists used were brilliantly vibrant, and have lasted remarkably well over thousands of years. Different minerals were used to make different colours – carbon for black, ochre for red and yellow, and azurite and malachite for green and blue.

- **Teams of master artists** worked on large wall paintings. They were planned on a board marked with grids. The wall was then marked with a scaled-up grid, and the painting was copied onto the wall at the enlarged size.

- **In Egyptian art**, figures are not usually depicted face on. A person's head is usually turned right or left. The eye is always shown in full frontal view.

- **As a result of this style**, paintings of figures were not very realistic, because a single portrait included a variety of viewpoints.

- **Paintings usually adopted a hierarchal scale**. If the king was featured, he would be shown much larger than his servants who were ranked in size according to their importance.

- **Some of the best-preserved paintings** are murals in the rooms that lead to tombs. The paintings and their accompanying hieroglyphics describe stories about the pharaoh's journey into the afterlife.

- **Ancient Egyptians made a distinction** between draughtsmen and painters. Draughtsmen were called *sesh kedut* – 'writers of outlines'.

▼ *Egyptian artists painted pharaohs, possessions, food and other items that the deceased might need in the afterlife on tomb walls.*

Mathematics

- **The Greeks are usually credited** with inventing mathematics. However, the oldest recorded evidence for the use of mathematics was found in ancient Egypt and dated back to around 2000 BC.

- **Reading and writing numbers** in ancient Egypt was relatively simple. It used a system of symbols. The higher number was always written in front of the lower number.

- **There was no sign for zero** in the Egyptian numerical system. Scribes sometimes left a gap between numbers where a zero should be.

- **The Egyptian decimal system** had seven different symbols.

- **Our knowledge of Egyptian mathematics** is based on a tiny number of texts. The only evidence found so far comes from four papyri, a leather scroll and two wooden tablets.

- **The Rhind Mathematical Papyrus**, found in a tomb in Thebes, is packed full of fractions and complex calculations relating to the volumes of triangles, rectangles and pyramids.

- **Despite the dry mathematical nature of the text,** the last problem posed in the Rhind Mathematical Papyrus may be an Egyptian joke. It asks how much corn might be saved if 343 mice were eaten by 49 cats in seven houses!

- **The Egyptians used mathematics** in calculating how to set out the great pyramids. By working out the area of a circle according to the length of its diameter they could calculate the volume of a pyramid.

- **The ancient Egyptians** had no abstract formulae like the Greeks. Instead, they tackled mathematical problems by a series of smaller calculations.

MATHEMATICAL SYMBOLS

1 was shown by a single stroke.

10 was represented by a hobble for cattle.

100 was represented by a coil of rope.

1000 was represented by a lotus plant.

10,000 was represented by a finger.

100,000 was represented by a tadpole or frog.

1,000,000 was represented by a figure of a god with arms raised.

● **Scribes learned mathematics** by copying set examples and replacing figures with their own answers. Archaeologists have discovered ancient exercise sheets, with teacher's markings on them.

Craftwork

- **The ancient Egyptians** were extremely skilful carpenters. They could fashion tables, chairs and boxes with joints similar to those in use today.

- **Very little timber** was readily available in Egypt. Apart from a few acacia trees, tamarisk and willow, most of the wood was imported from Lebanon.

- **An adze** was used for carving and planing. It had a wooden handle and a blade fitted at the top. Early forms of drills were rotated by an implement like an archer's bow.

- **Carpentry was a demanding trade**. The excerpt below from a scribe reveals just how arduous this type of work could be: 'Every carpenter who picks up the adze is more tired than a peasant... There is no end to his labour. He has to work more than his arms are capable of.'

- **The tomb of Rekhmire at Thebes** contains a series of pictures of carpenters. These sketches reveal the wide array of tools they used to ply their trade.

- **A carpenter worked on rough wood** with an axe. Logs were split, and then chopped into smaller chunks. A saw was then used to slice into the wood.

- **Carpenters used a vice** to hold pieces of wood when sawing. The piece of timber was tied to a pole that was rammed into the ground, possibly with a weight attached to one end to keep the rope taut.

- **Bones were ground** to make a natural glue. An early form of plaster was also used. Gesso was made by mixing whiting with glue. It was harder than plaster, stuck better to wood and was an excellent base for painting.

> ...FASCINATING FACT...
> Rulers were used to check that lines and edges were straight,
> and set squares were used to make right angles.

- **Stones were used** to scour wood to ensure there were no rough edges, a practice that continued on ships (holystoning) until the 19th century.

◄ *Craftworkers were responsible for designing the great buildings and monuments of the Pharaonic era. They also created the tools that were needed to fashion wood, stone and precious metals.*

Making fine things

- **Egyptian jewellers** made objects such as amulets, rings, necklaces and girdles using gold, silver and semi-precious stones.

- **By the Middle Kingdom**, gold was the most precious material in Egypt. The first ever geological map is a diagram of gold mines and quarries in the Wadi Hammamat.

- **The process of casting** was used to make many metal objects. Metal was heated until it became liquid and then poured into moulds.

- **The ancient Egyptians exploited the mines** between the Nile and the Red Sea coast. Gold was mined from both the Eastern Desert and from Nubia, where Egyptian inscriptions date back to 3100 BC.

- **In Nubia**, workers used two methods for extracting gold. Rocks were smashed and the lumps of gold ore removed. More gold was washed out and caught in a sieve – possibly made out of a sheep fleece.

▶ *Most gold arrived in Egypt from Nubia. When it arrived it was weighed before being sent to workshops where goldsmiths made it into statues, jewellery and other beautiful objects.*

- **The technique of welding** was used by jewellers from the Middle Kingdom onwards. Different metals were heated until they became workable. The whole artefact was then joined over a ceramic furnace and a blowpipe used to increase the heat until the two pieces were welded together.

- **The technique of soldering** was in use from the 4th Dynasty onwards. Hard-soldering was preferred to soft-soldering as the artefact could be reheated without the bond melting.

- **The best example** of the goldsmiths' art are the funeral masks of pharaohs. Tutankhamun's beautiful death mask is a wonderful testament to their skill and ingenuity.

- **The first glass beads** were made in Pre-dynastic times. In the Old and Middle Kingdoms, artists made glass amulets, animal figures and other items. In the reign of Tuthmosis I in the New Kingdom, the first glass vessels were made.

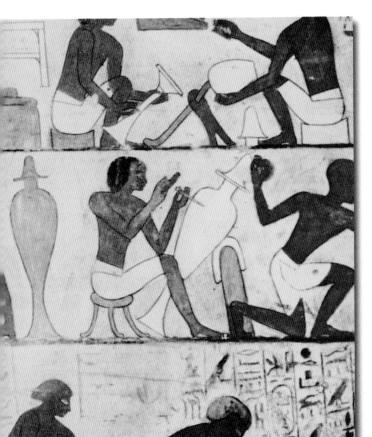

- **Most of the pottery** was made from reddish-brown clay, and is called Nile silt ware. It was not highly valued and was left without decoration.

151

The land between the rivers

- **Mesopotamia was an ancient region** covering the area that is now eastern Syria, southeastern Turkey, and most of Iraq. The name 'Mesopotamia' means land 'between the rivers'. The two rivers referred to are the Tigris and Euphrates, and the central part of Mesopotamia lay between them.

- **The Tigris and Euphrates rivers** originate in the southern mountains of modern-day Turkey and flow southeast. They join to form one river, which runs into the Persian Gulf.

- **Before 5000 BC**, the rivers did not join together. The area that is now dry land north of the Persian Gulf was once a vast area of marshland.

- **The valley** through which the two rivers flow is wide and flat, with mountains to the north and east and deserts to the south and west.

- **Silt and sediment** from the floodwaters of the rivers produced fertile soils, providing rich farmland.

- **Before 7000 BC,** people lived in Mesopotamia because the rich, fertile plain provided plants, which attracted animals that could be hunted.

...FASCINATING FACT...

Today, the area that was Mesopotamia is divided between the countries of Turkey, Syria and Iraq. These countries have existed for less than 100 years. Before that Mesopotamia was home to many nations.

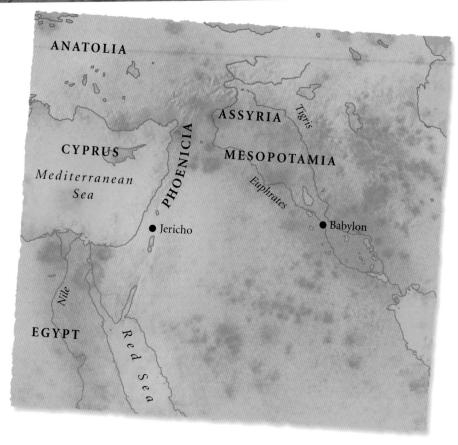

▲ *Mesopotamia, the land around the twin rivers Tigris and Euphrates, formed part of a 'fertile crescent' of good farming land that stretched west to the shores of the Mediterranean Sea, then south to Egypt.*

- **The first people to farm animals and crops** lived in the hills of the Middle East around 10,000 BC. They began to live on the plain around the two rivers 3000 years later.

- **The climate in Mesopotamia** is hot and dry. Early settlers had to irrigate the land (deliver water to it by digging ditches or canals) along the river banks in order for plants to grow.

- **These early farmers** kept sheep, goats and cattle. They grew barley, millet and emmer wheat.

153

The first cities

- **One of the earliest farming villages** found by archaeologists is Catal Huyuk in southern Turkey, northwest of the historic area known as Mesopotamia.

- **Houses were made of mud brick** – mud mixed with straw that has been dried hard in the sun. The flat roofs were made of wood and straw. Mesopotamian houses continued to be built in this way for thousands of years.

- **The land around Catal Huyuk** was fertile and the rivers provided water for farming crops. By around 5000 BC, much of this land was occupied.

- **Around 5000 BC, farmers moved** to the areas that did not lie alongside the rivers. Although the land was fertile, it sometimes flooded or dried out, so crops did not grow easily.

- **Farmers discovered** that if they dug water channels and irrigation ditches, they could divert flood water away from their fields, and then bring in water from the rivers during dry spells.

- **Digging channels and ditches** required large numbers of men to work together, which small villages did not have. By around 4000 BC cities of several thousand people began to develop.

- **The first cities** included Ur, Kish, Uruk and Lagash in southern Mesopotamia. Each city controlled large areas of farmland and many nearby villages.

- **In small farming villages** each person had to make their own tools, pottery and clothes. In cities, people could specialize – tailors could make clothes, potters could make pottery and other craftsmen could make goods for sale.

- **This specialization of labour** was a key development and ensured that the cities continued to grow larger and more prosperous.

- **Soon the cities were home** to thousands of people. They were surrounded by tall walls to defend themselves against other peoples who might want to steal the wealth of the city.

◀ *The small town of Catal Huyuk began as a village of farmers living in flat-topped houses, but grew rapidly.*

155

Gods and ziggurats

- **The Mesopotamians** were a very religious people. The citizens of each city believed that any good luck or success they had was due to their gods. They offered prayers and sacrifices to the deities.

- **The Sumerians believed** that the gods were led by Enlil, the god of storms and winds. It was Enlil who sent good or bad weather to help or damage the crops. His wife was Ninlil, the queen of the gods.

- **An important task of Enlil** was to choose rulers for the cities. When a ruler died his successor had to go to the temple of Enlil to be approved by the god.

- **The moon god**, Sin, was an old man with a blue beard. He measured the passing of time and judged disputes between the other gods. Sin was married to Ningal, the Sky Lady. He was worshipped with great fervour in Ur.

- **Shamash the sun god** was the son of Sin and Ningal. He was a brave and strong young god who watched over the doings of humans and punished criminals.

- **The great goddess, Ishtar**, was the daughter of Sin and Ningal. She fought wars for the gods, riding in a chariot pulled by seven lions and shooting arrows at the enemy.

- **Ishtar was also the goddess** of growing crops and rich harvests. She was linked to the planet we call Venus, and farming activities were timed to take place according to the movements of this planet.

156

▲ *The cities of Mesopotamia were built around a temple*
that took the form of a massive artificial hill called a ziggurat.

- **Most Mesopotamian temples** took the form of a ziggurat. This was a huge artificial hill made of layer upon layer of mud bricks. A staircase ran up one side of the ziggurat to a small shrine at the top. Some ziggurats were more than 30 m in height.

- **The ziggurats were surrounded** by offices and sleeping quarters for the priests, and by storerooms for grain and the other wealth of the city. Most government administration was done by the priests.

- **Writing was invented** around 3300 BC by priests in Mesopotamia to record and communicate information. They used writing to keep records of taxation, wealth and work that needed doing.

Farmers and hunters

- **The earliest cities** emerged in southern Mesopotamia, an area known as Sumer. Elsewhere in Mesopotamia there were only scattered villages where people hunted as often as they farmed.

- **Around 3000** BC, the cities had spread north to the area known as Akkad. New cities such as Uruk, Larsa, Nippur, Sippar and Babylon were founded and grew quickly.

- **The people of Akkad** spoke a different language to the people of Sumer. Although they copied many aspects of Sumerian culture, they had their own gods and systems.

- **Gilgamesh was an early ruler** of Uruk. He enlarged the area ruled by the city, converting wild lands to farming lands. The Akkadians preferred to be ruled by kings, such as Gilgamesh, instead of priests as in Sumer.

- **An epic poem** was composed about Gilgamesh. It became the most popular legend of Mesopotamia and was still being told 3000 years after he died.

- **The legend tells how** Gilgamesh fought against a wild man named Enkidu who lived by hunting animals. Enkidu then joined Gilgamesh in many adventures. The legend reflects how the early rulers of Akkad merged farming technology with hunting peoples to produce a new form of civilization.

- **By around 2900** BC, the Akkadians were using the plough to improve their harvests. They caught fish in the rivers and hunted animals in the hills for meat.

- **Around 2236** BC, Sargon became King of Kish. He soon united all of Akkad under his rule. Then he invaded Sumeria and conquered the cities of southern Mesopotamia.

- **The Empire of Sargon** survived for 100 years. During this time the peoples of Akkad and Sumer merged so that one culture dominated all of Mesopotamia.

- **The city of Ur** emerged as the richest city in the world by around 2000 BC, but the city of Babylon was also growing quickly.

▲ *According to legend, Gilgamesh defeated the giant Humbaba because he wanted to be remembered as one of the greatest heroes ever to have lived.*

159

The lawgivers

- **The great city of Babylon** was conquered around 2000 BC by a group of people from the west called the Amorites. The invaders founded a new warrior dynasty, but retained the prosperous culture of the city.

- **In 1711 BC** Hammurabi, King of Babylon, completed the conquest of the whole of Mesopotamia. He combined the culture of Mesopotamia with the warrior code of his own people.

- **Hammurabi believed** that he was partly divine, and that his leadership was approved by the gods. His power was absolute and to disagree with him was not only treason, but sacrilege (an insult to the gods) as well.

▶ *The Sumerians invented a form of writing, shown here, that used ideographs (pictures to represent objects or ideas). These were slow to write and were eventually replaced by cuneiform, a combination of pictures and symbols. Cuneiform remained in use for 3000 years.*

...FASCINATING FACT...

Government records were inscribed on wet clay tablets, which were then dried in the sun to become permanent records. Archaeologists have found thousands of these in Babylon and across Mesopotamia.

- **Hammurabi used the Sumerian language** to communicate with all the peoples of Mesopotamia. He devised a law code, and laws were written on stone pillars that were set up in the different cities.

- **The 282 laws of Hammurabi** set down rules about how people should live, as well as imposing penalties for theft and other crimes. The peoples of Mesopotamia believed that Hammurabi was given the laws by the god Shamash.

- **Contracts between merchants** and craftsmen had to be made according to the law, and written copies had to be kept.

- **Each city elected an official** called the *rabianum* who was responsible for making sure that Hammurabi's laws were obeyed and that taxes were paid on time.

- **Babylonian officials** checked written accounts of taxes, government spending and other official accounts. The population of the city grew rapidly until more than 100,000 people inhabited Babylon.

- **Hammurabi died in about 1750** BC, but his ideas survived. For centuries monarchs in Mesopotamia ruled according to his concept of law and bureaucracy.

Assyrian might

- **In the north of Mesopotamia** lay the country of Assyria, based around the city of Assur. The country was conquered by Hammurabi, but kept its dynasty of rulers who copied many ideas from Hammurabi.

- **In 1112 BC**, the Assyrians conquered neighbouring areas of northern Mesopotamia. A few years later they conquered northern Syria.

- **The warrior king Tiglath Pileser III** captured Babylon in 730 BC and made Assyria the most powerful state in Mesopotamia. By 671 BC, Assyria had conquered all Mesopotamia, Syria, Palestine and Egypt.

- **The king Ashurbanipal** ruled the vast Assyrian Empire from 669 BC to 626 BC. He was the most powerful of the Assyrian kings.

- **The Assyrian government** was dedicated to raising and maintaining a large, powerful army with which to defeat all enemies. The roles of the bureaucracy and tax collectors were merely to fund the army.

- **The main wealth of Assyria** came from the farmers over which it ruled. The crops and livestock they produced were taxed for funds, while the farmers themselves were recruited into the army and government service.

- **The Assyrian kings** hired large numbers of mercenaries to serve in the army. These men fought for personal gain, not loyalty to the king.

- **The most effective Assyrian weapon in battle** was the chariot. This fast-moving vehicle was pulled by two horses and carried a driver, an archer and a spearman.

- **The Assyrians were renowned** as engineers. They built massive fortifications around their cities and fortresses, but were just as skilled at breaking down the defences of enemy strong points.

● **The wars that Ashurbanipal fought** made Assyria the largest empire Mesopotamia had known, but they exhausted their finances and manpower. By the end of his reign the empire was large, but weakened.

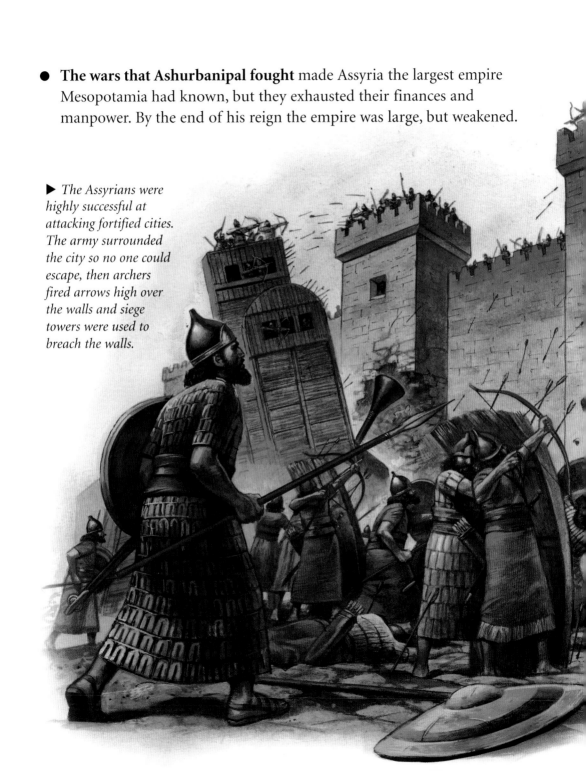

▶ *The Assyrians were highly successful at attacking fortified cities. The army surrounded the city so no one could escape, then archers fired arrows high over the walls and siege towers were used to breach the walls.*

Babylon

- **Babylon had remained** the largest, wealthiest and most prosperous city in Mesopotamia ever since the days of Hammurabi. Even when the Assyrian Empire was powerful, Babylon was richer.

- **In 616 BC**, Nabopolassar, a Babylonian nobleman, declared that the city was independent of Assyria and that he was the new ruler of the city. Other areas of Mesopotamia hurried to join him.

- **The Babylonians formed an alliance** with the Medes, a mountain tribe from an area that is now Iran. In 610 BC the Medes and Babylonians crushed the Assyrian army and destroyed the Assyrian Empire.

- **Mesopotamia was united** under Babylonian rule, which also extended to Syria and Palestine. The city of Babylon soon became larger and richer than ever before.

- **Nebuchadnezzar, son and successor** of Nabopolassar, became the richest and most powerful man in Mesopotamia. He ruled Babylon from 604 BC to 562 BC and rebuilt much of the city.

- **The walls around Babylon** were rebuilt to be stronger and wider. The mighty Ishtar Gate, faced by glazed tiles and sacred to the goddess Ishtar, was excavated by archaeologists *c.* 1900–1914.

...FASCINATING FACT...

The Hanging Gardens of Babylon were built by Nebuchadnezzar to remind his beloved wife, Amytis, of the sloping hills of her home in Media. The terraced gardens were so fantastic that they became known as one of the Seven Wonders of the World.

► *The beautiful Ishtar Gate of Babylon was not only a powerful fortification, but was also decorated with glazed tiles to show the wealth of the city to visitors.*

- **Peace and prosperity in Babylon** continued for more than 70 years. The patron god of Babylon, Marduk, became recognized as the most important deity across much of Mesopotamia.

- **After 550 BC the king Nabonidus** abandoned the worship of Marduk for the god Sin. The move was very unpopular.

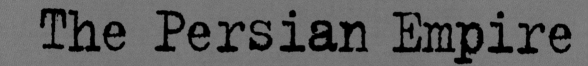

The Persian Empire

- **The Persians** were a fairly small tribe from what is now Iran. In 549 BC, the Persians merged with the more powerful Medes through a royal marriage.

  - **Cyrus, the new ruler** of the Persians and Medes, conquered what is now Turkey. Many Greek cities along the coast submitted to Cyrus, but were allowed to rule themselves.

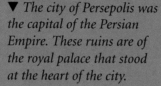

▼ *The city of Persepolis was the capital of the Persian Empire. These ruins are of the royal palace that stood at the heart of the city.*

- **In 539** BC, Cyrus marched on Babylon. He announced that he had come to restore the god Marduk to his position as chief god in the city. The Babylonians opened their gates to Cyrus.

- **Egypt was conquered by Cambyses,** son of Cyrus, in 524 BC. By this date the Persian Empire was larger than any earlier state, reaching as far east as the Indus river.

- **The vast Persian Empire** was divided into 20 districts, called satrapies. Each satrapy was ruled by a satrap, appointed by the Persian ruler, or King of Kings as he was known.

- **The satrap had total power** over justice, taxation and government within his satrapy, but had to submit regular accounts to the King of Kings. Most satraps chose to respect local laws and gods to keep peace.

- **The Persian army** was under the direct rule of the King of Kings, and only Persians or Medes could be officers. The army was used to enforce Persian rule within the empire as well as to fight foreign enemies.

- **In 490** BC, Persia invaded Greece, but was defeated at Marathon. A second and larger invasion in 480 BC was defeated at Thermopylae and Salamis.

- **In 334** BC, a Greek army led by Alexander the Great, King of Macedon, invaded the Persian Empire. In a campaign lasting 11 years, the Persians were defeated, but Alexander died and his generals could not hold down the vast area they conquered.

- **By 200** BC **a new dynasty,** the Parthians, had taken over Mesopotamia and most of the Persian Empire. They preserved and modified the culture of Mesopotamia until the Middle Ages.

The Mycenaean Period

- **By about 1750** BC, the most important city in Greece was Mycenae. Modern historians refer to this period of Greek history as the Mycenaean Period. This lasted until around 1150 BC.

- **Other important cities** at this time included Iolkos, Tiryns, Pylos, Dyme, Delphi, Athens, Thebes and Orchomenos. Each city was independent of the others, and there may have been over 100.

- **Cities were surrounded** by strong walls made from large, irregular-shaped blocks of stone. These provided defence against attack. Some cities had spectacular gateways.

▲ *A golden mask found in a royal tomb at Mycenae dating to about 1400 BC. Mycenae was one of the largest and most powerful cities in Greece at that time.*

- **Most people lived** on the land as farmers or herdsmen, and many fishermen lived along the coast. Few people earned a living by making things to sell.

- **There was no money** in Mycenaean Greece. Instead, people swapped what they had for things they wanted. For example, a farmer might have swapped a quantity of food for a vase.

- **During this time**, the Greeks appear to have lived only along the coasts of the southern and eastern parts of what is now Greece, and also on some of the nearby islands.

- **Around 1450 BC**, the Greeks developed a system of writing. The early script they used is known as Linear A, but it is unlike later Greek script, and has not yet been fully deciphered.

- **People used** pointed pieces of wood to carve letter symbols into small tablets of wet clay. The clay could then be smoothed over and used again if necessary.

- **From about 1080 to 750 BC**, Greece entered a period now referred to as the Dark Age. During this time the history of the Mycenaean Period was lost. Later legends preserve stories about these times, some of which were probably based on fact.

. . . FASCINATING FACT . . .

If a clay tablet needed to be kept permanently it was fired like a pot. Some tablets were preserved accidentally after they became fired in a burning building.

The bull of Minos

- **During the Mycenaean Period** on mainland Greece, a different civilization flourished on the island of Crete. This civilization is known as Minoan, from the name of a legendary king of Crete – Minos.

- **The most important palace** on Minoan Crete was Knossos in the north. Other palaces included Kydonia in the west, Phaistos in the south and Kato Zakro in the east.

- **Temples and other important buildings** of Minoan Crete were decorated with pictures and sculptures of bull horns. It is thought that these people may have worshipped a bull god.

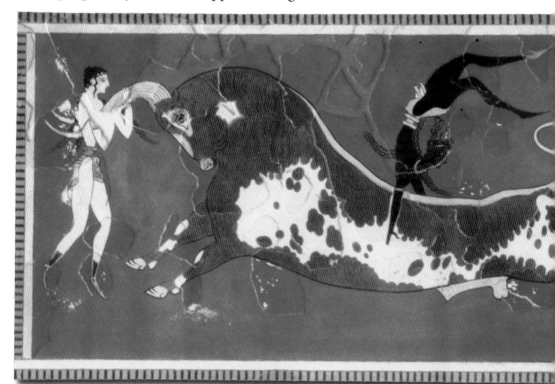

- **One fresco shows** young men jumping over the back of a charging bull. This may have been a dangerous sport, or some form of worship of the bull god.

- **Merchants from Crete** sailed to Syria, Egypt and mainland Greece to trade for goods such as bronze tools, olive oil and papyrus (a form of paper). The Minoans grew rich as a result.

- **Minoan merchants** also traded with other travellers who had come from further away. They imported amber from the Baltic Sea and ivory from Africa.

- **The Minoans** left writings in strange scripts, known as Linear A and Phaistos Disc.

- **Both of these scripts** remain undeciphered today, so we do not know what the writings mean.

- **Around 1625 BC**, Crete was hit by a tidal wave caused by a massive volcanic eruption on the island of Thera. Many cities and homes were destroyed. It is possible that this eruption was the reason why the Minoan civilization went into decline.

- **About the year 1450 BC**, Crete was taken over by Greek kings from the mainland. They introduced Mycenaean weapons and art styles, but also retained much of the Minoan culture.

◀ *A fresco (wall painting) found at Knossos, Crete. It shows a group of young men leaping acrobatically over a charging bull, an animal thought to be sacred to the Minoans.*

171

The Trojan War

- **Troy was a mighty city** in the country of Illios in what is now northwestern Turkey. It controlled trade routes to the Black Sea, becoming one of the richest cities in the ancient world.

- **Ancient records show** that the Trojans fought several wars against raiders from Mycenaean Greece. Archaeologists have found that the city was invaded and destroyed around 1180 BC.

- **According to later Greek legends**, Troy was destroyed after a war that lasted ten years. All the kings of Mycenaean Greece then joined forces to attack Troy, sailing across the Aegean Sea in a fleet of 1000 ships.

- **It was believed** that the Trojan War began when Paris, son of King Priam of Troy, fell in love with Queen Helen of Sparta. He abducted her and took her away to Troy. Helen's husband, King Menelaus, asked his brother, King Agamemnon of Mycenae, for help.

- **Agamemnon summoned** the Greek kings to attack Troy. Among those who came were Odysseus of Ithaca and the warrior-hero Achilles.

- **When Achilles fought**, the Greeks were much stronger than the Trojans, but after an argument with Agamemnon, Achilles stayed in his tent and refused to fight. The Trojans began to win victories.

- **When Achilles' friend Patroclus** was killed by the Trojan Hector, Achilles left his tent. He killed Hector in single combat then rejoined the fighting. The Trojans fell back behind their city walls.

- **Odysseus suggested** that the Greeks pretend to give up and go home, leaving behind a large wooden horse as a gift to the gods. In fact, the horse contained Greek warriors and the Greek army was only a short distance away.

172

- **The Trojans** pulled the horse into Troy. That night the hidden warriors leapt out and opened the city gates. Troy was captured by the Greeks.

- **After the war**, Helen returned to Sparta. Troy was later resettled, but was never again as rich and powerful as it had been.

◀ *Greek soldiers emerge from the wooden horse inside which they have been hiding. Legend says that the city of Troy was captured after a long war in about 1180 BC.*

The fall of the palaces

▲ *The entrance to a huge tomb just outside Mycenae, now known as the Treasury of Atreus.*

- **Around the year 1200 BC**, the eastern Mediterranean world entered a troubled time, and the cities of Mycenaean Greece began to decline.

- **Later Greek legends** blamed feuds within the ruling families of Mycenae and other cities for the economic decline.

- **Around 1190** BC, Egypt was attacked by a mass of invaders who arrived by sea from the north. At first, the Egyptians referred to the invaders as 'Sea Peoples', but later learned that the people referred to themselves as Sherdan, Peleset and Denyen.

- **Pharaoh Rameses III** defeated the first invasion by the Sea Peoples, but later invasions caused massive damage to Egypt.

- **Around the same time** the Hittite Empire collapsed. The Hittites ruled most of what is now Turkey. The collapse was so sudden that no records of the events survived.

- **In about 1120** BC, the city of Mycenae was destroyed by fire. After the fire, the city was abandoned completely, so it is possible that the destruction was caused by a war.

- **Many other cities** of Mycenaean Greece were also abandoned around that time. Some were left in ruins, while others, such as Athens, survived as smaller towns.

- **One document from Pylos** records that extra soldiers were sent out on patrol just before the city was destroyed. Few other written records from other cities survived the destruction.

- **Modern historians** think that a period of economic decline and poor harvest was followed by an invasion by a Greek-speaking people called the Dorians.

- **The kings** of Mycenaean Greece had failed in their most important duty – to protect their lands and people. The whole culture collapsed and a 'Dark Age' began in Greece.

The Dark Age

- **By about 1080** BC, the Mycenaean civilization had completely collapsed. There are no written records from this time and very few archaeological remains have been found. This period is known as the Greek Dark Age.

- **During this time**, small groups of people roamed Greece and nearby lands trying to find suitable areas for settlements. Some of these migrations formed the basis of later legends.

- **One group of Dorians** settled in the valley of the Eurotas River and became rulers of the city state of Sparta. Spartan records indicate that this happened in 1102 BC.

▶ *A large ornamental jar dating to the Dark Age of Greece. Decoration in horizontal lines was very popular during this period.*

- **Another group** of Dorians conquered Crete in about 1020 BC. They appointed themselves kings and nobles, and ruled over the native inhabitants.

- **A large number of Greeks** from around Athens fled from the Dorians. They settled on the western coast of what is now Turkey and called themselves Ionians after their first king, Ion.

- **Poetry was highly admired** as an art form during the Dark Age. Two long poems in the epic tradition dating from the Dark Age were later written down. They are called *Illiad* and *Odyssey*.

- *Illiad* and *Odyssey* are concerned with the Trojan War and its aftermath, and they were passed down through oral tradition for generations. They are traditionally considered to have been given their final form by a poet called Homer.

- **Homer** is believed to have lived in Ionia, possibly around 800 BC. Very little is known about his life, but it is traditionally thought that he became a poet as a way to earn a living because he was blind and unable to work at other trades. Some scholars deny that Homer ever existed.

- **During the Dark Age**, a new style of pottery developed in Greece. It featured simple patterns of squares, circles and straight lines and this style became known as Geometric. It was a departure from the earlier Mycenean style of pottery, which was more decorative.

- **Iron was introduced** to Greece during the Dark Age. At first, the metal was very expensive, so it was used only by kings and nobles.

Tyrants and lawgivers

- **By about 650** BC, many Greek cities were threatened with political crisis as a result of developments in battle techniques.

- **A new style** of fighting emerged. Lower class men began to fight in tight formations wearing hoplite armour of a shield, helmet, spear and sword. Using this method they were able to defeat the chariots of the aristocrats.

- **As a result** of their new success in battle, the lower classes wanted political power. The aristocrats thought the positions for lower class men should be restricted to part-time officials, and they refused to hand over power. Political disputes began, which sometimes turned into civil war.

- **Some cities** entered what the Greeks called *stasis*. This meant that the citizens were so busy arguing over who should rule the city that working and trading ground to a halt.

- **About the year 750** BC, a prince of Sparta named Lycurgos was given the power to reform the constitution of the city to solve the disputes between the aristocrats and the citizens.

- **While other cities** entered *stasis*, Sparta remained orderly and prosperous. The constitution invented by Lycurgos, and developed by later kings, ensured stability.

- **Other cities decided** to copy Sparta and appoint one respected man to reform their constitutions. These men became known as the lawgivers.

- **In 594 BC**, Athens appointed a poet named Solon as their lawgiver. Solon was so effective that he later travelled to other cities to give advice on lawmaking.

- **In other cities**, the disputes led to violence and bloodshed. Sometimes individuals would illegally seize power and rule without respect for the old laws. These people became known as tyrants.

- **Some tyrants** were aristocrats who crushed the hopes of poorer people. Others were poor men who smashed the power of the aristocrats.

▼ *Draco and Solon were both lawgivers in Athens. Draco drew up his laws in around 620 BC, to impose order on the city. Solon reformed the laws in about 560 BC, once order had been restored. Most of Solon's punishments are less severe than Draco's.*

CRIME	DRACO'S PUNISHMENT	SOLON'S PUNISHMENT
MURDER	DEATH	DEATH
BANKRUPTCY	SLAVERY	GRADUAL PAYMENT OF DEBT
SACRILEGE – EXTREME DISRESPECT FOR SOMETHING SACRED	DEATH	NO PUNISHMENT
REFUSAL TO JOIN THE ARMY	DEATH	BRANDING WITH HOT IRONS
BREAKING A CONTRACT	DEATH	MONEY FINE
PERSISTENT DRUNKENNESS	DEATH	BANNED FROM PUBLIC OFFICE

Colonies overseas

- **During the Dark Age** and the time of the tyrants and lawgivers, Greece's population grew, which led to economic problems in some places.

- **The governments** of many cities decided to solve the population problem by planting colonies – founding new cities outside Greece.

- **Some colonies** were founded as a result of political disputes. The losers of the dispute would be told to leave on ships and found a colony.

- **In about 680** BC, the pharaoh of Egypt asked Greek merchants to establish a colony near the mouth of the River Nile. The resulting settlement was called Naukratis, and became one of the richest cities in Egypt.

- **New colonies** were independent of their parent cities, but most maintained strong links by way of trade and friendship that lasted for generations.

- **Corinth founded** the colonies of Korkyra, Corfu and Syracuse, Sicily. Massalia (now Marseilles), in France, was founded by colonists from Phocea.

...FASCINATING FACT...

In the 5th century BC, the island of Thera was hit by famine. The government responded by sending some of its people to found a colony in North Africa, telling them that if they returned they would be executed.

- **The coasts** of Sicily and southern Italy were favoured for colonies between 800 and 600 BC, as the land and climate were similar to those of Greece.

- **Between 700 and 500** BC, many colonies were founded around the coasts of the Black Sea. At the same time, other colonies were founded in the western Mediterranean in what is now France and Spain.

- **Some colonies** became wealthy. Sybaris in Italy, was situated on a very fertile plain, and as a result rose quickly in power and opulence.

▼ *A Greek temple at Syracuse, Sicily.*
Greek colonies on Sicily were very wealthy.

The power of Persia

- **In 546 BC**, the Persian emperor Darius crushed the kingdom of Lydia that had ruled most of what is now Turkey. Darius already ruled a vast empire that stretched from Egypt to India.

- **Many Ionian Greek cities** had paid tribute or had treaties with King Croesus of Lydia. Darius demanded that these cities should pay tribute to him instead. Most of the cities complied with his demands.

- **In 500 BC**, the city of Miletus refused to pay a new tribute that was higher than the original requests. Soon, other Greek cities joined the revolt against Darius. Sardis, the capital of Lydia, was captured and the Persians were killed or expelled.

- **Miletus** and other Ionian cities were colonies of Athens, and Athens sent out a fleet to help the revolt. The revolt was crushed by the Persians at the Battle of Lade in 494 BC.

◀ *Rich carvings adorned the walls at Persepolis – the great city and palace of Darius' reign.*

- **Darius was determined** to punish Athens for aiding the Ionian revolt. In 490 BC, he sent a fleet and an army to attack Athens.

- **The Persian fleet** sailed first to the cities of Karystos and Eretria on the island of Euboia, which had also helped the revolt. Karystos and Eretria both surrendered. They were made to pay a heavy tribute, and the Persians burned down their temples.

- **The Persians then landed** at Marathon near Athens, with an army of over 20,000 men. They found the road to Athens blocked by an army of around 8000 Athenians.

- **The citizens of Sparta** promised to send an army to help Athens, but they could not do so until they had finished celebrating the religious festival of Carneia, during which no fighting was allowed. They said they would come in three days time.

- **When the Persian army** marched out of its camp, the Athenians launched a direct attack, hitting the Persians before they were properly in formation. The Persians were heavily defeated.

- **The Persians returned** to their ships and sailed back to the ports of the empire. The Spartans arrived in Athens the following day and congratulated the Athenians on their victory. Darius of Persia swore that he would have revenge on Athens and Sparta.

▶ *Darius, ruler of the Persian Empire, wanted to conquer Greece, but died before he could launch a major invasion.*

The Greek League

- **In 486 BC**, Darius, emperor of Persia, died. In 481 BC, his son Xerxes, began gathering a vast army.

- **Xerxes sent messengers** to every Greek state, demanding that they surrender and become part of the Persian Empire.

- **Sparta and Athens** announced that they would form a Greek League, made up of all of the cities that would agree to fight against Persia.

- **With an army** of about 200,000 men and a fleet of 700 warships, Xerxes arrived in northern Greece on 1 July 481 BC. The cities of Thessaly and Boeotia surrendered.

- **An army of 300 Spartans** and 6000 others, stood in the Pass of Thermopylae, a route through a narrow gap in the mountains, while the Greek fleet waited offshore in the narrow channel of the Euripus.

- **King Leonidas** of Sparta and the Athenian admiral Themistocles hoped that in the narrow space of the pass they could halt the Persian advance.

- **The Greeks held out** for three days. Then the Persians found another pass through the mountains, and King Leonidas and his Spartans were killed.

- **Xerxes captured Athens** and several other cities. After further advances he reached the Isthmus of Corinth, a narrow strip of land, surrounded by water on both sides, which was blocked by a new, larger Spartan army.

- **At the Battle of Salamis** (480 BC), the Greek fleet destroyed the much larger Persian fleet. Xerxes returned to Persia, and at the Battle of Plataea (479 BC) the Greeks defeated the rest of the Persian army that Xerxes had left behind.

- **The Persian Wars** continued for many years, but the Persians never again tried to invade Greece.

▼ *The Battle of Plataea, in which the Greek alliance defeated the invading army of the Persian ruler Xerxes.*

The might of Athens

- **After the Battle of Plataea** in 479 BC, the Greek league broke up. The Persian invasion had been defeated, and Sparta and some other states argued that the need for the league was over.

- **Some Greek states**, led by Athens, wanted the league to continue. They wanted to attack the Persian Empire and help the Ionian Greek cities break free from Persian rule.

- **In 477 BC**, representatives of the states wanting to continue the war met on the island of Delos. The meeting place was chosen because it was believed that Delos was an island sacred to the gods Apollo and Diana.

- **The states agreed** to form the Delian League with the objective of continuing the war against the Persian Empire. They asked the Athenian general and nobleman Aristeides to draw up rules for the league.

- **Aristeides was famous** for his honesty. He drew up a list that stated how much money each state had to pay to the league treasury to help fund the war.

- **The Persians** were driven out of the Aegean Sea in 476 BC. Ten years later the Delian League defeated the Persian fleet at the Battle of Eurymedon.

- **In 454 BC**, the treasury of the Delian League was moved to Athens by the Athenian politician Pericles. The power of Athens within the league began to increase, and Athens started to take money for its own use from the treasury.

- **Pericles and the Athenians** used the money of the Delian League to build beautiful new temples and strong walls to replace those destroyed by the Persians in 480 BC.

- **The peace treaty of Kallias** in 449 BC ended the war with the Persians, but the Athenians refused to disband the Delian League. Athens used its powerful fleet and army to defeat those that wanted to leave the league.

- **By the year 440 BC**, the Delian League had fallen completely under Athenian control.

▼ *The Parthenon as it looked when it was first completed. The mighty temple was the crowning glory of Athens in the 5th century BC.*

The Peloponnesian War

- **The Peloponnesian War** began as a minor dispute between Corfu and Corinth, but it escalated rapidly after Athens interfered, and soon affected nearly all of Greece.

- **In 432 BC**, Korkyra failed to send a religious tribute to Corinth, its founding city. When Corinth sent ships to Corfu, the Korkyran fleet attacked and captured them.

- **Fearing the Corinthian response**, the Korkyrans sent ambassadors to Athens to ask for help. Led by the politician Pericles, the Athenians declared war against Corinth.

- **Sparta, Thebes and other cities** were worried about the growth of Athenian power, and did not want Corinth to fall to Athens. Sparta sent ambassadors to Athens to seek peace, but they were insulted and thrown out.

▶ *Although he was one of ten generals, Pericles was referred to as the leader because his military record commanded such respect.*

- **The powerful armies** of Sparta and Thebes gradually gained a series of victories that gave them control of the land. The Athenian fleet and its allies gained control of the sea.

- **Athens tried to break** the stalemate by sending a fleet and army to capture Sicily in 413 BC. The expedition was a disaster and ended with the destruction of the Athenian fleet.

- **The Persians joined the war** on the side of Sparta. With Persian money and advisors, Sparta built a fleet of warships with which they blockaded Piraeus, the port of Athens. By 404 BC, Athens had run out of food and its people were starving. Athens surrendered to Sparta and Thebes and war ended.

Alexander the Great

- **King Philip of Macedon** was assassinated in 336 BC and the throne passed to his 20-year-old son, Alexander. The new king at once announced that he would continue with his father's plans to rule Greece and invade the Persian Empire.

- **Thebes led a revolt** against Alexander in an attempt to free Greece from Macedonian rule. Alexander quickly captured Thebes and sold the entire population as slaves.

- **After the destruction** of Thebes, the other Greek states accepted Alexander's leadership and sent troops to join his army as it invaded the Persian Empire.

- **In 334 BC**, Alexander marched into Persia with 35,000 men. At the Battle of the Granicus he defeated a local army, then marched on into the Persian Empire.

- **At the Battle of Issus** in 333 BC, Alexander defeated Darius, emperor of Persia, and his army of around 100,000 men. He then marched south to occupy Syria, Palestine and Egypt.

- **In Egypt**, Alexander founded the city of Alexandria and was declared to be a god by the priests of the supreme Egyptian god, Ammon.

◀ *Alexander the Great, king of Macedonia, is widely recognized as having been the greatest soldier in the ancient world.*

▲ *Alexander covered almost 32,000 km in the creation
of his massive empire. His route is shown in red.*

- **In 331 BC**, Alexander marched his army into Mesopotamia to face
  the main Persian army at the Battle of Gaugamela. Despite being
  outnumbered by about five to one, Alexander won the battle.

- **After capturing the cities** of Babylon and Persepolis, Alexander
  marched east to occupy the rest of the Persian Empire. He then
  invaded northern India, defeating King Porus at the Battle of
  Hydaspes in 326 BC.

- **Alexander turned back** to Babylon where he began the task of
  organizing a government for his conquests. He appointed Macedonian
  officers in government positions and told them to marry local wives.

- **At the age of just 32**, Alexander died in Babylon of a sudden fever.
  He is widely recognized as one of the finest military commanders of
  all time and is generally known as Alexander the Great.

The Hellenistic world

- **When Alexander the Great died** in 323 BC, his son Alexander was barely a year old. The Macedonian generals decided that Alexander's half-brother Antigonus should govern for the boy until he was old enough.

- **At once**, the generals divided up Alexander's vast empire between themselves, while claiming to rule the provinces on behalf of the infant Alexander.

- **Egypt and Palestine** were given to Ptolemy, Macedonia was taken by Antipater and Seleucus took control of Syria, Persia and the eastern provinces. Other smaller areas were grabbed by lesser generals.

- **Within five years**, the generals were at war with each other for the possession of disputed territories.

- **The generals appointed** Macedonians and Greeks to senior government and military positions in their territories. The Greek term for themselves was Hellenes, so this period is known as the Hellenistic Age.

● **The Hellenistic Kingdoms** introduced Greek language and culture across the Middle East. Local people adopted Greek ways of life.

● **As the power** of the Hellenistic Kingdoms declined, many countries made themselves independent. These included Pontus, Bithynia, Cilicia, Cappadocia, Galatia, Armenia and several of the Greek states.

● **In Egypt**, Ptolemy and his successors introduced new technologies that made Egypt one of the richest countries in the world. They continued to rule Egypt until 30 BC when Cleopatra VII was defeated by Rome.

● **The Seleucid Kingdom** gradually declined and by 65 BC it covered only part of Syria. The last king, Antiochus X, was deposed by the Roman general Pompey, who made Syria a Roman province.

◀ *The area of the world known to the Greeks around 200 BC. The rest of the world was thought to be inhabited by barbaric, uncivilized tribes.*

193

Houses

- **In ancient Greek cities**, houses were built close together, and some even shared walls. City houses did not have gardens.

- **Houses were built** on foundations of stone. The walls were mostly built of sun-dried mud bricks, as they were cheap to make and easy to repair.

- **Most houses** had two storeys, though some were taller than this.

- **Roofs were made** by laying wooden timbers across the mud-brick walls at an angle to form a slope. The timbers were covered by a layer of twigs and dried reeds and pottery tiles were laid on top. The tiles were waterproof and the slope allowed rainwater to run off easily.

- **Every house** had its own front door, which opened onto the street.

- **The walls** that faced onto the street were plain, with only a few small windows. There were no obvious outward indications of how simple or luxurious a house was inside.

- **Most families** lived in houses with about 12 rooms. Poor people lived in houses that may have had just two rooms, while rich families might have had up to 30 rooms.

- **Houses were often built** around an open-air courtyard that was surfaced with cobblestones. Balconies ran around the courtyard on the upstairs level.

Bedrooms were upstairs

Slaves cooked in the kitchen

194

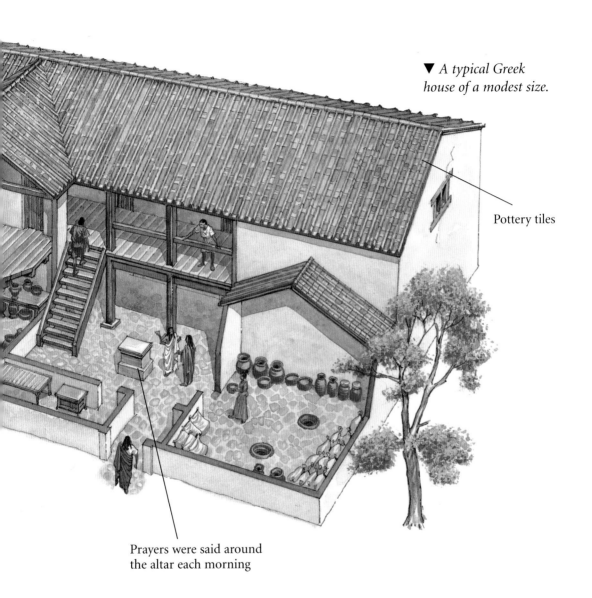

▼ *A typical Greek house of a modest size.*

Pottery tiles

Prayers were said around the altar each morning

- **The floors on ground level** were often tiled and sometimes had colourful mosaics. The floors of upper storeys were made of wood.

- **Most dining rooms** were brightly decorated, and were used to entertain friends and visitors.

195

City life

- **The streets** of most Greek cities were built in a grid pattern. This meant that they were straight and met at right angles. They were usually paved with cobblestones.

- **Most city streets** were wide enough to allow a cart to pass along it. The widest streets allowed two carts to pass going in opposite directions. Narrow alleyways just wide enough for a person to walk along ran behind houses.

- **Most cities** had a fortified hilltop site in, or near, the city centre. This was known as the *acropolis*, which means 'high town'.

- **The *acropolis*** was the area where important temples and public buildings were most commonly built.

- **There was usually** a large, open public space in the city called an *agora*. This was the market place where traders could meet to do business. It was also a place of assembly for the citizens.

- **All cities** had wells or fountains to provide water for their inhabitants. Wells drew their water from underground, beneath the city, while fountains spouted water that was brought along pipes from natural springs outside the city.

...FASCINATING FACT...
Large storehouses were used to keep grain, olive oil and other foodstuffs. These were maintained by the government so that the citizens had enough food in the event of famine or a war.

▲ *Palace pithoi (storage vases) at Knossos, the chief centre of the Minoan civilization. A storage area in a Greek city relied on vases to store liquids and grains. Other objects were kept in stone-lined pits in the ground.*

- **Waste food**, human sewage and other rubbish was dumped in specially marked areas outside the city walls. Poor people carried their own waste in buckets, rich families had servants or slaves to do this work.

- **Strong defensive walls** surrounded every city. Even in peacetime, the city gates were closed at night to keep out wolves and bandits.

- **Public buildings** such as temples, theatres and courtrooms were usually built of stone. This showed how important they were as stone would last for many years longer than the mud-brick of private houses.

Furniture and pottery

- **Most furniture** was made of wood and fairly simple in design. The most common piece of furniture was a stool called a *diphros* that had four legs and a seat covered with leather.

- **The furniture of rich people** might have been carved with decorations, or inlaid with coloured woods, stone or ivory.

- **At mealtimes**, people lay on couches rather than sitting upright. Couches had four legs and were usually covered with a padded cloth mattress.

- **Cupboards and drawers** had not been invented, so most clothes and other objects were stored in wooden chests. Kitchen equipment and household tools were hung on hooks on the wall.

- **Only the rich had baths** because water was heavy to carry into the house. Most people washed using a wide, shallow bowl of water set on a wooden stand.

◀ This detail from a painted amphora *(a vase used for fermenting and storing wine) shows a table, stool and footstool.*

▶ *A black-figure vase from about 500 BC, probably made in Corinth. These pots were the finest ever produced in Greece.*

- **Greek pottery** was made from fine clay that was fired to produce objects that were practical for everyday use.

- **Pottery decorations** usually consisted of pictures or abstract patterns. The earliest pottery had black designs on a reddish background. After about 530 BC, potters learnt how to decorate pots with red figures drawn delicately onto a black background.

- **Wide, rounded pots** with two handles and a narrow neck were called *amphorae*. These were used to store food and drink for long periods of time, or for transport. These were the most numerous types of pot.

- **Drinking cups** were in the form of a wide, shallow bowl with two handles, set on a circular stand. Some people preferred large cups that could be passed around to share drinks.

- **The most impressive pots** were *kraters*. These were large upright vases decorated with elaborate pictures of gods or heroes. They were used at parties to store wine and water before it was served to guests.

199

Clothes and fashion

- **The warm Greek climate** meant that clothes were only necessary for warmth during the winter months. Most of the time the Greeks wore clothes only for modesty.

- **The cheapest fabric** was usually wool, which was woven into cloth at home. Linen was slightly more expensive but was much more comfortable to wear in hot weather. Only the richest people could afford to wear cotton or silk.

- **Men usually** dressed in tunics. These were made of two squares of fabric, which were fastened together at the shoulder and held in place at the waist with a leather belt.

▲ *Greek clothes were loose and flowing, for comfort in the hot summer months.*

200

- **There were two types** of cloak for men. The *chlamys* was a square of cloth that was worn over one shoulder and reached to the knee. The larger *himation* was rectangular in shape and could cover the entire body to the ankles.

- **Sandals made of leather** were the most common footwear, although many poor people walked barefoot. In winter, leather ankle-length boots might have been worn.

- **Men tended to wear** their hair short and grow full beards. By the time of the Hellenistic period, men grew their hair longer and shaved off their beards.

- **Hats were made** of leather or wool. They usually had a low crown and a wide brim to provide protection from the summer sun.

- **Women often wore** a piece of clothing called a doric *chiton*. This consisted of two large squares of fabric, folded over at the top and joined by brooches at the shoulders. It was gathered at the waist by a cord.

- **After 500 BC**, the ionic *chiton* became fashionable for women. This consisted of two pieces of material about 1.6 m sq, that were sewn together down the sides and linked across the top, leaving a hole for the head. It was gathered around the waist or across the bust with straps and belts.

- **Women wore** their hair long, and tied it up with ribbons or scarves into a variety of styles.

Family life

- **The senior man** in a family was the head of the household. He was responsible for the actions of everyone in his family and other members of his family asked his advice before making decisions.

- **Most Greeks** lived in family groups that consisted of a married couple and their children. Sometimes, the parents of the married couple would also live in the same home.

- **The men worked** to support the family. It was considered a great humiliation if a man could not earn enough money to feed and clothe his family in accordance with his position in society.

- **When a baby was born**, the mother showed it to the father. If the baby was weak or sickly in some way, the father could refuse to accept it into the family and the baby would be left to die.

- **Until the age of about seven**, both girls and boys were brought up in the family home.

- **From the age of seven** onwards, children were prepared for adult life. Girls stayed at home to learn domestic skills from their mothers and boys went to school.

- **Children often stayed at home** with their parents until they got married, or could afford a home of their own.

- **Weddings were** usually arranged by the parents, although sometimes the views of the couple getting married were taken into account.

- **Weddings were celebrated** by the families of the couple. After sacrifices were made to the gods, the bride was led in a procession to the home of the groom. The couple then shared their first meal, at which point they became married.

▲ *A Greek vase painting showing the marriage of the gods Jupiter and Juno. In ancient Greece, the bride and groom were married in their best clothes, and crowned with wreaths of leaves.*

...FASCINATING FACT...
Girls were considered to be adults from the age of 15, while boys were not thought to reach adulthood until the age of 18.

Women in society

- **Women in ancient Greece** spent their entire lives under the protection and control of a male relative. At first, this was the woman's father, and after marriage, her husband. Widows remained under the protection of their eldest male relative.

- **The man who was responsible** for a woman was called her *kyrios*. The *kyrios* had complete control over any property owned by the woman and he could spend her money as he chose.

- **If a married woman** inherited property, her cousin or uncle could go to court to force her to divorce her husband. The inherited property would then go to her new *kyrios* – her cousin or uncle.

- **Women were not allowed** to own land or buildings. They were only allowed to own clothes, jewellery and personal slaves.

- **Women who were citizens** were not allowed to go outside of the city unless they were accompanied by a man. Many *kyrios* did not allow their women to walk about the city alone, either.

- **Most houses** had rooms that were reserved for women only. They were usually those at the back of the house, so that the women were hidden from visitors.

- **Special religious festivals** were reserved for female citizens only. At such times, women could gather without their *kyrios* being present.

- **Poor women** actually had more freedom than rich women. They had no slaves, so they had to shop for food and fetch water from the communal well themselves.

◀ *A vase painting showing a woman sitting outside on a folding stool. A pale complexion was thought to be a sign of nobility, so she holds a parasol to protect her skin from the sun.*

- **Domestic skills** such as spinning, weaving or cleaning were considered to be suitable occupations for rich women.

- **In Sparta**, women were allowed to own property, run farms or businesses and wander around the country freely. Other Greeks often used this as an example of how odd the Spartans were.

205

Education and schools

- **Boys attended school** from the age of seven. Schools charged fees that were paid by the father of the boy.

- **As soon as they had learnt the basic skills** such as reading and writing, boys from poorer families left school. From the age of 11 they helped their father at work, and learnt his trade.

▼ *A vase painting from around 500 BC illustrating the various lessons, such as music and writing, that were given at a school in Athens.*

- **Boys from wealthy families** stayed at school until they were 18. They were escorted to and from school by a slave.

- **Education was divided** into three subjects, the most important being literature. Basic literature meant being taught to read and write, and being able to use grammar properly.

- **More advanced literature** involved reading famous books – especially the works of poets, such as Homer. Boys were also taught rhetoric – the ability to write and deliver good speeches.

- **Physical education** was the second subject. This involved learning to play different sports, as well as military training, which included practising using weapons.

- **Music** was the third subject. Boys were expected to learn how to play several musical instruments and to sing.

- **At the age of 18**, boys joined the state gymnasion. This was where philosophers, mathematicians and historians taught. There were no formal courses, so men could drop by as they pleased if they wanted to listen to a lecture or talk to a teacher.

- **Girls did not** attend school. From the age of seven, they were taught domestic skills, such as spinning and weaving, to prepare them to become good wives. Most girls were not taught how to read and write.

- **Education in Sparta** was different. Girls were taught how to read and write and they received an education similar to that of boys, although they did not take part in military training.

Leisure time

- **Most people** in ancient Greece worked longer hours than the average person today, so they had less time for leisure activities.

- **The centre** for most leisure activities was the gymnasion, which was often the largest and most ornately decorated building in a city. All adult men belonged to the gymnasion.

- **At the gymnasion**, men could listen to famous teachers, play sports or simply sit about and talk. Rich men went to the gymnasion every day, but poor men had to work long hours and may have gone only once in a month.

- **Rich men** would also attend the gymnasion to play music, sing and dance. By contrast, poorer men could use their musical skills to earn money by becoming professional musicians.

- **Board games** were a popular pastime in ancient Greece. One such game was played on a marked board that may have been rather like modern draughts. They also played dice games.

- **The Greeks** liked to hold dinner parties. Most houses had a dining room or *andron*, and at normal meal times the whole family ate there. In poorer houses, the *andron* might also be used as a bedroom. Some were richly decorated with mosaics and wall paintings.

- **Women and children** sat on stools or chairs, but men reclined on couches to eat. Food was served on low tables in front of them. Two or three men could share a couch.

- **Wealthy families** hired musicians and dancers to perform during dinner, while slaves served the food and drink.

▶ *A carving of a horse, probably from Athens. Riding and chariot racing were popular sports to watch, though only rich men could afford to take part.*

- **After the meal** was over, the women would leave the table. At this point the men would often hold a political or philosophical discussion called a *symposion*.

- **Some *symposions*** were less sophisticated affairs where men drank too much and played a game called *cottabos*, which involved flicking wine dregs from their cup at a chosen target.

Country life

- **In most Greek states**, about 20 percent of the population lived in the main city, and another 20 percent in other towns. However, the vast majority of the population lived in villages and on farms.

- **People who lived** in the country worked the land, growing crops and raising animals. Most farmers owned small farms, and the few that could afford larger areas of land hired servants or bought slaves to do the work.

Figs

- **The most important grain** crops were wheat and barley, which could only be grown on flat, fertile ground. Large plots of land were needed for grain crops as the ploughs needed room to work properly.

- **Smaller patches** of land were used to grow fruits and vegetables. These crops could be cared for by hand and so could be planted in the smallest plots of fertile land.

- **Grape vines** could grow on the worst soil and steepest slopes. Some grapes were eaten as fruit, but most were turned into wine.

▶ Fruits were popular foods in Greece, and were eaten both fresh and dried. Some fruits were preserved by being sealed in jars filled with honey.

Grapes

Pomegranate

- **Oxen were used** to pull carts and work machinery. These cattle were expensive so sometimes several farmers owned a pair jointly, or a farmer hired them from a more prosperous neighbour.

- **Olives were** an important crop. Like grape vines, olive trees can grow on poor soil and steep slopes. Olives were eaten, and were also crushed to produce olive oil.

- **Farmers kept some of their produce** for themselves to feed their families, and spare produce was taken to the nearest town or city to be sold at the *agora*.

- **People who lived on the coast** often worked as fishermen. They went out in small boats equipped with nets and spears to catch fish and other types of seafood.

- **If they were struck** by disease, or if there was not enough rain, the crops might fail. Famines sometimes killed thousands of people.

211

Food and drink

- **The basic food** of ancient Greece was grain. Wheat was usually ground into flour and then baked into bread. Barley was crushed and boiled to make porridge.

- **Meat was eaten** by rich people, or on special occasions. Roasted lamb was a favourite meat, but boiled mutton or goat might be served instead.

- **Sea fish** was eaten in quantity. Tuna, mackerel, snapper, octopus and squid were favourites. Sea urchins, mussels and clams were all considered to be delicacies.

- **Cucumbers, lettuces and onions** were used in salads, which were often served dressed with olive oil.

- **Vegetables eaten** included peas, artichokes, leeks, beans, turnips and carrots. These could be served raw and thinly sliced, but were more often boiled to make a thick broth.

- **Milk was not often drunk** as it would go sour in the hot weather quickly. Instead, it was made into cheeses, which could be stored for long periods of time.

◀ *Olive trees flourished in the dry, rocky terrain of ancient Greece, and oil made from the crushed fruit was used widely.*

- **Water was obtained** from natural springs. Wealthy people had spring water brought to their houses in large pots if there was not a spring nearby.

- **Greek wine** was heavy and sweet. It was stored in vats smeared with pine resin, which gave it a distinctive flavour. Wine was usually watered down before it was drunk.

- **The Spartan diet** was different. Men ate food thought to make them fit for battle. The main meal consisted of barley bread and vegetable broth, followed by cheese and figs.

▲ *The main course was followed by figs, grapes, cheese and nuts, such as almonds (above).*

...FASCINATING FACT...
An invitation to a Spartan military meal was considered an honour, but the food was so dull it caused one Athenian to remark, "Now I understand why the Spartans do not fear death."

Craftsmen

- **Greek craftsmen** produced goods made of pottery, metal, wood and leather that could then be sold for cash.

- **Early craftsmen** worked in their own homes, usually at the front of the house so that customers could easily do business with them without passing through the rest of the house.

- **Later craftsmen** set up shops to work in, which might have been on the ground floor of their house, or in a separate building.

- **Younger male relatives** would sometimes assist the craftsmen, learning the trade in the process. Slaves could be bought to help with non-skilled parts of the work.

- **Some craftsmen** set up their relatives, or even a slave, in a business of their own. The craftsman would expect a share of any profits in return.

- **One of the most important crafts** in ancient Greece was pottery manufacture. Greek pottery was of a high quality and was exported all over the known world.

◄ *A pair of Greek earrings made from thin sheets of gold, which were carefully hammered into shape.*

◄ *A red figure vase carefully painted to show a warrior putting on his armour. Such exquisitely-made ornamental vases were very expensive.*

● **Some potters** were talented artists, able to decorate their pots with scenes from everyday life, or pictures of gods, goddesses and heroes.

● **Carpenters** produced furniture for houses, and handles for tools and weapons. Many were also employed to build houses, temples and public buildings.

● **Bronzesmiths** were highly regarded. They produced bronze helmets and other weapons in large quantities. Some specialized in making statues for temples and public buildings.

● **Blacksmiths** produced iron and steel used for making weapons or tools. Ancient Greeks could produce only small pieces of iron at a time, so it was used only for smaller objects.

Slaves and slavery

- **It is thought** that between one-quarter and one-third of the population of ancient Greece was made up of slaves.

- **Slaves had no rights** at all. They were regarded as 'living tools' for their masters. A master could order his slaves to do whatever he liked.

- **If a slave was injured** by someone, the perpetrator was expected to pay compensation. The money was not paid to the slave, but to the slave's owner, whose property had been damaged.

- **The poorest citizens** did not own slaves, but most families owned at least one slave to help them with their work or with domestic jobs, such as cooking and cleaning.

- **Rich families** might own up to 40 slaves. Male slaves were often employed as doorkeepers, while female slaves usually worked in the kitchen.

- **Some men bought slaves** to work in workshops. A man named Lysias (c. 440 BC–c. 380 BC), who lived in Athens, owned 120 slaves who worked in his shield business.

- **Slaves were expected** to stand aside to allow citizens to pass in the street and never to look a citizen in the eye. If a slave broke such rules he could be beaten.

- **People who had been captured** during a war were sometimes sold into slavery. It is also thought that some people sold their children as slaves to pay off heavy debts.

◀ *A plate decorated with a scene from a dinner party. A slave girl dances to amuse her master.*

- **Slaves were allowed** to own money and personal effects, but they were not allowed to own land or buildings. It was usual to pay a slave a small tip when you visited a friend's house.

- **Slaves could buy their freedom** if they managed to save up enough money, but only if their owner agreed to sell them. Sometimes slaves were freed when their master died.

Trade and merchants

- **Merchants earned a living** by buying and selling goods. They might buy pottery in Athens, take it to Sicily and sell it in exchange for wheat that they would then take back to sell in Athens.

- **Merchants relied** on the fact that goods could be bought for less money in one place, and sold for more somewhere else. For example, grain could be bought cheaply in Syracuse because of its large, productive farming system, but it was much more expensive in Athens because there was a lack of good farming land.

- **Before trade became common**, all Greek communities were self-sufficient, each producing all the food and goods necessary for its own survival. Farmers provided a full range of food crops, and craftsmen of every type lived within a city.

- **As trade became more common**, people began to specialize, producing a smaller variety of goods and concentrating on quality. For example, Athens was close to good clay, so its craftsmen could make quality pottery at reasonable cost.

◀ *A pair of gold rings decorated with lapis lazuli, a semi-precious stone. The gold came from local sources, but the beautiful blue stone was imported from Afghanistan.*

▶ *Greek coins were made from precious metals such as gold or silver. The design on this coin shows the head of Alexander the Great.*

- **Soon the people of Athens** were producing vast quantities of pottery that they then exported. In return, the Athenians were able to import food that they were not able to grow on the local poor soils.

- **Coins made trading** much easier, allowing merchants to carry a small bag instead of bulky goods. It also made it easier to compare prices of goods in different cities and countries.

- **Some merchants** became incredibly wealthy, but most earned a reasonable living that was only marginally better than that of a farmer or a bronzesmith.

- **The status of merchants** in ancient Greek society was not very high. Aristocrats and politicians preferred to earn their money by owning farms or renting out houses. Haggling over prices was not thought to be very dignified.

- **Some cities** had special areas of the *agora* where merchants from other cities were allowed to trade.

- **Merchants had to pay taxes** before they were allowed to bring goods into a state to sell them. Some cities grew very rich on these taxes.

Travel and exploration

- **Most Greeks** did not travel much. They visited the main city of their state and may have journeyed to a neighbouring state, but few people ventured much further.

- **Travel was expensive**. Time spent travelling meant a loss of income. Only men who could afford to hire others to do their work in their absence could afford to be away for any length of time.

- **Most people travelled** on foot over land, sometimes carrying a stick for support and a folding stool to sit on when resting. Rich men could afford to ride a horse or travel in a chariot.

- **Men serving** in the army or navy might travel long distances to attack enemies or to help friends. Many young men got to see foreign places in this way.

◄ *A Greek merchant ship from about 400 BC. Ships such as these could only travel downwind, so crews sometimes had to wait weeks for a favourable wind.*

...FASCINATING FACT...

Around 350 BC, Pytheas, a Greek merchant from Marseilles, sailed around Britain. He then sailed further north to an island he called Thule (thought to be Iceland). No other Greek had ever travelled this far from Greece.

- **Travelling was part** of a merchant's job. Merchants trading overland used donkeys or mules to carry goods because most roads were too narrow or bumpy for carts.

- **Most merchants** preferred to trade by sea. They used ships that were about 15 m long and 4 m wide. They were powered by a single square sail, although some larger ships had two masts.

- **Merchants only sailed** in the summer months, as winter storms could blow up without warning to make sailing dangerous.

- **Around 1000** BC, Greeks only knew about the eastern Mediterranean Sea, but by 700 BC, they were trading throughout the entire Mediterranean and the Black Sea.

- **After about 500** BC, Greeks began to sail beyond Gibraltar, which they called the Pillars of Heracles, to trade with the people of western Spain, western France and northwestern Africa.

Heroes in chariots

- **During the Mycenaean Period** of about 1800–1150 BC, warfare was carried out by kings and their bands of professional warriors. Only rich men could afford the expensive weaponry needed for warfare.

▼ *A scene from the 2004 movie* Troy *(Warner Bros. Pictures). Chariots carrying the heroes advance in front of the main army.*

- **The richest nobles** fought from chariots. These were two-wheeled vehicles pulled by two ponies, which could carry a driver and a warrior into battle. The warrior had throwing javelins and a sword.

- **Armour was made** of bronze. Horizontal bands of shaped bronze covered the body from the neck to the knees, while hinged plates covered the shoulders and upper arms. Famous warriors could be recognized at a distance by their armour.

- **Helmets were often made** from sheets of bronze held together by leather straps. Some were made of boar tusks stitched on to a leather cap.

- **Leading noblemen** often challenged each other to single combat before a battle. They began by throwing javelins, then they would rush at each other to fight with swords at close quarters.

- **Noblemen who won** a single combat fight sometimes celebrated by tying the body of their opponent to the back of their chariot and dragging it around the battlefield.

- **Some noblemen** led groups of elite warriors into battle. If the leading nobleman was killed, the warriors would flee the battle.

- **Most ordinary warriors** did not wear metal armour. Instead, they used large shields that were up to 1.8 m tall and shaped like a figure-of-eight. Their main weapon was a heavy spear.

- **Warriors fought** in groups with their shields overlapping.

- **Some places**, such as Knossos, Crete, could put hundreds of chariots onto the battlefield. It is likely that all warriors from Knossos fought from chariots instead of on foot.

Early hoplites

- **Warfare in ancient Greece** underwent dramatic changes between about 800 and 700 BC. From being dominated by noblemen on chariots and sieges of cities, an entirely new style of fighting developed.

- **The new style** of fighting depended on armoured men called hoplites, fighting in a formation called a *phalanx*.

- **The purpose** of the *phalanx* formation was to defeat the chariots of the noblemen. Chariots were very effective when used to attack other chariots, or when charging infantry in the sort of loose formation used in Mycenaean times.

▶ *A Corinthian-style helmet. These were hammered out of a single sheet of bronze, which made them extremely strong.*

- **In the *phalanx* formation**, rows of infantry soldiers stood very close together with their shields overlapping. This exploited the fact that horses will not run straight into a large solid object. They will shy off at the last minute and turn aside.

- **Horses would not charge** at men on foot standing close enough together to look as if they are a large, solid object, so the *phalanx* adopted this formation. The chariots of the noblemen soon became useless when confronted by a solid line of men.

- **At first**, the men were equipped in a similar fashion to the Myceanaeans. They had large shields, two throwing spears and a sword.

- **Around 750** BC, the city of Argos introduced a new type of shield. This was round, about one metre across and made of layers of laminated wood fronted by a thin sheet of bronze.

- **The Argive shield** was lighter to use in battle, but still large enough to protect both the man who carried it and the man to his left. Soon, all the armies in Greece were using the Argive shield.

- **The throwing spears** were replaced in about 730 BC by a single 2-m-long thrusting spear with a large, heavy spearhead.

...FASCINATING FACT...
At first, men still carried swords, but in later years these were abandoned by all but the most professional soldiers.

Peltasts

- **Every adult citizen** was expected to serve in the army when ordered to do so during wartime. However, the poorer citizens could not afford to buy the heavy armour needed to be a hoplite. These men served as peltasts instead.

- **Peltasts were a type of soldier** named for the type of shield they carried, the *pelta*. This was about 50 cm across and was made of wickerwork covered with leather or linen.

- **The weapons** of the peltasts varied. Most carried a number of lightweight throwing javelins that were about 1.2 m in length. Each man might have carried up to ten javelins when on campaign.

- **Other light infantry** used slings. These shot a lead pellet that weighed about 50 g. A skilled slinger could send a pellet up to 100 m. A pellet could break the bones of an unarmoured man, and even stun a man wearing a helmet.

- **Few Greek soldiers** used the bow and arrow. Greek bows were relatively weak, shooting an arrow only about 150 m. Only the men of Crete were skilled in archery.

- **No armour** was worn by the peltasts because they could not afford it. This meant that they could not fight in the *phalanx*. Instead, they developed their own methods of fighting.

- **In battle**, the peltasts assembled in loose groups of about 100 men. They would run forwards to throw spears or slingshot at the enemy army as it advanced.

- **Once they had thrown** their weapons, the peltasts would retreat, as they were no match for the hoplites in close combat. They would stand back at the rear to watch the clash between the main forces of hoplites.

- **After the hoplite battle**, the peltasts might be brought in to pursue a defeated army. They were also sometimes used by the losing side to delay the winning army from chasing the fugitives.

- **Peltasts were also used** to scout out enemy positions and to search the countryside for food and other items that could be used by an army.

◀ *The peltasts were lightly armoured and carried several light throwing javelins into battle.*

227

The phalanx

- **The key tactical formation** of the ancient Greeks was the *phalanx*. This formation was made up of armoured hoplite infantry men and could be adapted to include as many men as the army contained.

- **Each city** had its own variation on *phalanx* formations and manoeuvres, but the basic unit was the *lochos*, made up of 144 hoplites, divided into four *enomotia* of 36 men each.

- **On the march**, each *enomotia* was formed three abreast and 12 deep. The commanding officer, the *enomotarch*, led the right-hand file of men. His second in command was at the rear of the left hand file.

- **The front *enomotia*** was commanded by the man who led the entire *lochos*. This man had the rank of *lochagos*.

- **To form a *phalanx*,** the four *enomotia* assembled side by side. This produced a formation 12 men deep and 12 men wide. If the formation needed to cover a wider frontage, it would rearrange to six men deep and 24 men wide.

- **The front four ranks** of men held their spears overhead, pointing forwards over the tops of their shields. The rear ranks held their spears upright.

- **At the start of a battle**, the men would sing war songs and march into position. Then they would march towards the enemy.

- **When the two *phalanxes*** were about 100 m apart, the men would run forwards, keeping in formation. The two phalanxes would crash together when they met.

- **The men at the front** would use their spears, while the men at the back pushed forward with their shields. If a man fell in battle, the man behind stepped forward to take his place.

- **Eventually**, one *phalanx* would begin to give way. Once this happened, the *phalanx* would break up and the men would fall back quickly.

▲ *Most Greek battles involved rival* phalanxes *fighting each other at close quarters.*

Early warships

- **During Mycenaean times,** warships were not dissimilar to merchant ships, but they had oars so they could travel even if there was no wind.

- **When Mycenaean warships met,** the crews would first throw spears at the rival ship. When the ships manoeuvred closer to each other, the men would leap across to attack the enemy crew with swords.

- **One tactical aim** was to trap an enemy ship between two of your own. That way you would have twice as many men boarding the enemy as the enemy had to defend their own ship.

- **The *pentekonter*** was a new type of warship that was invented around the year 900 BC. Instead of boarding the enemy, the *pentekonter* crew would try to ram and sink the enemy ships.

- **Pine was the traditional material** used to make a *pentekonter*, and spruce was used for the oars. The strength of the ship came from three timbers that ran the length of the ship. The planks that formed the hull were attached to these timbers with wooden pegs.

- **A *pentekonter*** was about 20 m long and just 1.2 m wide. It was powered by 50 men rowing, arranged in 25 pairs sitting side by side. Each man used an oar about 4 m long that was held in place by leather straps.

- **A narrow walkway** ran between the rowers, connecting two larger areas of deck at the front and back of the ship.

- **The captain stood** at the back of the deck, along with a man who steered the ship using two large paddles, one either side, and a drummer who beat out a rhythm to keep the men rowing in time.

▲ *In Mycenaean times,*
warships carried large crews.
If they successfully boarded an
enemy ship they would attack
the crew with swords.

- **Men armed with javelins** stood at the front of the ship, ready to
  hurl them at the oarsmen on enemy ships. This would slow the enemy
  down and make them vulnerable to attack.

- **At the front of the ship**, a long metal-covered spike, or ram, projected
  forwards about 2.5 m. This ram was able to smash through the flank of an
  enemy ship.

Later warships

- **A new type of warship**, the *bireme*, was invented around 700 BC. This ship had two banks of oarsmen on each side, sitting one above the other.

- **The *bireme*** had a greater number of men rowing for the size of the ship, so it was able to move faster than the *pentekonter*, giving it an advantage.

◀ *A modern replica of a Greek* trireme *shows how the three banks of oars were organized.*

- *Biremes* **often had a mast** and a sail to help the ship move quickly if the wind was in the right direction. They were not used during battle.

- **Around 550 BC**, a new type of warship appeared – the *trireme*. It was very similar to the *bireme*, but it had an extra bank of oarsmen sitting above the existing two on lightweight benches that projected over the sides of the ship.

- **By 500 BC**, all Greek navies were equipped with *triremes* as their main type of warship. A few *pentekonters* were kept for use as messengers and scouts.

- **A typical *trireme*** would be about 40 m long and 3 m wide, though the upper benches might increase the width to around 5.5 m.

- **The crew** included 170 oarsmen, arranged with 54 on the lower and middle banks, and 62 on the upper bank. There was also a captain, a steerer and a musician who kept time for the rowers. In addition, each vessel carried about 15 soldiers.

- **The *trireme*** could move faster than any other warship and so it was able to ram with greater force. The ram had an upright pole, or bulge, to stop it driving too far into an enemy ship.

- **The ram** was made of bronze-covered wood, and often shaped so that it had three sharp prongs facing forward just below the waterline.

- **Around 380 BC**, ships were made wider so that more than one man could pull on each oar. A typical *quinqereme* had two banks of oars, with two men pulling on each lower oar and three men on each upper oar.

Siege warfare

- **In Mycenaean times**, siege warfare involved bombarding city gates with rocks and axes. The city walls were too tall and strong for the armies to break through with hand weapons.

- **Between 1000 and 450 BC**, the Greeks did not lay siege to cities. During this time, city defences were very strong and Greek armies were made up of part-time soldiers who were ill-equipped to fight a long, drawn-out battle.

- **After about 450 BC**, the Greeks began to learn siege tactics from their Persian enemies, and developed ideas of their own. At the same time, some armies were made up of full-time soldiers, so lengthy sieges were more practicable.

- **One new tactic** was to surround the city, cutting it off from any sources of food or supply. A large army was necessary to keep a good watch for anyone trying to bring supplies to the city.

- **In 429 BC**, a small Spartan army built a wall of brick and timber all the way around the city of Plataea to stop supplies getting into the city.

- **A battering ram** consisted of a bronze-tipped tree trunk suspended from a wooden cage on wheels. This could be swung repeatedly at the city walls to smash through them.

...FASCINATING FACT...

An assault ramp consisting of earth packed between timber piles could be built against the city walls. This allowed troops to storm up and over the wall.

▶ *The catapult was first used in Greece around 400 BC. It was built of wood and used twisted strips of rawhide or sinew for power. It could hurl a stone or bolt about 600 m.*

- **Defenders could counter** a battering ram by shooting the men working it. Alternatively, they could lower large hooks over the walls, catch hold of the ram and pull upwards to overturn it.

- **During Hellenistic times,** siege techniques advanced rapidly as the kings fought for control of the rich cities in what had been the Persian Empire.

- **Hellenistic siege engines** included wooden towers up to 40 m in height, which allowed attackers to target men on the city walls. They also featured catapults that were able to hurl projectiles that could destroy buildings, armoured wooden huts containing ballistae (a powerful ancient crossbow that shot giant bolts), and many different devices for drilling and tunnelling.

King Philip's army

- **Around the year 350** BC, King Philip of Macedon completely reformed the army of his kingdom.

- **With his improved equipment** and tactics Philip conquered Thrace and most of Greece, while his son, Alexander, defeated the Persian Empire.

- **The core** of the new Macedonian army was the *syntagma*, a unit of 256 infantry, which marched, camped and fought together as a compact unit.

- **All the men** in the Macedonian *syntagma* were equipped identically. The infantry were recruited from peasants, so the weapons and armour were supplied by the king.

- **Each man** wore a bronze helmet and carried a shield that was about 60 cm across and made of wood faced with leather. The men in the front ranks wore a bronze *cuirass* and bronze greaves, but the men to the rear wore linen *cuirasses*.

- **The key weapon** was the *sarissa*. This was a heavy pike up to 7 m in length, which had an iron spearhead and a heavy iron butt so that it balanced neatly at the rear.

- **The front five** or six ranks held their *sarissa* pointing horizontally forwards at waist height. This produced a solid hedge of long, iron-tipped spears that prevented their enemy from getting anywhere near them.

- **The men further back** held their *sarrisas* sloping forwards over the heads of the men in front. This produced a dense cover that could break the impact of javelins and arrows.

- **In battle**, each *syntagma* formed a square that was 16 men deep and 16 men across. They were trained to march forwards, sideways and backwards as a group.

- **In 334 BC**, the Macedonian infantry consisted of 50 *syntagma* – about 13,000 men. There were also about 7000 infantry armed with javelins or slings, who were probably peltasts.

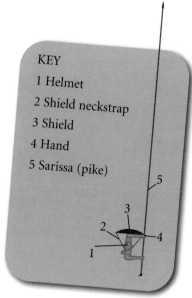

KEY

1 Helmet

2 Shield neckstrap

3 Shield

4 Hand

5 Sarissa (pike)

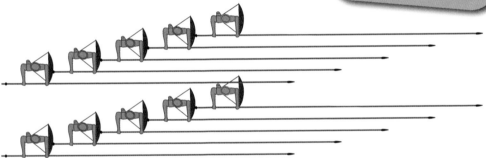

▲ *The 'closed order' position was used when the* syntagma *was advancing. The soldiers' shields had neckstraps because both hands were needed to support the* sarissa.

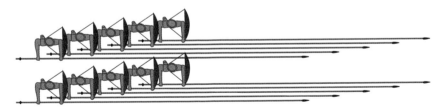

▲ *When the* syntagma *was on the defensive, the soldiers took on a 'locked' position, each one pushing his shield up against the man in front to provide a solid defensive wall.*

237

Companions on horseback

- **The success of the Macedonian army** on the battlefield was due to the careful combination of the *syntagma* with heavy cavalry, called Companions. While the *syntagma* held an enemy army, the Companions would charge through and sweep to victory.

- **The Companion cavalry** were recruited from noblemen and rich families. It is possible that each man may have paid for his own horse and equipment.

◄ *This Roman mosaic is thought to depict Alexander the Great's defeat of the Persian army at the Battle of Issus, in 333 BC. This detail shows King Darius in his chariot. His driver is desperately trying to turn as they face Alexander leading his cavalry.*

- **The armour consisted** of a bronze cuirass and bronze greaves, as well as flexible armour that protected the groin and thigh areas. No shields were carried.

- **The helmet** most commonly worn had a round crown with a flared brim that bent down over the ears. This was known as the Boeoetian helmet, and it gave good protection while still allowing excellent vision and hearing.

- **The main weapon** was a long, heavy spear, which was about 3 m in length. Each man also carried a heavy sword for use in case his spear broke in battle.

- **The cavalry fought** in formations known as *ilai*, which consisted of either 210 or 300 men.

- **When charging**, the cavalry formed a wedge shape, with the point facing toward the enemy. The impact of this formation when moving at speed was so immense that it could drive a hole through most infantry formations.

- **After the cavalry** had created a gap, other troops would pour through, then turn to attack the enemy from the flank and rear.

- **Alexander won** the battles of the Granicus, Issus and Gaugemala when he led his Companions in a charge that broke a gap in the Persian line.

- **The Macedonians** also had light cavalry called *prodromai*. These men wore no armour other than a helmet. They were used for scouting and for pursuing a retreating enemy.

War elephants

- **In 326 BC**, Alexander invaded India and fought the Battle of Hydaspes against King Porus. The Indian army included war elephants, and this so impressed Alexander that he started to use them in his own army.

- **Specially trained** Indian elephants were used in battle. They were controlled by riders who sat on their shoulders.

- **Each elephant** carried a wooden box on its back, held in position by strong chains. Inside the box crouched two archers and a man armed with a *sarissa*.

- **The archers** could use their high position to fire over the top of enemy defences. They also had a better view of enemy commanders or other high-value targets.

- **The man wielding the *sarissa*** was expected to drive off any enemy troops who attempted to attack the elephant. His armour was heavier than that of the archers.

- **War elephants** were trained to trample men underfoot, or kneel down and crush them with their tusks. They could also lift men in their trunks and throw them aside.

- **Siege work** required elephants that had been specially trained. They were equipped with metal plates on their foreheads with which they could push in the gates of a fortress.

...FASCINATING FACT...

Many horses were frightened of elephants, so a line of elephants would often stop a cavalry charge in its tracks.

- **Although they were difficult** to kill, javelins and heavy arrows could wound elephants badly. Wounded elephants were difficult to control and could inflict as many casualties on their own side as on the enemy.
- **Elephants could** be stopped by throwing planks studded with upward pointing nails on the ground, because these hurt their sensitive feet.

▼ *A scene from the 2007 movie 300 (Warner Bros. Pictures) showing a Persian war elephant in action. Elephants were powerful weapons, but could be unreliable.*

Kings and palaces

- **During the Mycenaean Period**, each city state was ruled by a king, and had several families of wealthy nobles.

- **Written records** from this period are rare, and those that have survived are usually lists of goods being stored or sold. Little is known for certain about the system of government during this period.

- **It is thought that the king** had total power over the city and its inhabitants, and could make laws and order punishments as he wished.

- **It is likely that the nobles** advised the king during councils, which were held to discuss important issues. However, it was the king who had the final say in any decision.

- **Kings often made alliances** with each other. Marriages between royal families were a common way to make an alliance more formal.

- **Every city** was dominated by a large palace where the king lived and worked. The palace also contained storerooms that housed food and other goods.

- **A king** would have kept all his valuables in the storerooms within his palace. Money had not yet been invented, so wealth was measured in terms of precious objects.

- **Laws were made by the kings**, who also acted as judges in legal disagreements. People brought their disputes before the king and he decided who was in the right and what punishment the lawbreaker should be given.

- **Part of a king's duty** was to be brave and successful in warfare. Kings had to protect their city and lands from other kings and their armies, and from raiders.

● **When a member of the royal family died**, they were buried in a large underground tomb filled with rich treasures. At Mycenae, the kings had gold masks placed over their faces before burial.

▼ *A section of the palace at Knossos on the island of Crete. A succession of powerful kings ruled a rich and populous kingdom here.*

The polis

- **The ancient Greeks** lived in separate communities, each usually based around a single city. A community such as this is known as a *polis*, translated as 'city-state'. The number of *poleis* in Greece varied, but usually numbered well over 100.

- *Poleis* **were independent** of each other The people of ancient Greece recognized that they all shared a common culture when compared to foreigners such as Persians or Romans, but they did not see themselves as part of a single nation.

- **The *polis*** was defined as a group of people living in a particular area, who ruled themselves and did not answer to any outside authority.

▼ *The Acropolis in Athens was the central part of the city-state. It was where elections were held and meetings took place.*

In 427 BC, the Spartans destroyed the *polis* of Plataea. The Plataean citizens that survived moved to Athens. More than 50 years later, Plataea was rebuilt and the citizens returned.

- **The centre of a *polis*** was usually a city. This was where the law courts and the most important temples were situated, and where the business of government was carried out.

- **The land** that a *polis* covered varied from largely barren and empty, or rich and dotted with farms and villages. Sometimes a *polis* would encompass more than one city.

- ***Poleis* ranged in size** from communities with only a few hundred citizens, to some with tens of thousands. They also varied widely in their wealth and culture.

- **Only adult men** were considered to be full citizens. Women and children from families that had citizen status still did not have the same rights as male citizens.

- **Not all *poleis*** were completely independent – some had to pay tribute to a more powerful *polis* nearby. Sometimes *poleis* would voluntarily join together to form a league or alliance.

- ***Poleis* that had joined together** would sometimes gradually lose their individuality. The territory of Attica contained several towns, but they all belonged to the *polis* of Athens.

The rule of the tyrants

- **The tyrant** Kypselus of Corinth took power with the backing of the hoplites of the citizen army. He proved to be very popular and was even able to go about Corinth unarmed and without a bodyguard.

- **Kypselus used the slogan** 'give justice to Corinth' throughout his rule. His first act to was ensure that all citizens were viewed as equal in the law courts – aristocrats and citizens were given the same punishments for the same crimes.

- **The key to Kypselus' success** was probably that he listened to the needs of ordinary citizens. It is thought that he called meetings of the citizens to discuss key decisions.

- **Kypselus was so popular** that when he died, his son, Periander, was immediately installed as the new tyrant of Corinth.

- **The city of Sicyon** appointed a tyrant called Orthagoras in 650 BC. He quickly gained a reputation for being honest and impartial, but he imposed severe penalties on anyone who broke his laws.

- **Orthagoras and his descendants** ruled as tyrants of Sicyon for more than 100 years.

- **The laws of Pittakos**, tyrant of the city of Mytilene on Lesbos, were biased against the aristocrats. For example, if an aristocrat committed a crime while drunk, he had to suffer double the penalty that anyone else would have been given.

- **Pittakos resigned his position** as tyrant in about 570 BC. He set up a constitution by which the citizens could elect government officials.

- **By about the year 500** BC, the rule of the Greek tyrants was ending. Most had either died, resigned or been ousted from power.

- **Tyrants continued to rule** in the Greek cities of Sicily and southern Italy after 500 BC.

Name	Details	Known for...
Peisistratos	Tyrant of Athens 560–527 BC	Patronizing the arts.
Gelon	Tyrant of Syracuse 491–475 BC	Defeating Carthage at the Battle of Himera (480 BC).
Hieronymos	Tyrant of Syracuse 216–211 BC	Patronizing science and employing Archimedes.
Anaxilaos	Tyrant of Rhegium d. 476 BC	Never executing anyone for any crime.
Phalaris	Tyrant of Agrigentum d. 552 BC	Building the Brass Bull of Sicily statue.
Phintias	Tyrant of Agrigentum d. 282 BC	Organizing the best parties in the world.

Lawgivers

- **Lawgivers were appointed** in some Greek states instead of tyrants. Lawgivers did not rule the state, but set up rules and constitutions that were designed to end disputes between aristocrats and citizens.

- **One problem in many states** was that it was the responsibility of the family of the victim to choose and enforce the appropriate punishment for the criminal.

- **Feuds developed** between different families and clans over arguments about legal punishments, and could become violent. Fighting in the streets was common and many men were killed as a result.

- **All lawgivers** sought to establish a method by which punishments could be decided and agreed upon by everyone. Some specified particular punishments for various common crimes, while others set up panels of judges to review each crime and give out appropriate punishments.

- **In some states**, the laws were not made public by the aristocrats. Lawgivers usually published their laws and decisions so that even the poorest knew what they were or were not allowed to do.

- **Getting into debt** was a common problem for the poorer people of ancient Greece. In some cities, men who had got into debt were sold as slaves, but this led to a decline in the numbers of citizens.

- **Slavery as a punishment for debt** was made illegal by most lawgivers. Instead, they introduced limits on how much interest a money lender could charge and set up different ways that a debt could be paid off.

- **Some of the laws** that were brought in by the lawgivers seem very strange to us today. In Athens, idleness was made a crime, so if a man did not have a job, he could be prosecuted in court and punished.

▲ *A modern reconstruction of the Stoa of Attalos in Athens. It was originally used as a market and meeting place, but is now a museum.*

- **Lawgivers also affected** the way states were run. In Athens, the lawgiver Solon established a council called the *boule* that ran the day-to-day affairs of government in Athens.

- **Not all Greek states** consulted a lawgiver. Some states continued to abide by traditional laws and ways of doing things.

The growth of democracy

- **The word democracy** is based on two words from ancient Greece. *Demos* means citizens who are not aristocrats, while *kratos* means power. Effectively the word democracy means 'people-power'.

▼ *Voting followed strict procedures, and varied from city to city. In Sparta, men raised their hands to vote, elsewhere they put coloured balls in pots.*

- **Both tyrants and lawgivers** sought to solve social problems by removing legal restrictions that the public objected to.

- **Democracy began to be seen** as a possible way to solve social and legal problems. If the ordinary people had some way to change laws and government policy, they would be less likely to cause trouble.

- **Solon, lawgiver to Athens**, began this process. He arranged that only aristocrats could serve as government officials, but that they had to be elected by the Assembly of all citizens.

- **When an official retired**, he could be appointed to join the *Areopagus*, a panel of judges, by his fellow aristocrats. This panel dealt with serious crimes, deciding if a person was guilty and what his punishment should be.

- **The Council** was a group of men elected by the Assembly. It decided how often the Assembly met and how votes were to be conducted. Aristocrats were not allowed to serve on the Council.

- **In 546 BC**, a rivalry between the citizens of Athens and the surrounding towns and the poor farmers living inland, led to a tyrant named Peisistratus taking power in Athens.

- **Peisistratus reformed** taxation laws but made few changes to the constitution of Solon.

- **After Peisistratus died**, Cleisthenes, a nobleman, used support in the Assembly to introduce radical new government structures that put even more powers into the hands of the ordinary citizens.

- **Cleisthenes set up new systems** for local and national government that allowed ordinary citizens more rights and power. For the first time, people began to talk about 'democracy'.

Archons and councils

- **Records of the government structures** of most Greek *poleis* have not survived, but it is accepted that the system in Athens was much admired, and parts of it were copied elsewhere.

- **In Athens**, the most important government officials were the nine archons, who were elected annually. The archons looked after law and order throughout the *polis*.

- **The most senior** was known as the Archon *Eponymous*. He dealt with disputes about inheritance, land ownership and the care of orphans. The second archon, the *Basileus*, dealt with disputes about religion.

- **The other archons** kept order in the streets. They hired men to arrest criminals and to make sure that everyone obeyed the laws of Athens.

- **Athens also had** ten *strategoi*. These men were also elected by the Assembly, but they were not necessarily aristocrats. At first, the *strategoi* were generals, each in command of one-tenth of the Athenian army.

- **Around 485** BC, many powers were transferred from the archons to the *strategoi*, and many of the activities of the aristocratic archons became largely ceremonial.

- **Lesser officials** in the government looked after basic administration and the day-to-day business.

- **Before Cleisthenes**, the lesser officials were unpaid, so only wealthy aristocrats could afford to do these jobs. After Cleisthenes, they were paid a basic salary. Even the poorest citizen could then become a government official.

▲ *An Archon in Athens judges a dispute between two foreign merchants about a business deal. The Archons were aristocrats elected by the Assembly.*

- **The Council** that decided how the Assembly worked was elected at the start of every year. The *polis* was divided up into 500 areas, each of which elected one Council member.

- **By 480 BC**, a motion could be put to the Assembly only if the Council had first agreed to it. This gave the Council a great deal of power.

253

Assemblies and voting

- **Every adult male citizen** was a member of the Assembly in their *poleis*. The way the Assembly functioned varied from state to state.

- **Assemblies usually met** in the open air so that there was enough room for all citizens to attend. At Athens, the Assembly met on the slopes of a small hill called the Pnyx.

- **Under the rule** of the aristocrats, most Assemblies were summoned so that the nobles could announce their policies. Men at the Assembly could applaud, or not, to show approval, but they did not have the power to change the decisions.

▶ *In Athens, men wrote down the way they were voting on pieces of broken pottery called* ostraka, *and handed them in to the officials.*

...FASCINATING FACT...

The word 'ostracism' means 'broken pottery'. The vote got this name
because people had to write their vote on a piece of broken pottery.

- **In some *poleis*,** Assemblies could vote on proposals put forward by the aristocrats. Assemblies could only approve or reject ideas, they could not come up with ideas themselves.

- **Votes were usually decided** by a show of hands. A formal vote would only be held if there was no clear majority.

- **One system of voting** was to give each man two clay discs. A disc with a hole in meant yes, one without a hole meant no. Each citizen dropped his chosen disc into a box to vote.

- **The vote** could be kept secret. If a citizen did not want anyone else to know which way he was voting, he could put his thumb over the centre of the clay disc to hide if there were a hole or not.

- **Tyrants often allowed Assemblies to vote** on proposals. Most tyrants wanted to be popular with the large number of poorer citizens, and allowing them to vote freely often ensured this.

- **In Athens,** the assembly voted once each year on ostracism. This meant that they voted to exile a person that they did not like from the *polis*. If anyone got enough votes they had to leave Athens for ten years.

Citizens and strangers

- **Only citizens** were able to take part in the government and public life of a *polis*. Being a citizen of a *polis* was considered a great a honour.

- **Citizens were usually men** aged over 18. In some states, men had to be over the age of 21, or had to have served in the army to be considered citizens.

- **At the time** of the aristocrats, a man could become a citizen by living in a city for a certain number of years, or by a decree from the government.

- **The right to citizenship** passed from a man to his sons, but did not pass through a woman to her children.

- **By about 400** BC, a boy could become an Athenian citizen only if his father was a citizen and his mother was the daughter of a citizen.

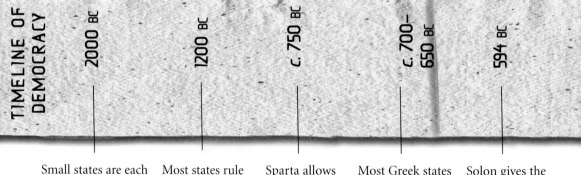

TIMELINE OF DEMOCRACY

2000 BC	1200 BC	c. 750 BC	c. 700– 650 BC	594 BC
Small states are each ruled by a king – some by force, others by consent. Most kings inherit power, but some seize it with armed men.	Most states rule by oligarchies – groups of noblemen who impose their rule on the state.	Sparta allows citizens to elect a new king when one dies, but they must choose from within the royal family.	Most Greek states allow all male citizens to vote in elections, but their power is usually limited.	Solon gives the Athens assembly new powers. The word 'democracy', is coined.

- **People outside of this criteria** had to be given citizenship by a vote of the Assembly, which very rarely happened.

- **The children** of a citizen and an outsider, or foreigners who had come to live in the *polis*, were non-citizens. They were usually called freemen.

- **Men who were not citizens** were allowed to own property and enforce contracts on citizens. They were also protected by law against fraud and theft.

- **Non-citizens** could not attend the Assembly or appear in court. If they were involved in a legal dispute, they had to get a citizen to appear in court on their behalf.

- **Slaves had almost no rights** at all. A slave who gained his freedom could become a freeman, but he was never allowed to become a citizen.

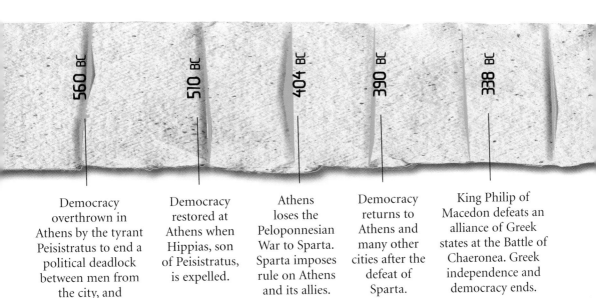

560 BC	510 BC	404 BC	390 BC	338 BC
Democracy overthrown in Athens by the tyrant Peisistratus to end a political deadlock between men from the city, and farmers.	Democracy restored at Athens when Hippias, son of Peisistratus, is expelled.	Athens loses the Peloponnesian War to Sparta. Sparta imposes rule on Athens and its allies.	Democracy returns to Athens and many other cities after the defeat of Sparta.	King Philip of Macedon defeats an alliance of Greek states at the Battle of Chaeronea. Greek independence and democracy ends.

The law

- **During the Mycenaean Period**, the word of a king was law. It is thought that there were no written laws at all, just customs and an agreed moral code that decreed some things, such as theft, to be wrong.

- **If one person** had a complaint against another, for instance that he had stolen something, the two people went to the king. The king then decided if a crime had been committed and, if so, what the punishment should be.

- **During the time of aristocratic rule**, the aristocrats acted as judges to decide whether or not someone was guilty and what their punishment should be. Some *poleis* had written laws, but these were not usually made public.

- **A key demand** of ordinary citizens in most cities was that laws should be stated publicly, so that everyone knew what they were and what the punishments for breaking them would be.

- **In Athens** and some other cities, a stone tablet was set up in the *agora* and was used to list the most important laws. New laws had to be announced in the *agora* and then a written copy was put up so everyone could read it.

- **Some cities had armed police** to arrest criminal suspects and take them to court. Other cities did not, and it was the citizen's responsibility to arrest anybody he thought had committed an offence against him.

- **In democratic systems** the judges were elected, usually by the Assembly, to serve for a fixed amount of time. If people thought a judge did not reach fair decisions, he was replaced.

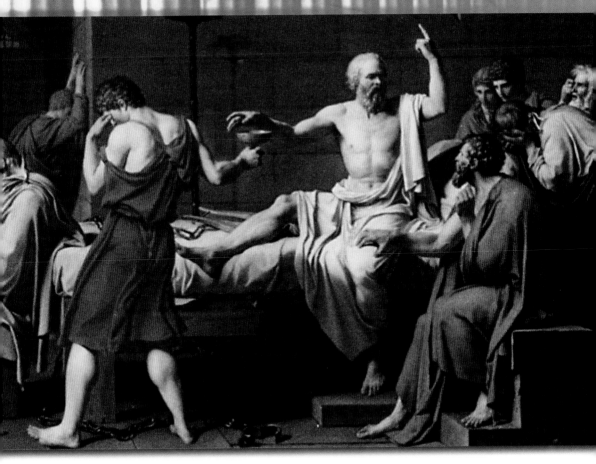

▲ *The philosopher Socrates was accused of corrupting young minds by the Athenian government and condemned to death. French artist Jacques-Louis David painted* The Death of Socrates *in 1787. It shows Socrates about to drink the poison that will end his life.*

- **Citizens had to present their own cases** in court. However, they were permitted to hire lawyers and speech-writers to help them make their case.

- **Citizens were only allowed** a limited amount of time to present their case. Speeches were timed using a water clock.

- **Allegations of treason** were heard in front of the Assembly. Since the crime was against all citizens, it was thought fair that all citizens should act as the jury.

259

Lesser officials

- **Every Greek *polis*** employed officials who ensured the smooth running of the government – enforcing laws, gathering taxes and keeping records.

- **In smaller cities**, these officials were often unpaid, and worked part-time. In larger cities, the officials worked full-time and most were paid a salary.

- **The *gymnasiarchos*** was in charge of the maintenance of the state gymnasion – the institution for education and sport.

▶ *The* Hoplomachoi *(centre) was an official who trained the citizens to fight in wars.*

- **Another task** of the *gymnasiarchos* was to find exceptional athletes among those who attended the gymnasion, who could represent the *polis* at festivals and games. If such a person were found, he may then have been paid a wage so that he could train full-time.

- **The *hoplomachoi*** was a key official in most cities. His main role was to train the soldiers. He also inspected the town walls and gates to make sure that they were in good condition.

- **Another official** kept a detailed record of all citizens. This office became increasingly important as citizens' rights increased. By about 400 BC, the citizenship records were updated regularly and were available to the public.

  - *Taxiarchs* **kept records on all citizens** containing details of whether men were fit and able to march with the army in the event of a war.

    - **The *agorarchon*** was responsible for regulating the market, or *agora*. Part of his job was to ensure that the scales that were used by all the traders weighed goods accurately.

      - **Most cities** levied taxes on goods that were imported or exported. A special official had the task of calculating the tax and making sure that it was paid.

      - **Harbour masters** had to ensure the smooth running of the port. He decided which ship should dock where, supervised dock workers and collected fees from shipowners.

The kings of Sparta

- **The *polis* of Sparta** was unique in ancient Greece. It had a system of government quite unlike any other, and had customs and social rules that other Greeks found very strange.

- **The Spartan system** of government was designed by Lycurgos around 700 BC. In devising his system, Lycurgos had to decide how to regulate the Spartan kings.

- **Sparta was unusual** in that it was still ruled by kings, but aristocrats and ordinary citizens wanted the kings' powers to be limited.

- **The problem** was complicated by the fact that the royal family had two branches, the Agiads and the Eurypontids, both of which claimed to be the true royal family.

- **Lycurgos decided** that there should be two kings, one Agiad and one Eurypontid. One should command the army and the other should deal with religious and domestic affairs.

- **Five officials** called *ephors* were elected each year by the Assembly of citizens, to ensure the kings obeyed the law and spent state money wisely.

- **The *ephors*** even had the power to put the kings in prison. In 427 BC, King Agis of the Eurypontids was imprisoned by the *ephors* for a crime of sacrilege (disrespect for something sacred).

- **The Spartan kings** sat on the senior council, the *gerousia*, which dealt with the running of the government. The other council members were men aged over 60, elected by the Assembly.

● **Each Spartan king** was allowed to have a bodyguard of 300 soldiers that he kept with him at all times.

...FASCINATING FACT...
The most famous Spartan king was Leonidas, who was killed fighting the Persians at the Battle of Thermopylae (480 BC). A modern statue of the king stands at Thermopylae in Greece.

▶ *King Leonidas of Sparta, as depicted in the 2007 movie, 300. Leonidas was one of the most famous warriors of ancient Greece.*

Leagues and alliances

- **Greek *poleis*** operated independently of one another, but they sometimes formed leagues and alliances. Some were based on religion, others were military in nature.

- **The majority of leagues** were organized to serve a particular purpose. For example, a number of small states would sometimes form a league in order to fight against a single, larger state.

- **The story of the Trojan War** was remembered in legend. It was fought by a league of Greek states against Troy, a city in what is now western Turkey.

- **The oldest known league** was the Amphictyony (group of neighbours) of Anthela, which was formed some time before 650 BC. It included *poleis* from Thessaly, Locris, Boeotia and Phocis.

- **The Amphictyony of Anthela** was dedicated to the defence of the sacred temple to Apollo at Delphi. It continued until about AD 300, but by then was a religious organization only.

- **The unity of all Attica** as the *polis* of Athens by 600 BC is thought to have been based on an earlier league between the then independent cities of Athens, Marathon, Aphidna, Eleusis, Thoricus and Rhamnus.

- **The city of Thebes** joined with other nearby cities to form the Boeotian League. None of the states in the League could go to war without the permission of the others.

- **By about the year 400 BC**, Thebes had come to dominate the Boeotian League, which increasingly behaved as if it were one state when it came to foreign policy.

▲ *The Hellenic League (shown in blue) included most of the states in southern Greece.*

- **The most famous league** was the Hellenic League. This was founded in 481 BC to oppose the Persian invasion of Greece.

- **The last league** was the Achaean League of cities in the Peloponnese. It was crushed by the Roman Empire in 146 BC.

265

Greek architecture

- **In the Mycenaean Period**, the Greeks built strong defensive walls of stone around their cities, although most houses and other buildings were made of wood.

- **Until about 650** BC, the Greeks built all of their buildings out of wood or brick, using thatch for roofs. A few roughly shaped stones were used for foundations and around doorways.

- **When the Greeks** began to build in stone, they based their designs on the wooden structures that the new stone buildings were replacing. For example, their new temples had stone columns that were based on pillars carved from single tree trunks.

- **At first**, the Greeks only used stone for temples, but later it was used for many different types of public buildings.

- **There were three** basic styles, or orders, of Greek architecture. Some buildings were built using just one order, others combined two or even all three.

- **The Doric order** developed in mainland Greece around 650 BC. Doric columns had a plain square capital (top), and did not have bases. The space above the columns had small sculptures.

...FASCINATING FACT...

Most stone buildings were square because it made them easier to build. However, a few temples, called *tholos*, were round.

- **The statue of Zeus** at Olympia was Phidias' greatest work. It survived until AD 475, by which time it had been moved to Constantinople. It was destroyed in an accidental fire.

- **It is thought** that Phidias had a team of junior sculptors who followed his designs and did most of the more basic work.

- **The sculpture** of Hermes and Dionysus, found by archaeologists at Olympia, is almost certainly the original work by Praxiteles.

- **Phidias later moved** to Lemnos, where he produced dozens of bronze and stone sculptures. He died in about 415 BC.

- **Praxiteles lived** around the year 350 BC. He specialized in nude figures, and his Aphrodite of Cnidus was considered to be the finest statue of a naked woman, in the world.

- **Lysippus of Sicyon** produced more than 600 statues throughout his career. Alexander the Great commissioned him to produce the only official statues of himself.

- **Lysippus was famous** for his unusual compositions. His best-known work showed a man getting out of a bath, but he also produced conventional statues of gods and men.

The tragedies

- **The tragedy** is a grand drama doomed to end unhappily for the hero. The form was created by Greek dramatists such as Aeschylus, Euripides and Sophocles.

- **The earliest Greek plays** were performances of sacred songs and dances that were held in honour of the god Dionysius every spring. These were staged in the *agora* and were performed by a chorus of 15 men.

▼ *The Temple of Herodes Atticus in Athens was built about* AD *160, with banks of seats and a tall stage set.*

- **Around the year 540** BC, Peisistratus, tyrant of Athens, introduced a drama competition. Each year, three writers were asked to put on plays during the spring festival to Dionysus. The man who wrote the best play was given a prize.

- **The first performance** by an actor as a character in a play was around 510 BC. His role on stage was to ask questions, which the chorus would answer. Dramatists used the actor to set the scene and create emotions.

- **By about 500** BC, plays were being staged in purpose-built theatres. These were made by building seats into the side of a hill and erecting a stage in front of the seats.

- **From about 483** BC, the writer Aeschylus wrote a series of plays that won the drama competition for several years running. He used up to three actors on stage, in addition to the chorus. Seven of his plays have survived and are the oldest known dramas.

- **When Aeschylus staged** three connected plays, called the *Oresteia*, in 458 BC, he introduced masks and costumes. The play told the mythical story of the revenge of Orestes and was so powerful that people in the audience fainted.

- **Sophocles first** won a drama competition in 468 BC. He introduced the idea of irony – when a character does not realize the significance of what he says, but the audience does.

- **Aristotle and other Greeks** believed that the play *King Oedipus* by Sophocles was the greatest tragedy ever written.

- **Euripedes wrote** 92 plays between 441 and 406 BC. His work was very popular and his plays continued to be staged long after his death.

The comedies

- **The satyr plays** began to be staged by about 490 BC. These were rude comedies that featured forest spirits called satyrs, and they were intended to provide light relief between tragedies.

- **Some satyr plays** poked fun at real people, such as politicians and rich noblemen, although care had to be taken to not offend anyone important. Aeschylus was prosecuted for sacrilege for the content of one of his plays.

- **Comedy plays** first appeared in 488 BC, when a prize was given at the spring festival to Dionysus for the best comedy. At first, comedies took the same form as tragedies, with two actors and a chorus.

- **The earliest comic playwright** to become famous was the Athenian Cratinus, who specialized in puns. He wrote a serious of crude plays about men who drank too much and chased women.

- **A new comic writer** put on his first successful play in 424 BC. This was Aristophanes, who specialized in making up words by combining two existing words and using it as part of a joke.

- **Aristophanes also gained fame** by dressing his chorus in elaborate costumes to resemble animals or objects.

- **Around the year 410 BC**, a young poet named Plato began writing comedies. He became very famous, but none of his work has survived.

. . .FASCINATING FACT. . .
The only complete play by Menander was found written on some sheets of papyrus in an Egyptian tomb in 1958.

▶ *A typical theatre, such as the theatre of Dionysus in Athens, seated 14,000 people. Greek actors wore masks with exaggerated painted features so that the audience could clearly see what sort of character they were playing.*

- **In around 320** BC, the writer Menander developed a new type of comedy. Menander's plays focused on ordinary people's reactions to events that could take place in real life.

- **Many of Menander's** plays were love stories. Misunderstandings and mistakes lead to all sorts of comic circumstances that almost always end happily for all characters concerned.

275

The early philosophers

- **The sophists** were men who, from around 700 BC, would move around the cities of Greece holding lessons on morality, truth and other subjects. The word 'sophist' means wise man.

- **One of the most famous sophists** was Protagoras, who died in about 415 BC. He taught that 'man is the measure of all things', and believed that it was humans, not gods, who should decide what was good or bad.

- **Pythagoras of Samos** was a mathematician and sophist. He believed that all animals, including humans, were essentially the same. He thought that souls were reborn after death in a new human or animal.

- **In about 530 BC**, Pythagoras and his followers moved to southern Italy. At Croton, he set up a small community of men and women who devoted themselves to learning.

- **Empedocles lived in Sicily**, and died in about 433 BC. He believed that everything on Earth is composed of four elements – earth, air, fire and water. This idea remained influential for over 2000 years.

- **Socrates was the son** of an Athenian stonemason, and fought in the army when he was young. Around the age of about 35, he gave up work and devoted himself to ideas and morality.

...FASCINATING FACT...
Socrates married a woman named Xanthippe, then spent the rest of his life complaining about her bad temper.

▲ *A painting from the Italian Renaissance of the school of Athens.*
The philosophers of Athens are shown debating the eternal truths of existence.

- **Socrates said "virtue is knowledge"**, by which he meant that before people can be good they must first understand what 'good' means.

- **Socrates often used his knowledge** to show how little wealthy or important people knew. He would ask them a questions designed to show that their assumptions and behaviour were based on false knowledge.

- **In 399 BC**, the rulers of Athens put Socrates on trial for sacrilege and condemned him to death. Socrates was forced committed suicide.

The Academy

- **Plato was a pupil** of Socrates. He expressed ideas by writing dramas based around philosophical conversations. Much of what we know about Socrates comes from the work of Plato.

- **In *The Republic*,** a series of ten books, Plato proposed a system of government. He said there should be a class system and that the ruler should be a philosopher-king, wise enough to rule in the interests of all.

- **The education** that the philosopher-king should receive was described as being based on physical exercise, artistic appreciation and philosophy.

▶ *Plato was one of the greatest of all Greek philosophers and founder of the Academy. His works have remained influential into the 21st century.*

- **After travelling** to many Greek cities, Plato produced a new book called *Laws*. In this, he abandoned the idea of a philosopher-king and said there should be joint ownership of all property by the citizens.

- **When he returned** to Athens, Plato bought a field called Academus that lay just outside Athens. He set up a school in the field, called the Academy, where he taught his ideas.

- **Plato died in 347** BC, but his Academy survived until AD 529. Thousands of men were educated there and Plato's ideas have remained important up to the present day.

- **Aristotle was a pupil of Plato** at the Academy. He was hired as the tutor to the young Alexander the Great and travelled widely around the Mediterranean.

- **Aristotle believed** that the education at the Academy was too narrow, so he set up a rival school called the Lyceum. Lessons at the Lyceum included all types of science and mathematics as well as philosophy and the arts.

- **The teachings of Zeno** of Citium became known as stoicism because he would often sit in a porch – 'stoa' in Greek – to teach. Stoics believed that the world is ruled by divine reason, and that humans should accept this and be indifferent to success or hardship.

- **Epicurus of Samos** came to Athens in about 300 BC. He caused scandal by allowing women and slaves to attend his lessons. Epicurus taught that people should seek happiness by renouncing greed and desire.

Archimedes and mathematics

- **Pythagoras of Samos** was a philosopher and mathematician. He was fascinated by numbers and believed they could be applied to many different aspects of life. Around 530 BC he worked out the precise lengths of strings on a lyre needed to produce accurate musical notes.

- **Pythagoras** measured the movements of the planets. He found that they were closely related to the measurements of the lyre strings, so he developed a theory of divine tunes that he called the music of the spheres.

- **The best-known work** of Pythagoras is his theorem concerning the relationships between the measurements along different sides of triangles.

- **In about 300 BC**, King Ptolemy of Egypt hired a man named Euclid to teach mathematics to the court. Euclid insisted that he would not teach anything until he had proved that it was true.

- **Euclid wrote 15 books** about geometry. In them he developed a systematic method of proving mathematical propositions.

- **Archimedes of Syracuse** was generally recognized to be the greatest mathematician of ancient Greece. He was able to apply mathematical theory to solve practical problems.

. . .FASCINATING FACT. . .

One of the many earlier theories that Euclid was able to prove was that of Pythagoras. As a result, some people prefer to give the credit for the discovery to Euclid.

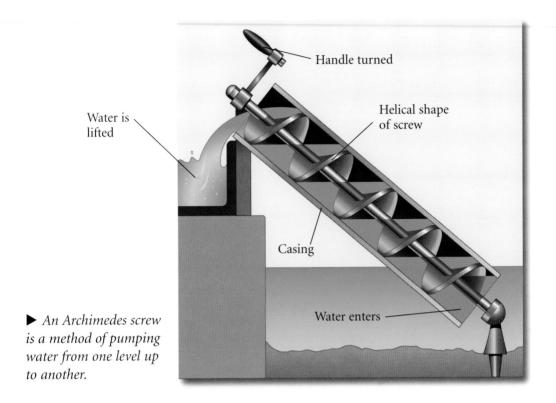

Handle turned

Helical shape
of screw

Water is
lifted

Casing

Water enters

▶ *An Archimedes screw is a method of pumping water from one level up to another.*

- **King Heiron of Syracuse** asked Archimedes to work out if a jeweller had used pure gold to make a crown. This meant calculating the density of the metal, and Archimedes needed to know the volume of the crown to do this.

- **When getting into his bath**, Archimedes noticed that some of the water was displaced by his body and flowed over the edge of the tub. He realized that if the crown was pure gold it would displace the same volume of water as an equal weight of pure gold. By putting the crown in water and measuring the volume of water, he could solve the problem.

- **Archimedes was so excited** that he leapt out of his bath and ran to King Heiron shouting "Eureka", meaning 'I have got it'. Not until he met the king, did Archimedes realize he was not wearing any clothes.

281

The invention of history

- **During the Mycenaean Period**, it is thought that each king employed a man whose task was to compose poems about the great deeds of the king and his ancestors.

- **Some of the events** of the Mycenaean Period were still known during the Dark Age. The poet Homer used these to produce his great epic poems about the Trojan War, the *Illiad* and the *Odyssey*.

- **Around 570 BC**, Anaximander of Miletus wrote a book called *On Nature*, which was a description of the various countries of the world, but which also included sections on their recent past.

- **Hecataeus of Miletus** wrote a book called *Genealogies* in about 500 BC, in which he attempted to trace the history of Greece back to the Mycenaean Period. However, most of his material came from legends and folklore and not from official records.

- **In about 460 BC**, Herodotus of Halicarnassus decided to record a history of the wars that took place between the Greek cities and Persia. The men who fought as soldiers in the wars were growing old and Herodotus thought the story of the war should be preserved for future generations and not forgotten.

- **The *Histories* of Herodotus** was the first book in which the writer not only records what happened, but also tries to explain why it happened. Herodotus has been called 'the father of History'.

- **In the years** after Herodotus produced his work, many histories of many other *polis* were recorded. Few of these have survived, and some recorded as much legend as fact.

- **In about 404 BC**, Thucydides of Athens wrote a history of the Peloponnesian War. He produced a coherent account that included analysis of the events and their causes as well as the speeches of famous men.

- **Thucydides' style of writing** was much admired. For the 1000 years, it was used by historians as a model.

- **During the time** of the Hellenistic Kingdoms, historians were hired by kings and nobles to write about events as they happened. As a result, many of these were complimentary to the kings who paid for them.

◀ *The great warrior Achilles as depicted in the 2004 movie Troy (Warner Bros. Pictures). Achilles was a legendary hero who may have been based on a real person.*

283

Doctors and healing

● **According to the poet Homer**, the first Greek doctor was Asclepius who lived in the Mycenaean Period. Asclepius taught that sick people should rest in a temple of Apollo and pray for a cure.

● **Later Greeks** believed that Asclepius was the son of Apollo, and a god. If they recovered from a serious disease they would sacrifice a cockerel to him.

● **Around 450 BC**, Hippocrates of Cos began working as a doctor at the shrine of Asclepius. He advocated that doctors should keep records of the symptoms suffered by patients so that they could recognize different types of disease.

◀ *A doctor cares for a patient, as seen in an ancient carving. The Greeks were the first people to keep records of diseases and how to cure them.*

- **Over the next 150 years**, the doctors that followed Hippocrates at Cos kept detailed records of the diseases they recognized and what they did to try to cure them.

- **The books** produced at Cos include instructions for carrying out surgery, and recipes for producing medicines using herbs and plants. Thousands of doctors were trained at Cos.

- **Herophilus of Chalcedon** was interested in the effects of drugs on the body. From about 270 BC, he tried giving herbs and plant extracts to people and then studied what happened.

- **Herophilus was the first doctor** to take a patient's pulse to study how his heart was working.

- **In 260 BC**, Eristratos of Ceos began to cut up the dead bodies of condemned criminals to examine internal organs.

- **Eristratos identified many organs** in the body and their jobs. He thought that the body was like a complex machine and that sickness happened when the machine broke down.

Technology

- **The oldest Greek clock** was installed in Athens, in about 350 BC. It consisted of a stone tower that was filled with water. In the water was a float supporting a pole. As the water flowed out of a hole at the bottom of the tower, the pole fell.

- **Ctesibus of Alexandria** was the son of a barber who, in about 290 BC, invented a mechanism by which his father could move all the mirrors in his shop at the same time. He was at once hired by King Ptolemy II to make gadgets.

- **The** *clepsydra* (water clock) developed by Ctesibus, consisted of a pot of water that dripped slowly onto a series of wooden wheels. The wheels moved a small statue that pointed to the correct time on the clock face.

- **Around 100 BC**, a Greek ship sank at Antikythera. In 1901, the wreck was excavated by archaeologists who found a large number of bronze gearwheels. It was not until 1951 that anyone realized what they were.

- **They realized** that the Antikythera Device, as it was known, was a mechanical computer for calculating the movements of the Sun, Moon and several stars.

- **Written accounts** from ancient times record devices like that found at Anitkythera. Poseidonius of Rhodes was said to have such a device that was in the shape of the Earth, with the Moon going around it.

- **The ancient Greeks** had some knowledge of electricity. They knew that if they rubbed a piece of amber with fur, it gave it the power to attract seeds and pieces of paper.

- **The word 'electricity'** is derived from the Greek word 'electron', which means amber, because amber attracts seeds by static electricity.

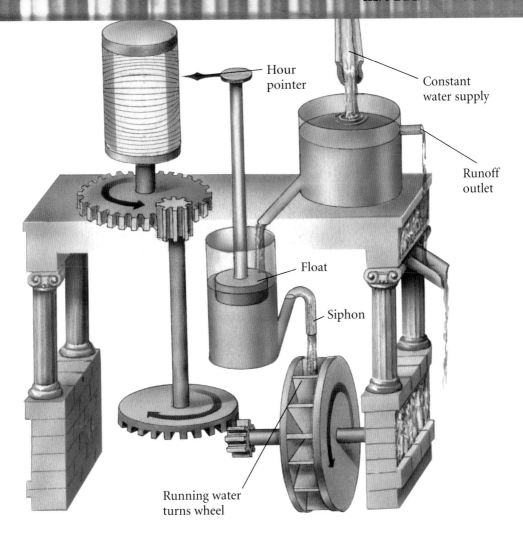

Hour pointer

Constant water supply

Runoff outlet

Float

Siphon

Running water turns wheel

▲ *A reconstruction of an ancient water clock. As the water level falls, the upright rod descends, moving the hand around the dial.*

- **Some shrines** dedicated to the sky god Telchines were said to bring lightning down to earth. The metal spears on top of the shrines may have been early forms of lightning conductor.

- **Around 500 BC**, the Athenians invented a way to refrigerate wine. They made vases at sizes that could sit inside each other, with a gap in between. The wine was placed in the inner jar and snow was put in the outer jar.

The Olympian gods

- **By about 500 BC**, most Greeks believed that there were 12 gods and goddesses that were more important than all the others. They thought these deities lived in magnificent palaces on Mount Olympos, so they were known as the Olympians.

- **Zeus was the king of the gods**. He could hurl thunderbolts to Earth and control the weather. He sometimes fell in love with human women and the children he had with them became heroes.

  - **Hera was the queen of the gods**, and Zeus' wife and sister. She was the goddess of marriage and motherhood, and the protector of women. She often quarrelled with Zeus.

    - **Athene was the goddess of wisdom**, and of craftsmen. She was the patron goddess of Athens, which was named after her, and she protected Athenian soldiers in battle.

◄ *A bronze statue of Zeus. The eyes would originally have been filled with semi-precious stones.*

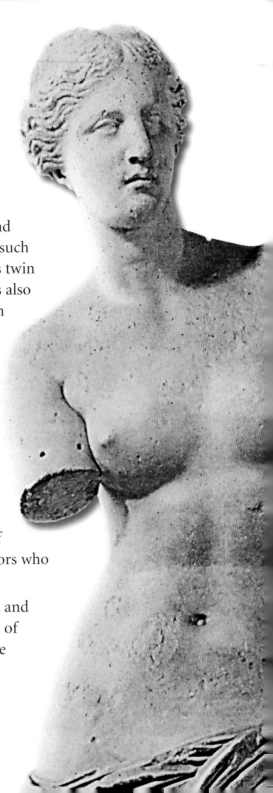

▶ *A statue of Aphrodite, the goddess of love and desire, carved in marble.*

- **Apollo was the god of the sun**, music and the arts. He was also linked to livestock, such as sheep and cattle. Artemis was Apollo's twin sister, and goddess of the moon. She was also the goddess of wilderness and the patron of hunters.

- **Aphrodite was the goddess of love**. She was in love with Ares, god of war. He loved bloodshed, courage and bravery, and was said to have a ferocious temper.

- **Hephaistos the Lame** made the weapons of war, and was the god of smiths.

- **Poseidon was god of the sea** and also of earthquakes. He was worshipped by sailors who greatly feared his anger.

- **Hermes was the messenger** of the gods, and patron of travellers. He was also the god of merchants. Hestia was the goddess of the hearth and of home life.

- **Demeter was the goddess of farming**, and of all plants that could be eaten.

Lesser mythical figures

- **The Olympian gods** were the most important and powerful of the Greek gods, but there were also many others.

- **Themis was a female Titan** who had helped Rhea hide Zeus from Kronos. She was the goddess of justice, and acted as the judge in disputes between the various gods.

- **Iris served the Olympian deities**, especially Zeus and Hera. She brought messages from the gods down to Earth by sliding down the rainbow.

- **Hebe was the goddess of youth**. Together with her handsome young brother Ganymede, she carried out the tasks on Olympos that were the job of unmarried girls in Greek families.

- **Boreas was the god of the north wind**, and loved creating storms. Zephyros was the god of the gentle west wind, while Notus was god of the south wind and Eurus was god of the east wind.

- **The Harpies** were evil creatures. They had the faces of old women and the bodies of birds. They destroyed crops with disease and brought famine to the Earth.

- **The Tritons and Nereids** were the servants of Poseidon. They were believed to be friendly to sailors and fishermen.

...FASCINATING FACT...
The Greeks thought that there was one thing more powerful than all the gods put together – destiny. Even Zeus did not argue with destiny.

- **Nymphs were female spirits** who guarded rivers, springs and other sources of fresh water. They were believed to be very beautiful, and every water source had an attendant nymph.

- **Eunomia, Dike and Irene** were the three Horae. They controlled rainfall on Earth and controlled the growth of plants.

▶ *Sea sirens were beautiful women who sang songs to lure sailors to sail closer to the rocks, causing their boats to crash.*

Deities of
the world

- **The goddesses Gaea and Rhea** were probably worshipped by the Mycenaean Greeks, but by about 900 BC, they were no longer to be powerful deities.

- **Demeter was the goddess of grain** and the harvest. She was worshipped most on Crete, and in the Peloponnese and Attica. Her temples were always surrounded by trees.

- **Kore was the daughter** of Demeter. She was the goddess of corn, and was worshipped on Sicily, the main grain-producing region of the Greek world, and in Attica.

- **Dionysus was first worshipped** in Thrace, and became popular in Boeotia before spreading to the rest of Greece. He was the god of wine.

- **As the son of Zeus** but with a human mother, Dionysus was only a demi-god. He wandered across the world to see its marvels. Later, he was made into a true god by his father.

- **The Satyrs** were a semi-divine race of woodland spirits. They looked like hairy men with pointed ears and the hindquarters of a goat. They loved to play tricks on humans who wandered into the forests.

- **Pan was a god of the Peloponnese**, who was particularly revered by the shepherds of Arcadia. He was a piper, and was often depicted in a similar way to the satyrs, with the horns, ears and legs of a goat.

- **Aristaeus** was a god from Thessaly. In his home territory, he was thought to protect all domestic animals, but elsewhere in Greece he was most associated with bee-keeping.

◀ *Atlas was one of the Titans. He was given the task of holding up the sky to stop it falling on Earth. The sky is symbolized here by a globe.*

- **Ate was a daughter of Zeus** who was thrown out of Mount Olympos for causing too many arguments between the gods. Instead, she wandered the world encouraging men to take irresponsible decisions, and causing conflicts.

- **Zeus regretted his decision** to inflict Ate on the world, so he sent another daughter, named Lita, to track her down. Lita was the goddess of compromise and fair dealing, but she never managed to catch up with Ate.

Heroes and legends

- **To the ancient Greeks**, heroes were not just brave or wise men, they were believed to be partly divine. Most Greek states had an ancestral hero.

- **Theseus was the principle hero** of Athens. He was said to have been the son of King Aegeus of Athens, in about 1230 BC. Many legends tell of his stupendous strength.

- **The greatest exploit** of Theseus was to slay the Minotaur, a terrible half-man, half-bull monster that lived on Crete.

- **Corinth had two great heroes**. The first, Sisyphus, was said to have founded the city in around 1300 BC.

- **Sisyphus cheated death**. When he died, he tricked Hades, god of the underworld, into letting him return to Earth.

- **The second hero of Corinth** was Bellerophon, grandson of Sisyphus. Legends tell that with the aid of his flying horse, Pegasus, Bellerophon killed the terrifying monster, the Chimaera.

- **Perseus was the hero of Argos**, and son of Danae and Zeus. He was believed to have killed the Gorgon. It was said that looking at the face of a Gorgon could turn the viewer to stone.

- **Perseus avoided** looking at the Gorgon by using the reflection from the polished inside of his shield to see where he was striking.

- **Jason was a hero from Thessaly**. He was deprived of the throne of Iolkos by his uncle, King Pelias, who had secretly murdered Jason's father.

- **King Pelias sent Jason** to retrieve the golden fleece (the coat of a winged ram), believing he would not return. Departing in his ship, the *Argo*, Jason managed to obtain the fleece and took it back to Thessaly in triumph.

▲ *Theseus confronts the monstrous Minotaur in the labyrinth of the palace of King Minos of Crete.*

The cults

- **In addition** to the official Olympian gods and the public ceremonies carried out at temples, the Greeks also had a number of cults.

- **A cult** was a club or society that was dedicated to the worship of one particular god. Membership of these societies was often kept secret. Many had specific rituals and beliefs that were unknown outside the cult.

- **The wine god**, Dionysus, was the focus of a very popular cult. Dionysus was officially worshipped only once a year, at the Dionysian festival in the spring, but his cult continued all year round.

- **Women took part** in the cultic ceremony of Dionysus. They would meet in a wood, where they drank large quantities of wine, and danced. After this, they ate a meal of raw meat.

- **The women's cultic ceremony** of Dionysus was based on a legend of semi-divine women, called Maenads, who were said to follow the god in a wild dance. It was believed that they would tear to pieces anyone who did not worship the god.

In 331 BC, Alexander the Great visited the Egyptian temple of Ammon. The temple priests declared him a god, and some cities set up a cult of Alexander. Other Hellenistic kings later claimed that they were gods too.

- **Men who took part** in the Dionysus cult attended ceremonies held in private houses. These usually involved drinking huge quantities of wine.

- **During the Hellenistic Period**, the Persian god Mithras became the focus for a new cult. Mithras was a sun god who helped crops grow, and was linked to fertility.

- **The cult ceremonies** of Mithras took place in caves or underground rooms, in which a statue of Mithras killing a bull was placed. Rituals included sacred meals of roasted meat.

- **The Egyptian goddess**, Isis, was the centre for a cult in Greece that appears to have catered mostly for women and travellers.

◄ *Isis was a goddess in Egyptian mythology, where she was worshipped as a wife and mother figure. She became the centre of a popular cult in later Greek times.*

The oracle of Delphi

- **At Delphi**, on a mountainside overlooking the Gulf of Corinth, stood a temple to Apollo that was one of the most famous and respected in the whole Greek world.

- **The fame of Delphi** was due to the fact that the chief priestess was believed to be able to talk directly to Apollo, to ask him questions on behalf of the humans who visited the temple.

- **A place** where humans could talk to the gods was known as an oracle. The oracle at Delphi was considered to be the greatest in the world.

◀ *A small shrine at Delphi, where the god Apollo was thought to answer questions posed by humans.*

- **According to legend**, Apollo killed a terrible serpent named Python at Delphi. To celebrate this feat, he set up an altar to himself and persuaded a group of sailors from Crete to settle there as his priests.

- **People who wished** to consult the god at Delphi had to climb the mountain and bathe in the waters of a sacred spring. They were then allowed into the sacred precincts of the temple.

- **After waiting for the chief priestess**, the Pythia, to announce she was ready, the men were led into the temple and through to a small, dark room near the back. Here, they told the Pythia the question that they wanted to ask Apollo.

- **The Pythia** then stood on a three-legged stool that spanned a crack in the rocks, from which came volcanic gasses. The Pythia fell into a trance, during which she was believed to become possessed by Apollo.

- **The Pythia's answer** came in one of several forms. Sometimes she answered the question in verse, sometimes in ordinary speech and sometimes by incoherent rantings, which were translated by a priest.

- **The answers given** by the oracle at Delphi are often said to have been either obscure or to have two meanings. King Croesus was told that if he invaded Persia he would destroy a mighty kingdom. He did, but the kingdom that was destroyed was his own, and not Persia.

- **Some answers were very clear**. In 480 BC, the oracle told a representative from Athens, "pray to the winds". The Athenians did, and a storm destroyed much of the Persian invasion fleet.

The Olympic Games

- **The most important** shrine to Zeus was at Olympia in the western Peloponnese, between the Kronos hill and the river Kladeos.

- **Once every four years**, men from all Greek *poleis* gathered at Olympia to watch or take part in athletic competitions, which were held in honour of Zeus. Physical prowess was believed to be a gift from the gods.

- **Some ancient Greeks** believed the Olympic Games were founded in about 1480 BC by Zeus, while others thought they were started by Heracles in 1222 BC.

- **The first recorded games** were held in 776 BC. There was only one event, a foot race, which was won by a man named Coroebus of Elis.

- **For many years** the foot race was the only event, but gradually other contests were added. One of the most taxing events was the pentathlon. Contestants taking part competed in five different sports – running, wrestling, the long jump, throwing the discus and throwing the javelin.

- **Some popular events** were derived from warfare. Discus-throwing developed from throwing shaped stones in battle. Horse and chariot races were staged on a special track called a hippodrome.

- **The governments** of *poleis* gave rewards to citizens who won at Olympia. They might be freed from paying taxes for life, given money, or allowed to sit in the front row for all theatre shows and religious festivals.

...FASCINATING FACT...

The finest athletes from across the Greek world competed at the Olympic Games, and the prestige of winning was immense, but the only prize given was a wreath of olive leaves for the winner of each event.

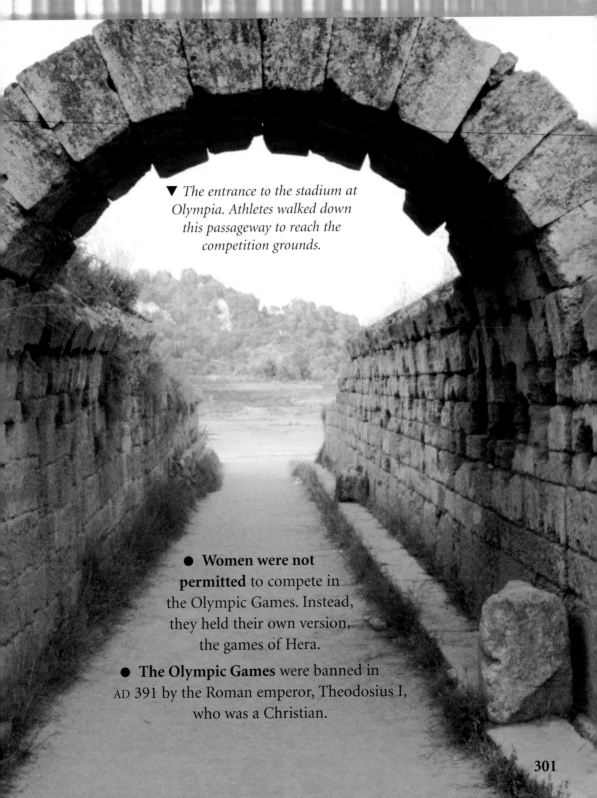

▼ *The entrance to the stadium at Olympia. Athletes walked down this passageway to reach the competition grounds.*

● **Women were not permitted** to compete in the Olympic Games. Instead, they held their own version, the games of Hera.

● **The Olympic Games** were banned in AD 391 by the Roman emperor, Theodosius I, who was a Christian.

The kingdom of the dead

- **Funerals in ancient Greece** could be very grand. The body was carefully washed, and dressed in a white robe. It was then laid out on a bed in a room of the house where the person had lived.

- **After one day**, during which friends and relatives could visit to pay their respects, the body was carried to the burial grounds. A rich person's body would be transported on a carriage.

- **The funeral procession** included musicians, and professional mourners who were paid to wail and weep as loudly as possible. The family and friends of the dead person followed behind.

- **Bodies were buried or cremated (burned).** Most families had a tomb in which the body or ashes of their dead relatives would be buried. The living relative would visit the tomb regularly to pay respects and make offerings to the dead.

- **The Greeks believed** that the souls of the dead went to the underworld, which was ruled by the god Hades.

- **To reach Hades**, the dead soul had to be ferried across the River Styx by Charon, the ferryman. Charon charged for the service, so most people were buried with a bronze coin.

- **Once past the River Styx**, a dead person had to get past the three-headed dog, Cerberus, which stopped the living entering the underworld, or the dead leaving.

- **On arrival into the underworld**, the soul was met by Hades, brother to Zeus and king of the dead. Along with Hades, were the souls of King Minos of Crete, and King Rhadamanthys of the Cyclades, both of whom had been famous for justice when alive.

- **Hades, Minos and Rhadmanthys** questioned the souls that came before them. Those who had offended the gods were imprisoned behind bronze gates, in Tartarus, where they were tortured for eternity. Most souls went to the underworld, which was a grey, dull place.

- **The souls** of those who had pleased the gods were sent to the Elysian Fields. This was a sunny, beautiful country swept by warm, gentle breezes, where good food and wine was plentiful.

◄ *The supernatural dog, Cerberus, had three heads. The Greeks thought that this dog guarded the entrance to the lands of the dead.*

Indus Valley

- **The mighty River Indus** flows from the Himalaya Mountains in a southwesterly direction, across what is now northwest India and Pakistan to enter the Indian Ocean.

- **Regular flooding from the river** deposits rich beds of silt across the plain. This silt produced rich, fertile soils, in which plants grew well.

- **Around 7000 BC**, the people of the Indus Valley began to plant barley, fruits, vegetables and cotton. They also kept herds of domestic cattle and pigs for meat and leather.

- **The main deity** of the Indus Valley was a mother goddess, although statues of a god with three heads and horns have also been found. It is thought that the elephant, tiger, rhinoceros and bull were also considered sacred.

- **By around 2500 BC**, towns had spread across the Indus Valley. A form of writing developed around 2600 BC, but it remains undeciphered.

◀ *The Indus Valley civilization is thought to have had up to 100 settlements. Harappa and Mohenjo-Daro were two of the largest.*

▼ *The ruins of Mohenjo-Daro lie in Pakistan on the edge of a desert area, but in ancient times the region was watered by the Indus River.*

- **It is thought that most of the Indus Valley cities** were centred on a large and luxurious citadel.

- **There were no large temples** in the cities. Instead, religious activity may have taken place in people's houses.

- **Many historians think** that the Indus Valley cities were run by a small group of noble families who cooperated to make decisions affecting the city.

- **The most important building** in most cities was a granary for the storage of grain and other foods from the fields around the city.

- **It is thought** that the organization of communal farming activities and the storage of food for times of famine or poor harvests formed the basis of Indus Valley civilization.

Harappan urban centres

- **Harappa was the first large city** of the Indus Valley civilization to be discovered by archaeologists, so the culture is sometimes known as Harappan. Around 50 cities have been found in total.

- **Mohenjo-Daro and Harappa** were both about one square kilometre and each was home to around 20,000 people. The port of Lothal was not as large, but had a large dock complex. The other cities were smaller.

- **The docks of Lothal** were more than 200 m in length. Archaeological finds show the ships sailed as far as Ur in Mesopotamia to trade.

- **The larger cities** were laid out on a grid pattern. The main streets ran north to south with smaller streets running east to west.

▲ *The cities of the Indus Valley were built on a regular street plan with roads running from north to south and alleys cutting across them.*

- **The houses** were two storeys tall. Each house had blank walls facing the street and only one entrance. Inside, the rooms had open windows and doorways that faced onto a courtyard.

- **In Egypt and Mesopotamia**, houses were built of bricks that had been left in the sun to dry. The Harappan people fired their bricks in kilns, so their buildings were stronger and more resistant to weather.

- **Houses had flat roofs**, and people used them as extra rooms in good weather, even sleeping on them. Drains ran off any water from the infrequent rains.

- **Each house** had an indoor bathroom, with an area for washing and a toilet. Water had to be carried in by hand, and waste was flushed out into underground drains.

- **Most cities** had a large open area that may have been used either as a market place or for holding assemblies.

- **At Mohenjo-Daro** there was a vast public bath 12 m in length and around 2 m deep. The water came from a well and was drained out through a tunnel 2 m in height.

Harappan rural society

- **The smaller towns and villages** of the Harappan civilization lacked the sophistication of the large cities. For example, they did not have underground drainage systems to get rid of waste.

- **Most of the Harappan population** lived in villages or smaller towns, and either worked in farming, or made tools for farmers.

- **The Harappans** were probably the first people to cultivate rice, which was grown in marshy coastal areas. The use of this plant later spread to China and to Mesopotamia.

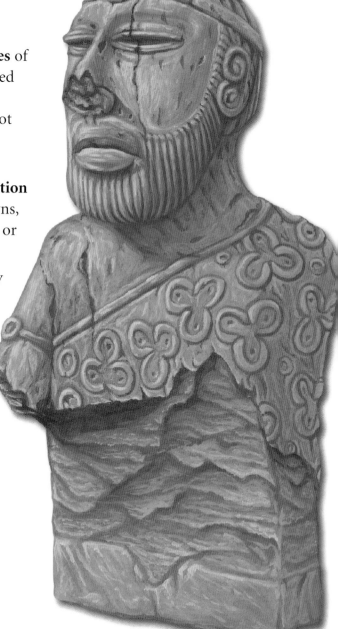

▶ *This statue from Mohenjo-Daro is thought to show a priest or noble at prayer.*

The Harappan civilization was smashed and the cities were abandoned. It was entirely forgotten until the early 20th century, when workmen building a railway found Harappa.

- **Cotton was grown** in quantity. This was woven into brightly coloured cloth that was probably exported to Mesopotamia, as well as being used locally.

- **Most of the farmland** was irrigated by water delivered along ditches and channels dug from a nearby river. If the flow of water in the river failed, the crops would not grow properly.

- **Statues indicate** that men wore a loose cloak fastened over one shoulder. Women are usually shown wearing brightly coloured, short dresses.

- **The Harappan civilization** relied upon the Indus River for water and transport. In around 1600 BC the Indus suddenly changed course. Land that had been fertile became desert or swamp.

- **The city of Harappa** was abandoned very quickly. Elsewhere the civilization survived, but economic decline, famine and a fall in population took place.

- **A wave of invading tribes** overran the declining Harappan cities around 1400 BC. These were nomadic Aryan peoples from central Asia who tended herds of cattle and goats, but planted no farm crops.

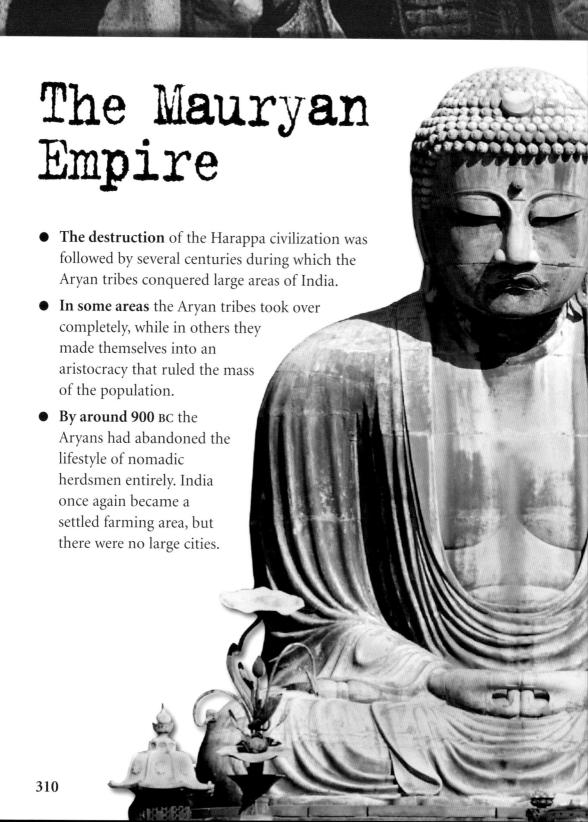

The Mauryan Empire

- **The destruction** of the Harappa civilization was followed by several centuries during which the Aryan tribes conquered large areas of India.

- **In some areas** the Aryan tribes took over completely, while in others they made themselves into an aristocracy that ruled the mass of the population.

- **By around 900** BC the Aryans had abandoned the lifestyle of nomadic herdsmen entirely. India once again became a settled farming area, but there were no large cities.

- **The Persians invaded** northwest India around 500 BC. They established provinces that owed allegiance to the King of Kings in Mesopotamia.

- **The Persians were defeated** in 327 BC by the Greeks of Alexander the Great. Alexander set up his own governors loyal to him. Both the Greeks and Persians brought new ideas and traditions with them.

- **Around 310 BC**, the ruler of Patna, Chadragupta Maurya, drove out the Greeks and united all of northern India under his rule. His grandson Ashoka Maurya expanded the empire into central India.

- **The Mauryans** were Buddhists. They followed the teachings of a prince named Siddartha Gautama, known as Buddha or 'enlightened one', who had been born in Nepal around 560 BC.

  - **Ashoka Maurya sent missionaries** to preach Buddhism in Sri Lanka, Egypt and southeast Asia.

  - **Ashoka imposed law and order** on his realms, encouraged merchants and built new and improved roads throughout the empire. He gathered huge sums in taxes, which he spent on the arts and on building beautiful temples.

  - **Ashoka died in 232 BC**, and around 50 years later the Mauryan Empire collapsed. Members of the royal family quarrelled and began a series of civil wars. Local governors rebelled. India became a mass of small, independent states.

◀ The Daibutsu Buddha in Kamakura, Japan. The statue has a serene expression, which reflects the Buddhist ideal of perfect peace.

The triumph of Hinduism

- **The fall of the Mauryan Empire** allowed the Parthian Empire to take over areas of northwest India. Then the Kushans, from the area that is now Afghanistan, invaded and took over the Indus Valley.

- **Around AD 320**, Prince Chandragupta became ruler of Pataliputra on the Ganges River. He united several nearby cities and states under his rule.

- **The Gupta empire was at its peak** under Chandragupta's grandson, Chandragupta II. By AD 400 the Gupta Dynasty ruled all of northern and most of central India.

- **The Guptas** were devout Hindus. They built great temples and lavished money on Hindu scholars and priests. Buddhism was ignored and soon died out in India, though it survived elsewhere.

- **Scholars working under the Guptas** discovered that the Earth is round and that it spins on its axis. They also invented the concept of zero and gave it the symbol '0', which later became known to Europeans via the Arabs.

- **Craftsmen perfected the process** of cleaning and spinning cotton yarn, and of weaving it into fine fabrics that were dyed brilliant colours.

- **The art of sculpture** was highly developed during the time of the Gupta Dynasty. Working in stone, ivory and bronze, the craftsmen produced beautiful statues, some of which are still used in Hindu temples.

- **Poetry flourished** during this period as poets were commissioned to write stories and fairy tales by the nobility. Many of these have survived and are still part of Indian culture.

▶ *A statue of a Hindu goddess, her many arms holding attributes of her power. The triumph of Hinduism in India followed the suppression of Buddhism.*

- **Around** AD **480,** a new invasion struck India. The YeTa tribes were probably related to the Huns, who were then destroying Roman Europe. The YeTa demolished cities, massacred entire populations and utterly destroyed vast areas.

- **The Gupta Empire collapsed** as the YeTa rampaged across northern India. But in AD 520 the YeTa retreated over the mountains to the north.

Early Chinese cultures

- **The vast valley** of the Hwang-ho (Yellow River) is an area with a mild climate, fertile soils and plentiful water. Before 6000 BC this land was inhabited by tribes of nomadic hunters.

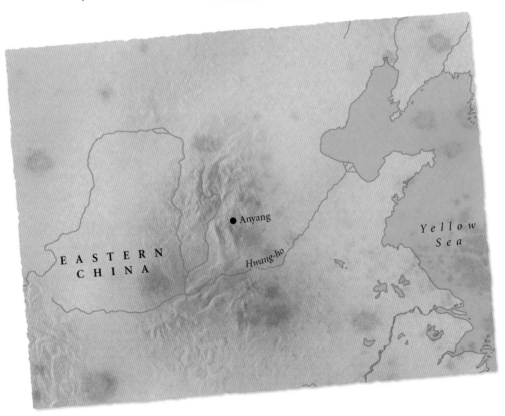

▲ *The earliest Chinese civilization grew up around the middle areas of the Hwang-ho River where fertile soils were well supplied with water.*

- **The first farmers** in China lived along the middle reaches of the Hwang-ho around 5000 BC. They raised cattle and sheep as well as growing millet. The fertile soil and river water made farming relatively easy.

- **The early Chinese people** soon began keeping silkworms from which they produced silk cloth. They also learned how to make pottery of a very high quality.

- **According to later accounts**, the various farming peoples of the Hwang-ho were united around 2200 BC by a ruler named Yu, who founded a family of rulers called the Hsia.

- **The Hsia organized the villages** into groups from which large numbers of men could be recruited to dig drainage ditches, build dams to stop floods and other work that extended the area of farming land.

- **Government officials** kept track of what work was being done and who was doing it. Pictographic writing began to develop in China began around 1400 BC, so bureaucrats were able to create accurate records.

- **The earliest Chinese peoples** used tools made of stone or wood, as they had not yet learned how to make and use metals.

- **The vast swamps** of the lower Hwang-ho began to be drained at this time, but the process would take many centuries to complete.

- **All the accounts** of the Hsia period were recorded several centuries later by bureaucrats who claimed to be translating the old pictographic writings, which were then lost. Nobody is certain how much of our knowledge of Hsia history is accurate.

The Shang Dynasty

- **The Hsia** was eventually overthrown by a nobleman named T'ang. The surviving records are confused so it is not clear when this happened, but it was probably some time between 1760 BC and 1550 BC.

- **The new dynasty** was named the Shang. Like the Hsia, the Shang ruled over all the farming peoples of the Hwang-ho Valley. The Shang encouraged farmers to settle on land south of the Yangtze Valley.

▶ *The Chinese first produced weapons and armour of bronze during the time of the Shang Dynasty.*

- **The Shang** built the first large city in China. It was named Yin, and stood on the north bank of the Hwang-ho. The city had no large temples or palaces, but hundreds of modest houses.

- **Around 1500 BC**, Chinese craftsmen learned how to cast bronze. They produced beautiful vases in the shapes of animals and imaginary monsters.

- **Bronze was mostly used** to make weapons such as helmets, armour, swords and spear points. This gave the Shang an advantage over neighbouring tribes that were still using only stone.

- **It was the bureaucrats** working in government for the Shang who developed the earlier pictographic writing. They used around 3000 different symbols, many of which were similar to modern Chinese signs.

- **The chief god** of the Shang was Shang-Ti, a divine ancestor who the people believed cared for them and their king. Other gods were thought to be in command of the rain, winds, harvest and other important features of life.

- **Human sacrifice** was performed by the Shang to appease the gods if they were thought to be angry. If the Hwang-ho flooded, humans were thrown into the waters to drown.

. . . FASCINATING FACT. . .

Priests used oracle bones to read messages from the gods. These were the shoulder blades of oxen or turtles that were heated up and then shattered. The way they broke revealed the message.

The Warring States Period

- **The tribes** living outside the realm of the Shang gradually learned how to farm and how to make bronze weapons. They grew in wealth and power and became rivals of the Shang.

- **Around 1125 BC**, the Chou tribe from the southwest invaded the Hwang-ho Valley. They defeated the Shang armies and took over the entire Shang Empire.

- **The amount of land** being farmed increased enormously under the Chou and China became a rich and heavily populated land. However the Chou failed to enforce peace and by 770 BC nobles were fighting each other.

- **The Chou emperor** ceased to have any real power from around 500 BC and became little more than a figurehead for rituals. Real power lay in the hands of nobles who divided China up into numerous small states. The following centuries are known as the Warring States Period.

- **Despite the turmoil and bloodshed**, China made dramatic advances in technology. Metalworkers learned how to make iron for weapons and household goods.

- **Chinese farming advanced rapidly** after the invention of the ox-drawn plough. The amount of grain that could be produced increased dramatically, allowing more people to live on a given area of land.

- **Around 550 BC**, a scholar named Lao-tzu reformed traditional Chinese religion. He imagined the gods and deities to be organized in a similar way to the Chinese system of government of the time.

- **Lao-tzu wrote a book** called *Tao-te Ching*, or 'the Way of the First Principles', and so the religion he described is known as Taosim. In this religion, there are hundreds of gods led by Yu-shang-ti, the Jade Emperor God.

- **Taoists believe** that when he grew old, Lao-tzu mounted a sacred ox and rode off to live a life of eternal harmony in the west.

▶ *The religion of China was reformed and systematically arranged by the sage Lao-tzu and his followers.*

319

The Han Dynasty

- **In 256 BC**, the Warring States Period came to an end when Prince Cheng of the Ch'in Dynasty defeated all his rivals and united all the Chinese peoples once again.

- **At this point in time**, China was larger and richer than it had ever been before. Due to the invention of the ox-drawn plough, the valleys of the Hwang-ho and Yangtze could be farmed quickly. Chinese farmers also spread north to the edge of the Gobi Desert and south to the coast.

- **To show his power**, Cheng took the title Ch'in Shih Huang Ti, meaning First Emperor of the Ch'in. He ordered the building of the Great Wall of China to form a defence against nomadic tribesmen from the north.

- **Huang Ti died** in 210 BC. Civil war engulfed China, but it was quickly ended by a peasant general named Liu Pang. He founded the Han Dynasty, which ruled China for 400 years.

- **The Han Dynasty** divided China into 13 provinces, but established a large bureaucracy in the capital of Ch'ang-an to keep a close watch over the provinces so that none could stage a rebellion.

- **During the long years of peace** under the Han, the population of China increased to more than 60 million people.

- **Farmers began** to grow new crops. Rice was imported from India and quickly became a major crop. Grapes, oranges and apricots were also introduced, as was tea.

- **Mining and industry** were kept under strict government control. The production of iron, lead and silver was directed solely to projects that helped the government.

▲ *The power of the first Ch'in Emperor is demonstrated by his vast tomb, guarded by an entire army of terracotta soldiers that was buried nearby.*

- **Scholars were paid** by the government to study astronomy, poetry, art and science.

- **After AD 150,** the Han emperors lost power to court officials and nobles who were more interested in their own wealth than the empire. Raids by nomads from the north became more frequent. In AD 220 a general named Tsao Tsao ousted the last Han Emperor and declared himself emperor instead.

Trade and prosperity

- **The prosperity** and booming population of China during the Han period was boosted by government action aimed at improving trade and wealth.

- **A great canal** was built to link the Yangtze and Hwang-ho rivers. This canal was used by merchants transporting goods between the two great rivers, in the valleys of which the majority of the population lived.

- **A network of roads** was built across the empire to link the capital of Ch'ang-an to all lands ruled by the emperor. The roads were built for government purposes, but they were open to merchants and other citizens.

- **Silk became the most important export** for China. Vast factories were established around Lin-tzu on the lower Hwang-ho to spin thread and weave high-quality cloth.

- **In AD 73**, the general Pan Tchao and his army were sent to explore and guard the trade route heading west along which silk was exported. He conquered as far as Kashgar.

◀ *Chinese silk was a valuable export for the Chinese Empire. The government established factories to produce the cloth using water power.*

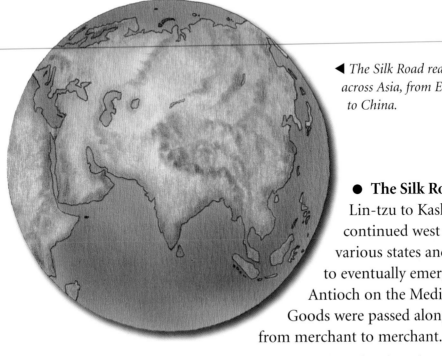

◄ The Silk Road reached across Asia, from Europe to China.

● **The Silk Road** from Lin-tzu to Kashgar continued west through various states and countries to eventually emerge at Antioch on the Mediterranean. Goods were passed along the road from merchant to merchant.

● **The empires of China and Rome** traded with each other along the Silk Road. Neither empire had much knowledge of the other, so wild rumours and legends spread.

● **Lacquer was produced** in huge quantities around Ku-mu. It was used as a waterproof covering on houses, boxes and storage containers.

● **The introduction** of bronze coins made trade much easier, as everyone knew the value of the various coins and trusted the purity of the metal.

● **During the Han period**, work began on a book called *Historical Memoirs*. Each year officials at the court compiled a record of government actions and decisions and entered them in the book. It continued to be added to each year until 1911.

Religion and society

- **The scholar and teacher** K'ung Fu-Tzu, often referred to as Confucius, was born around 551 BC. He rose to be a senior government official, but later retired to become a full-time teacher.

- **After his death**, the pupils of Confucius collected his sayings and writings together into a book called *Analects*. The book records the teachings of Confucius, and includes later additions made by other scholars.

- **The teachings of Confucius** and his followers gradually acquired the status of a religion. Confucianism became the official religion of the Chinese imperial government and remained in place until the revolution of 1911 ousted the imperial throne.

- **Confucius taught** that the moral values of kindness, loyalty, respect, reciprocity and hard work were the most important factors in leading a good and worthy life.

◄ *Confucius was a scholar and government official who set out to establish a code of rules to ensure efficient government and harmonious lifestyles.*

- **Confucius believed** that the status of people within society should be based on their ability. Everyone should respect the rights and duties of other people in society so that society was harmonious and peaceful.

- **The majority of Chinese people** respect Confucius, but do not follow the religion of Confucianism. Most prefer to follow the gods and spirits of the traditional religion formed by Lao-tzu.

- **By the time of the Han Dynasty**, a large minority of Chinese people were Buddhist. This religion was brought to China from India in the Warring States Period, but spread during the Han.

- **Buddhism had been founded** by an Indian prince named Siddhartha who became known as Buddha, the enlightened one, due to his learning and teachings.

- **Buddha taught** that life on Earth is miserable and full of suffering. True happiness can be found only in Nirvana, or freedom from existence. Only those that follow strict Buddhist rules will achieve Nirvana when they die, others will be reborn on Earth to suffer anew.

...FASCINATING FACT...

Knowledge of Confucianism became a requirement for service in the government around AD 200. Men could only enter or be promoted in the bureaucracy by passing exams on the teachings of Confucius.

The great rebellion

- **When the general** Tsao Tsao declared that he was emperor, another general named Souen Kiuan made himself emperor, while a junior prince named Liu Pei announced that, in fact, he was emperor.

- **The Yellow Turban religious movement** swept across China in a vast rebellion that aimed to alleviate the taxation and workload on the peasants. The unrest lasted for years.

- **A vast wave of nomadic barbarians** poured over the Great Wall in AD 311. Their ruler Liu Yuen was a skilled commander, but utterly ruthless.

- **Liu Yuen captured** all of China north of the Yangtze River. He burned the Chinese capital, slaughtered its population and allowed his men to take anything they wanted.

- **After Liu Yuen died** in AD 311, his army broke up into gangs of warriors who rode across northern China killing and looting at will. Total anarchy reigned, the harvest failed and millions died of starvation.

- **South of the Yangtze River**, the Tsing Dynasty built a new capital at Nanking. They managed to retain Chinese culture and civilization, but on a much reduced scale.

- **The wandering gangs** destroying northern China were defeated or absorbed by a new tribe of invaders, the Tobas, around AD 395. The Tobas decided to tax the peasants rather than slaughter them.

- **The Tobas were destroyed** by a fresh wave of invading nomads in around AD 540. These Turks pursued a policy of slaughter, but were disunited and their empire quickly fragmented into small states.

- **The Chinese peasants** were suffering terribly from barbarians in the north and from heavy taxation and dishonest officials in the south. In AD 618 a great rebellion began, organized by an army officer named Li Shihmin.

- **By AD 626**, Li Shihmin was the ruler of China. He established the Tang Dynasty, reformed taxation, sacked dishonest officials and re-established the teachings of Confucius.

◄ *The Great Wall of China was built to defend the farming lands in the south from nomadic barbarians.*

Romulus and Remus

- **The early history of Rome** is shrouded in myths and legends. Early Romans did not know how to read or write, so they passed down their history as oral tales and poems. Over the years these stories became rather mixed.

- **Later Romans** studied the old tales and legends, many of which were written, or strongly influenced, by the Greeks. They used these to put together an account of the first 300 years or so of the history of Rome. This helped to reflect Rome's growing importance.

- **According to legend**, Rome was founded by two brothers named Romulus and Remus in 753 BC. By that date, the brothers had already led exciting lives.

- **Romulus and Remus** were the grandsons and heirs of King Numitor of Alba Longa, an Etruscan city. When Numitor's brother, Amulius, grabbed the throne by force, he threw the baby brothers into the river Tiber to drown.

- **However**, the two boys were washed up on a sandbank where they were found by a she-wolf, which fed them on her milk. Eventually, the boys were found by a shepherd named Faustulus, who brought them up with the help of his wife, Larentia.

- **When they grew up**, the brothers lead the local shepherds. They founded their own state on the hill where they had been cared for by the wolf. This hill was the Palatine, by the river Tiber in the land of the Latins.

- **Romulus had the job** of building a wall around the hilltop. Remus said the wall was too low to keep out enemy soldiers. To prove this, Remus jumped over the wall in a single bound. Romulus was furious and killed his brother.

- **In this way**, Romulus became king of Rome. He then kidnapped all the unmarried women from the region of Sabina to be wives to his shepherds.

▲ *A famous legend tells how Rome was founded by Romulus and Remus, twin boys who had been suckled by a wolf.*

FASCINATING FACT

One day in 716 BC, Romulus was reviewing the Roman army when a thunderstorm appeared and the king was struck dead by lightning. He was buried beneath a black marble slab at the foot of the Palatine.

● **The Sabine men** marched to destroy Rome, but the Sabine women refused to let their fathers kill their husbands. A treaty was drawn up between Sabina and Rome.

The Roman kings

- **All of the early kings** are surrounded by myths. Historians think these may contain some clues as to what actually happened. According to myth, when Romulus died, he left no children so his role as king was taken by Numa Pompilius, a Sabine man.

- **As king**, Numa helped to establish a calendar that was unique to Rome. Certain days were set aside for religious activities, other days for government elections and festivals. Numa ruled Rome until 673 BC.

- **The third king** was Tullus Hostilius, who reigned for 32 years. He led Rome against Alba Longa, a city of Latium, which was conquered. Tullus was murdered by Ancus Martius, grandson of Numa Pompilius, who became the fourth king.

- **Ancus Martius** either conquered or formed alliances with other states in Latium. He built the port of Ostia at the mouth of the river Tiber and extended Rome to include the Aventine Hill and the valley between that hill and the Palatine.

◀ *King Numa, the second king of Rome. His reign was peaceful, and he helped to establish religious rites and ceremonies.*

- **When Ancus died** in 616 BC, his children were young, so an Etruscan named Tarquin the Elder was made guardian. Tarquin took the throne for himself, using his money to build new temples and public buildings.

- **Tarquin the Elder** was murdered in 578 BC by the sons of Ancus. The throne was then taken by Servius Tullius, who was married to Tarquin's daughter.

- **Servius Tullius reigned** until 534 BC. During that time he expanded Rome to include the Esquiline, Quirinal and Virminal hills, by which time the state had 84,000 inhabitants.

- **Servius was murdered** by his daughter Tullia and her husband Tarquin the Proud, grandson of Tarquin the Elder. Tarquin the Proud then became the seventh king of Rome.

- **Tarquin the Proud** built beautiful new temples on the Capitoline Hill dedicated to the Capitoline triad of deities – the three most important Roman gods. However he ignored the wishes of the people and tried to control the Senate (Roman council) by threats and bribery.

FASCINATING FACT
Another story says that In 510 BC, Sextus, son of Tarquin, attacked the noblewoman, Lucretia. Lucretia's husband, Collatinus, and his friend Brutus Lucius Junius, expelled Tarquin and his family from Rome. There were no more kings of Rome.

The early republic

- **After the expulsion** of Tarquin the Proud, a new form of republican government began to evolve in Rome. It was based on the idea that power should be in the hands of the people.

- **Tarquin the Proud** fled to his Etruscan relatives. He asked King Lars Porsenna of Clusium to lead an army to Rome to return him to the throne.

- **The invasion was halted** at the Sublician Bridge by the guard Horatius Cocles. He held the bridge alone until the Romans cut it down, then he swam back to Rome.

- **The various cities** of Latium formed the Latin League in 338 BC. The League fought a long series of wars against the Etruscans. These ended with the capture of the Etruscan city of Veii in 396 BC.

▶ *A bronze statue of an Etruscan warrior from about 400 BC. He carries a small round shield and has elaborate body armour made up of small plates of metal.*

- **In 451 BC**, the Romans appointed a board of ten wise men, the *Decemviri*, to review and reform the laws of Rome. This was in response to years of unrest by the citizens and the growing size of the city. The reformed laws were engraved on 12 tables of brass and set up where everyone could see them.

- **In 390 BC**, an army of Celts swept down the Po Valley, led by their king, Brennus. At the Battle of Allia, the army of the Latin League was defeated.

- **The Celts** captured Rome. Most people had fled, but a few held out on the Capitoline Hill to guard the temples. A sneak Celtic attack was defeated when the sacred geese in the Temple of Juno raised the alarm.

- **The Romans agreed** to pay the Celts to return to the Po Valley. When they complained that the scales used to weigh the gold tribute were unfairly weighted Brennus replied, "*Vae Victis,*" meaning 'Woe to the conquered'.

- **In 340 BC**, the Latin War began. Some Latin states tried to fight the power of Rome, others sided with Rome. After two years of fighting, the Latin League was replaced by Roman rule.

FASCINATING FACT
The Samnites were defeated at the Battle of Sentinum in 295 BC after a long war. Many Greek cities in southern Italy, and other states, also came under Roman rule after this.

War with Carthage

- **By 265** BC, Rome was the most powerful state in Italy. Other cities or states south of the Po Valley had either been conquered by Rome or were allied to Rome.

- **That year,** Italian mercenaries captured the city of Messana on the island of Sicily from Hieron, king of the independent city state of Syracuse. They asked Rome for help, while King Hieron asked for aid from his ally, Carthage

- **Carthage** was the most powerful city state in the western Mediterranean. It stood in North Africa, near what is now Tunis. The wars between Rome and Carthage are called the Punic Wars because the people from the area around Carthage were known as Punics.

- **The First Punic War** ended in 241 BC with defeat for Carthage. Rome now controlled Sicily and the west Mediterranean. Syracuse and other independent states in Sicily became allies of Rome.

- **The Second Punic War** began in 221 BC when Rome sent help to the city of Saguntum in Spain, which was rebelling against Carthaginian rule.

- **Hannibal**, the Carthaginian commander in Spain, crushed Saguntum but realized he could not defeat Rome in Spain. While Rome made preparations to invade Spain and Carthage, he led his army on the long march over the Pyrenees and Alps into Italy.

. . . FASCINATING FACT . . .

At the Battle of Cannae in 216 BC, Hannibal surrounded and massacred an army of over 70,000 Romans, only some 5000 of which escaped. However, Hannibal had no siege equipment and so could not capture Rome.

- **In Italy**, Hannibal was joined by the Celtic tribes of the Po Valley. He marched south, defeating a Roman army at the Battle of Lake Trasimeno, where 20,000 Romans were killed for the loss of 1000 Carthaginians.

▲ *Hannibal's army included war elephants, which were led over the Alps and into Italy where such creatures had never been seen before.*

- **Rome eventually defeated** Carthage at the Battle of Zama in 202 BC. Carthage was exhausted from the years of warfare and forced to surrender. Rome was now recognized as the most powerful state in the western Mediterranean.

- **The Third Punic War** began in 152 BC when King Masinissa of Numidia in North Africa, an ally of Rome, attacked Carthage. After a siege lasting six years, Carthage fell to the Romans. The city was destroyed and the population sold as slaves.

335

Growth of empire

- **When Rome was founded** it controlled about 15 square kilometres of territory. By the time the Republic was founded, this had grown to about 900 square kilometres. Rome was still a small country.

- **At the start** of the first Punic War, Rome controlled about 25,000 square kilometres of territory, with a population of around one million. Allies added another 100,000 square kilometres and an extra 2.5 million people.

- **By 260 BC**, Rome was the most powerful state in Italy. All states south of the Po Valley were either allied to Rome or had been conquered.

- **Conquered cities** and states of Italy were ruled directly from Rome. A few important men were made Roman citizens, but most people had few rights.

- **The allied states** were allowed to govern themselves and even to maintain their own armies. However they were not allowed to form alliances or start wars without permission from Rome.

- **After the First Punic War**, Rome took over Sicily. The former Carthaginian lands were ruled from Rome, but Syracuse, an independent state of Sicily, was treated as an ally.

- **In 238 BC**, Rome seized Corsica and Sardinia from Carthage. The islands were ruled by a Roman governor, and an army was stationed permanently on the islands to enforce his rule.

- **As a result** of the Second Punic War, Rome took control of all Carthage's lands in Spain. These were made into a province called Hispania Citerior (meaning 'nearer to Rome'). It was ruled by a governor sent from Rome.

- **After the Second Punic War**, Rome conquered the Celtic tribes of the Po Valley. Their land was made into the province of Cisalpine Gaul – meaning 'Celts this side of the Alps' – which was ruled by a governor sent from Rome.

● **Macedonia** in northern Greece was conquered in 148 BC and became a Roman province. In 133 BC, King Attalus of Pergamum (modern-day Turkey) died without an heir, so he left his kingdom to Rome. It became a new province called Asia Minor.

◄ *Roman ruins of Carthage in North Africa. The site was abandoned after its destruction and all its territories taken over by Rome.*

Social crises

- **The vast expansion** of Rome began to cause serious social problems within Italy. The problems set in motion a series of crises that would last for over a century and end with the destruction of the Roman Republic.

- **The army** was made up of Roman citizens and the citizens of allied states. These men served without pay for a few weeks each year, but were allowed a share of any treasure captured during a successful war.

- **The generals** were usually patricians, or noblemen. When they divided up the booty of war they usually gave the smallest amount possible to the soldiers. The rest was given to themselves and their friends.

- **The common citizens** (plebeians) were reduced to poverty. They flocked to Rome to live off state hand-outs. Meanwhile, the richer men became even richer and more powerful as they exploited the wealth of the new provinces.

- **By 140** BC there were very few citizens who owned their own farms or small businesses. These types of people had long been the main strength of the Roman army and state.

▶ *The Gracchus family. Although the Gracchi were rich, they put the interests of the poor first in their political campaigns.*

- **The nobleman Tiberius Gracchus** saw that the division of Roman citizens into very rich and very poor would cause serious problems. In 133 BC, he was elected to the post of Tribune and promised to solve the problems.

- **As Tribune**, Tiberius Gracchus introduced new laws. These distributed land owned by the government to the Roman citizens on condition that they lived there and farmed the land.

- **This state land** was taken from patricians who had been farming it with slave labour. When Tiberius Gracchus announced he would stand for election again, the nobles organized a mob to attack him. The attack turned into a street battle that left over 300 people dead, including Gracchus.

- **In 122 BC**, Gaius Gracchus, brother of Tiberius, was elected Tribune. He was murdered by the senator Lucius Opimius. Days of bloodshed followed as the supporters of both sides attacked each other. About 3000 people died on the streets of Rome.

- **After the death** of the Gracchi brothers, the patricians changed the laws to give themselves power in Rome. They used their power to make themselves rich and became notoriously corrupt.

Pompey vs Caesar

- **After Sulla's retirement** and death, power returned to the Senate. However corruption and intimidation were so widespread that real power lay with rich men and successful generals.

- **The most successful general** in Rome at this time was Gnaeus Pompeius Magnus, known as Pompey the Great. He was the son of a famous supporter of Sulla, Pompeius Strabo.

- **The richest man** in Rome was Marcus Licinius Crassus, who made a fortune by buying slaves, training them to be skilled workers, then selling them at a large profit.

- **Crassus and Pompey** ruled Rome. They bribed or attacked opponents so that only men supported by Crassus and Pompey were elected to government. In 70 BC both men had themselves elected as Consuls.

- **Pompey then left Rome** to fight a series of wars in the eastern Mediterranean. He defeated the rulers of Pontus and Armenia, adding those lands to the Roman Empire. He then conquered Syria and Judaea.

- **While Pompey** was in the east, a politician named Julius Caesar grew popular. Caesar was a member of the Julian family, which was one of the oldest in Rome, and claimed to be descended from the goddess Venus.

- **Julius Caesar** was also related by marriage to Gaius Marius. He was therefore popular with both the patricians and with the poorer plebeians.

- **At first**, Caesar, Crassus and Pompey worked together. Caesar conquered large areas of Gaul and even raided Britain. Pompey stayed in Rome. Crassus went to command in the east.

- **Crassus was killed** at the Battle of Carrhae in 53 BC, fighting the Parthians. Without him to act as intermediary, Pompey and Caesar began to quarrel.

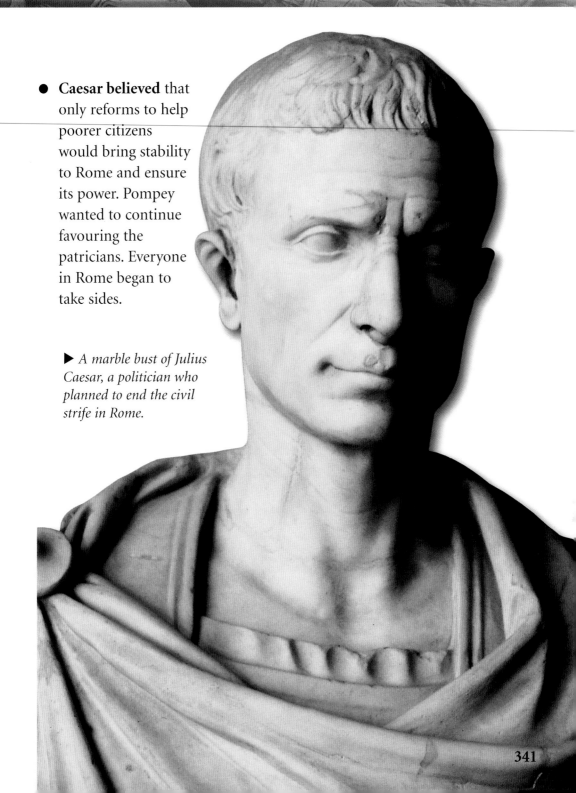

● **Caesar believed** that only reforms to help poorer citizens would bring stability to Rome and ensure its power. Pompey wanted to continue favouring the patricians. Everyone in Rome began to take sides.

▶ *A marble bust of Julius Caesar, a politician who planned to end the civil strife in Rome.*

341

The civil wars

▲ *Brutus was told by the ghost of Caesar that they would 'meet at Philippi'. Brutus was killed there in battle a few months later.*

- **In 49** BC, Julius Caesar was declared to be an enemy of Rome by the Senate, which feared he would introduce reforms in favour of the poor. The Senate then asked Pompey to capture Caesar.

- **Caesar asked his army** in Gaul for their support. They gave it. Caesar led his army over the river Rubicon that divided Gaul from Italy. He reportedly said, "*Alea jacta est,*" which translates as 'the die is cast', meaning that he had taken a step that he could not undo.

- **Pompey was taken by surprise**. He had a few soldiers in Italy, but most of the men loyal to him were in Spain and the eastern Mediterranean. He left a few garrisons in Italy, then went to Greece.

- **After defeating** Pompey's garrisons in Italy, Caesar led his army to Greece. At the Battle of Pharsalus on 9 August 48 BC, Pompey was defeated. He fled to Egypt, but was murdered by King Ptolemy XIII.

...FASCINATING FACT...

When Caesar arrived in Egypt he had King Ptolemy XIII killed and put the dead king's sister Cleopatra on the throne. Caesar and Cleopatra had a son together.

- **Caesar returned** to Rome and offered a free pardon to all supporters of Pompey, as long as they surrendered at once. Most did, but Pompey's sons raised a new army in Spain. Caesar defeated them at Munda in March 45 BC.

- **In 45 BC**, Caesar began reforming the government of Rome. But when he had himself declared Dictator for Life, many people feared that he wanted to become king. Even some close supporters turned against Caesar.

- **On 15 March**, 44 BC, Caesar was murdered by a group of senators. One of the conspirators was Marcus Brutus, a descendent of the man who had ousted King Tarquin the Proud.

- **A new civil war** broke out. The cause of Caesar's reforms was taken up by his nephew, Octavian Caesar, and by Julius Caesar's deputy, Mark Antony.

- **Brutus** and the conspirators were defeated at the Battle of Philippi in 42 BC. Octavian Caesar and Mark Antony returned to Rome to continue Caesar's reforms.

The first emperor

- **In 42 BC,** the three most powerful men in Rome were the general Mark Antony, the politician Marcus Lepidus and Octavian Caesar, nephew and heir to the popular Julius Caesar.

- **They realized** that urgent reforms were needed after years of civil war. Lepidus was put in charge of North Africa, while Octavius took Italy, Spain and Gaul. Mark Antony was given control of the eastern Mediterranean.

◄ *A statue of Augustus shown in the uniform of a senior military officer to emphasize his victorious career.*

- **In 34 BC**, the officials in North Africa asked Lepidus to resign due to his laziness, but he refused. Octavius crossed to Africa with a small army and forced Lepidus to retire to his country estates, where he lived in peace until he died in 13 BC.

- **Meanwhile**, Mark Antony had reasserted Roman control over the eastern provinces. He reformed the taxation system and repaired the defences against the powerful Parthian Empire (in modern-day Iran) to the east.

- **Mark Antony met Cleopatra**, Queen of Egypt, and was dazzled by her beauty, her intelligence and by the vast wealth of Egypt.

- **Cleopatra had several children** by Mark Antony, even though he was married to Octavia Ceasar, sister of Octavius.

- **Octavius thought** Mark Antony intended to set himself up as an independent ruler in the east. When Antony divorced Octavia and married Cleopatra, Octavius declared war.

- **At the Battle of Actium** in 31 BC, Octavius defeated the armies of Cleopatra and Mark Antony. Soon afterwards, Mark Antony committed suicide, followed by Cleopatra in 30 BC. Octavius made himself the new King of Egypt, then returned to Rome.

- **In 27 BC**, Octavius surrendered all his formal powers to the Senate and people of Rome. He said that the ancient Republic had been restored. In fact, he kept all real power informally in his own hands.

- **Octavius took** two new titles. He called himself Augustus, meaning 'exalted one,' and it is by this name that he is best known. He also called himself *Imperator*, meaning 'commander'.

The early emperors

▲ *Julius Caesar died in 44* BC. *His name was taken by all future emperors of Rome, including his adopted son and heir, Augustus.*

- **Augustus** was the first Emperor of Rome and ruled from 27 BC–AD 14. He completed the reform of the government of the empire and erected many new public buildings.

- **Augustus pushed** the Roman frontier to the river Danube and the river Rhine, and defeated the Parthians in the east. However, an invasion of Germany in AD 9, ended in disaster when three legions led by Quintilius Varus were wiped out.

- **Augustus' two grandsons** died before him, so he named his stepson, Tiberius, as his successor. Tiberius was a successful soldier and scholar, but he disliked ceremony and did not enjoy the public role of emperor.

- **Tiberius retired** from ruling in 26 AD. He appointed talented men to be governors and senior officials. However, Tiberius could be cruel, and he ordered the execution of several senators whom he suspected did not support him.

▶ *Nero was a talented artist and scholar, but a poor ruler. When he was murdered, the line of emperors from the family of Julius Caesar ended.*

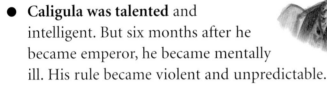

- **When Tiberius died** in AD 37, he was succeeded by his great nephew, Gaius Ceasar Germanicus, who is better known as Caligula, which means 'Little Boots'. The nickname referred to the fact that he spent most of his young life in army camps with his parents, and miniature soldiers' boots were made for him as a child.

- **Caligula was talented** and intelligent. But six months after he became emperor, he became mentally ill. His rule became violent and unpredictable.

- **Caligula** had himself declared a living god in AD 40 and began to order random executions. In January AD 41, Caligula was murdered by soldiers acting on orders of the army high command and some senators.

- **Caligula's uncle**, Claudius, became the next emperor. He proved to be a steady, if uninspiring, emperor. He worked hard to get rid of corrupt officials and conquered Britain in AD 43.

- **In AD 54**, Claudius was murdered by his wife, Agrippina, so that her son, Nero Claudius Caesar, would become the next emperor. Nero then murdered Agrippina. Nero proved to tyrant, and a persecutor of Christians.

- **The government** was almost bankrupt by AD 67. In that year, two provincial governors rebelled. Servius Galba, governor of Spain, marched on Rome. The Senate supported him and Nero committed suicide.

The adopted emperors

▶ *The emperor Trajan was the first of the adoptive emperors, starting a tradition that ensured stability for Rome.*

- **Chaos followed** the death of the Nero in AD 68. He left no legitimate heir to the wealth, power and offices that he had inherited from his ancestors. Instead, the governor of Spain, Servius Galba, marched an army to Rome and took power.

- **In AD 69**, there were no less than four emperors. Galba was murdered by his own bodyguards, the Praetorians, who made the rich nobleman, Marcus Otho, the next emperor.

- **Otho** committed suicide when the army on the Rhine made their commander, Aulus Vitellius, emperor. Then the armies in the east made their commander, Titus Flavius Vespasianus, emperor. In December they smashed Vitellius' armies, captured Rome and killed Vitellius.

- **Vespasian** was a tough soldier who came from a middle class background. He was not a nobleman from Rome, but was an able administrator and became famous for applying the law without favour or bias.

- **When Vespasian died** he left imperial power to his son, Titus, who died suddenly and was followed by Domitian, his brother. Domitian proved to be brutal and greedy. He was murdered by government officials.

- **After the death of Domitian**, the Senate chose the elderly lawyer, Marcus Nerva, to be emperor. Nerva had no children, so he adopted the able general Marcus Trajanus as his son.

- **The adoption** of Trajan began a period during which each emperor adopted a talented man as his successor. Trajan adopted Hadrian, governor of Syria, to be his son and heir.

- **Hadrian** became emperor in AD 117 and ruled until AD 138. He appointed as his adopted son and heir the wealthy senator, Antoninus Pius, who at once adopted Marcus Aurelius to be his son and heir. The rule of Antoninus was one the most peaceful and prosperous in the history of the empire.

▲ *A statue of Marcus Aurelius. He is usually regarded as one of the finest emperors that Rome ever had.*

- **Marcus Aurelius** became emperor in AD 161 and ruled for 19 years. He was a skilled military commander, talented government official and well-educated man. He left imperial power to his son, Commodus, who proved to be incompetent.

- **Commodus** was murdered in AD 193. The Roman Empire was torn apart by plots and coups from which the general Septimius Severus emerged as the new emperor. His family ruled until AD 235.

349

Highpoint of empire

- **The highpoint** of the empire was *c.* AD 160. During this period, the empire experienced a time of peace, and it also grew to its largest size.

- **In the south**, the empire covered the entire North African coast, from the Atlantic to the Red Sea. The fertile coastal areas and inland hills were divided into four provinces that reached as far south as the edge of the Sahara.

- **Egypt was kept** as a separate kingdom owned by the Roman emperor. The vast personal wealth gained from Egypt meant that the emperor was always the richest man in Rome.

- **The provinces** of Arabia, Judaea, Syria and Cappadocia bordered on the mighty Parthian Empire. For most of this period there were few major wars, but the Parthians were always a threat to Rome in the east.

- **The richest parts** of the Roman Empire were the provinces that covered what are now Turkey, Greece, Bulgaria, Serbia, Croatia, Slovenia and Montenegro. The cities in these areas produced great tax revenues for Rome.

- **The areas** that are now Austria, Switzerland, Belgium and the Netherlands were border regions. These areas had massive military bases and fortifications.

> ....FASCINATING FACT....
> The entire Mediterranean world was part of the Roman Empire. The
> Romans called the Mediterranean *mare nostrum*, meaning 'our sea'.

▲ *The Roman Empire during the reign of Trajan*
(AD 98–117). By this date most of the known civilized world
was ruled by Rome. The black lines indicate major roads.

- **The province of Britain** produced crops of grain and wool as well as producing valuable minerals such as gold and tin. Neither the north of Britain nor Ireland were ever conquered by Rome. Garrisons of troops were kept in Britain to protect it from invaders.

- **Gaul covered** what is now France. It was divided into three provinces. Gaul produced rich crops, but had few wealthy cities and did not have many troops stationed in it.

- **Spain was divided** into three provinces and, like Gaul, was the source of much agricultural wealth. Some of the mountain tribes in the north refused to accept Roman rule.

351

Imperial decline

- **In AD 235**, Emperor Alexander Severus paid a massive bribe to the German tribes to stop them raiding the Roman province of Gaul. This so disgusted the legions based on the German frontier that they murdered Alexander and made their own commander, Maximinus Thrax, the new emperor.

- **The new emperor** was the son of a barbarian from Thrace. He had risen to high command in the army because of his talents as a soldier, but he had never been to Rome and knew little about administration.

- **The reign of Maximinus** marked a new stage in the history of Rome. For the first time, a man who was neither Roman nor experienced in government became emperor because he had the support of the army.

- **After just three years as ruler**, Maximinus had spent vast sums of money. New taxes on all classes in the empire made him hugely unpopular. In AD 238, the tax collector in Africa was killed.

- **The governor of Africa**, Marcus Antonius Gordianus, announced that he was the new emperor. He and his son were killed by forces loyal to Maximinus 20 days later.

▼ *The Roman mob could overpower emperors. In* AD *69 Emperor Vitellius was murdered by an angry crowd.*

● **Meanwhile**, the Senate announced that Maximinus was no longer emperor. They elected two noblemen, Decius Balbinus and Marcus Pupienus, to rule instead.

● **The plebeians** refused to accept Balbinus and Pupienus. They elected Marcus Antonius Gordianus, grandson of the man killed in Africa. The Praetorian Guard declared for Gordian, then Maximinus was killed by his own officers.

● **The plots**, rebellions and murders continued. In just 50 years, Rome had 24 emperors. There were about 20 other men who began rebellions, which failed. For 15 years from AD 260, Gaul and Britain refused to be ruled from Rome, but had their own 'emperors'.

● **While generals and senators** fought for control, the empire was in decline. The economy failed and poverty was common. Provinces were lost in the east, and those to the north were raided by barbarians.

● **In AD 284**, Emperor Numerian was murdered by Aper, commander of the Praetorian Guard. Soldiers killed Aper and elected the general Diocletian as emperor.

The Tetrarchy

- **At the time** that he became emperor in AD 284, Diocletian seemed to be just another ambitious general. Nobody expected his reign to last very long.

- **Diocletian's first move** was to keep in office most of the officials who had served the previous emperor, Numerian. He announced that he would give positions to the person who was best able to do the job.

- **Diocletian's second move** was even more of a surprise to the Romans. He announced that he was making his friend and second in command, Maximianus, an emperor as well. Maximianus would rule in the west and Diocletian would rule in the east.

- **Maximianus accepted** that he was the junior emperor and never tried to oust Diocletian. The two men worked well together to try to solve the many problems facing the Roman Empire.

- **In AD 287**, Diocletian announced that he was a son of the god Jupiter and that Maximianus was a son of Hercules. The emperors were trying to inspire loyalty and respect.

- **In AD 293**, Diocletian and Maximianus introduced a radical new arrangement that became known as the Tetrarchy, or the Rule of Four. It was an attempt to recreate the peaceful years of the adopted emperors.

- **The successful general**, Julius Constantius, was adopted as son and heir by Maximianus, whose daughter he married. Meanwhile, Diocletian adopted another popular commander, Galerius, and married him to his daughter.

- **Galerius and Constantius** were each given the title of Caesar, indicating that they were junior to the emperors, but held some of their powers.

- **Diocletian** then reorganized the empire. He split it in half – east and west – and divided each province into two or more smaller provinces, and grouped them into 12 dioceses. The civilian government was in the hands of the provincial governors. The army was controlled by the emperors and caesars.

- **In AD 305**, Diocletian and Maximianus stood down as emperors. The two caesars became emperors, and each adopted a new caesar as his deputy and heir.

▶ *The Tetrarchy, or rule by four men, restored order in the empire. This statue shows Diocletian and Maximianus on the left with Galerius and Constantius on the right.*

Division of empire

- **The Tetrarchy** did not survive long after the abdication of Diocletian. Soon rival factions within the army would cause new civil wars.

- **Constantius was given** as his new caesar in the west, a man named Severus, who was close friends with Galerius, the new emperor in the east. Neither Constantius or his officers really trusted Severus.

- **In AD 306**, Constantius died at York, in Britain, while preparing a campaign against the barbarian Picts of northern Britain. His army at once appointed his son Constantine to be the new emperor.

▲ *Constantine the Great unified the empire under his sole rule.*

- **Galerius told Constantine** that he could be the new Caesar, but not the new emperor. Then Severus was defeated and killed by an army raised by Maxentius, son of Maximian.

- **Maxentius announced** that he was the new emperor in the west. Constantine accepted this and married Fausta, daughter of Maxentius. In AD 312, Constantine marched his army on Rome to attack his new father-in-law.

- **Constantine and Maxentius** met at the Battle of the Milvian Bridge in AD 312. Maxentius was killed and Constantine became sole ruler in the west.

- **In AD 324**, Constantine led a great army to invade the eastern half of the empire. He defeated Emperor Licinius at the Battle of Hadrianopolis, and soon afterwards had him killed. Constantine was now the sole emperor.

- **Constantine** was an able and efficient ruler. He ensured that the corruption and poor administration that had grown during the years of chaos were rooted out, but he did introduce new and severe taxes.

- **In AD 312**, Constantine became a Christian. In AD 324 he banned all pagan religious sacrifices and confiscated the treasures of the pagan temples. He spent some of the pagan money on building new churches.

- **In November**, AD 324, Constantine ordered that a new capital city for the empire be built on the site of the small Greek city of Byzantium (modern-day Instanbul). He called it Constantinople. The new city was to be capital of the eastern half of the empire, Rome was capital only of the western half.

▼ *The Battle of the Milvian Bridge. It is said that Constantine had a vision of the Christian cross superimposed on the sun, with the words* In hoc signo vinces, *meaning 'in this sign conquer'.*

The fall of Rome

▲ *Alaric the Goth captured Rome and stole as much gold and silver as he could find.*

- **When Constantine died** in AD 337, his three sons squabbled over power until Constantius II emerged triumphant. In AD 361, Constantius died and was replaced by his nominated heir, Julian.

- **The emperor Julian** was killed in battle against the Parthians in AD 363. He was succeeded by Jovian in AD 364, who ruled for just eight months. The army then appointed the general Valentinian as emperor. Valentinian at once appointed his brother Valens to be emperor in the east.

- **During this time**, the empire was again in decline. There had been a serious disease that killed thousands of people. The economy began to collapse in the west and became weaker in the east.

- **From about AD 350** onwards, the barbarian tribes on the northeastern frontiers became more aggressive and troublesome.

- **In August AD 378**, the combined forces of the Ostrogoth and Visigoth tribes crushed the army of the eastern empire at the Battle of Adrianople (in modern-day Turkey). The emperor Valens was killed along with his senior officers and most of his men.

- **The new eastern emperor**, Theodosius the Great, made peace with the Goths, but allowed them to take over part of the empire. He died in AD 395 leaving his 17-year-old son Arcadius to rule the east and his ten-year-old son Honorius to rule the west.

- **The success of the Goths** tempted other German tribes to attack the empire. In AD 406, the Vandals, Sueves and Alans poured over the Rhine, defeated the local Roman armies and plundered almost all of Gaul.

- **Alaric**, the new king of the Goths, invaded Italy in AD 408. He demanded payment of tribute from the emperor Honorius, but the Romans refused.

- **Rome fell** to Alaric the Goth in AD 410. The Goths rampaged through the streets, plundering, looting and killing.

...FASCINATING FACT...

Julian tried to restore the traditional pagan religion of Rome. He did not persecute the Christians, but did restore property to the pagan temples and once again permitted pagan sacrifices to take place.

◄ By around AD 300, most towns in the Roman Empire were protected by strong walls of stone or brick.

The last emperors

- **The Goths** did not stay in Rome for long after they had captured the great city in AD 410. They moved north out of Italy and then west to attack Spain.

- **The emperor of the west**, Honorius, was safe in the fortress city of Ravenna, but his control over the provinces had been shattered by the fall of Rome. Britain was abandoned and told to govern and defend itself.

- **Honorius** used the wealth of the African provinces to pay troops to try to control the barbarians in the provinces of Gaul and Spain.

- **When Honorius died** in AD 423, power was taken by his aunt Galla Placidia, who ruled in the name of her six-year-old son, Valentinian. Placidia hired the general Aetius to lead the Roman armies.

- **In AD 454**, Aetius defeated the armies of Attila the Hun at the Catalaunian Plains in Gaul. Valentinian, now aged 34, thought that Aetius was becoming too powerful so he had him killed. He was himself killed by men loyal to Aetius in AD 455.

  - **The wealthy** North African provinces had fallen to the Vandals, a German tribe, in AD 439. As soon as Valentian was dead, the Vandals invaded Italy. They captured Rome and sacked it.

  - **This second sack** of Rome destroyed the city as a centre for government, business or military activity. It became almost deserted and was only used as a centre for ritual ceremonies.

▲ *A pouch of Roman coins. The wealth of the empire lured the invading barbarians as they searched for money and land.*

- **Theodoric**, king of the Goths, sent an army to Italy to try to make his friend Avitus the next emperor. The Goths were defeated by an army of Suevians, a German tribe led by Ricimer, who wanted the Roman senator, Majorian, to be emperor.

- **The title of Emperor of Rome** was now little more than a mask behind which barbarian kings wielded power based on their armies. Nobody outside Italy took the title seriously any longer.

- **In** AD **476**, the German king Odoacer tired of the pretence. He told the 16-year-old Romulus Augustulus that he was no longer emperor. The boy retired to his family estates near Naples and vanished from history. Odoacer announced that he was now king of Italy.

▶ *The last Roman emperor, Romulus Augustulus, is forced to abdicate by Odoacer.*

The Seven Hills

- **When the first settlement** was established at what would become the city of Rome, the district was a wild and lonely place. There were no important roads through the area and few people went there.

- **The site** is where a range of hills from the east comes down to the banks of the river Tiber. Seven of these hills would later be included within the city which, therefore, became known as the Seven Hills of Rome.

▼ *The ruins of the Temple of Saturn overlook the Roman Forum. Modern Rome has been built on the ruins of the ancient city.*

- **Three of the hills**, the Quirinal, Viminal and Esquiline hills lie in the north of the city.

- **The Caelian Hill** lies in the southeast of Rome while the Aventine lies in the southwest of the city.

- **The two most important hills** stood close to the Tiber in the centre of the city. The Capitol Hill was the religious centre of Rome and on its summit stood the most important temples of the city.

- **The Palatine Hill** was where, legend said, Romulus built the first city of Rome. During the republic, this was the most fashionable residential area of the city and the emperors built their palaces here.

- **Archaeologists** working in the 1940s near the top of the Palatine Hill found a series of wooden post holes. These probably formed the foundations of three huts. These have become known as the 'Huts of Romulus'.

- **The area between** the Capitol and Palatine hills was known as the Forum, which means 'outside the walls'. At first it was a flat, marshy area, though it was later drained and built upon.

- **Between the Palatine** and Aventine hills was a straight narrow valley with a small stream running along it. In the earliest days of Rome, this 'circus', as it was known, was used for processions and games while the people sat on the slopes of the two hills.

- **North of the Capitol Hill** was an area of flat, dry land known as the Campus Martius – 'the field of Mars'. In the early days of Rome this area was used for army parades and for training young men in the manoeuvres used by the army.

City housing

- **Richer people** lived in two-storey town houses that were built around an open courtyard. There was often a small pool in the courtyard to catch and store rainwater that could then be used for cooking or washing.

- **Bedrooms** were located on the upper floor of the house. The doors from the bedrooms opened onto a balcony that ran around the courtyard. Stairs ran down one side of the courtyard.

- **On the ground floor** were the rooms where daily work was done and guests were entertained. These were often decorated with mosaic floors, statues and painted walls to show how rich the owners were.

- **The triclinium** was usually located next to the entrance to the house. This room was used as a dining room by the family, and was where visitors were entertained. Romans lounged on couches when eating or drinking.

- **The tablinum** was a study. This was where the head of the family kept his business records and private papers. Only very important business contacts or close friends would be invited to enter this room.

- **The kitchen** was located at the back of the house. It often had its own small door leading to a back alley, if there was one. This allowed supplies to be brought in and rubbish taken out without disturbing the family.

- **Very rich families** would have a small garden between the house and the street. A shady walkway ran around the garden, in which grew herbs and flowers. A tall wall was built between the garden and street to stop passersby looking in.

- **Poorer families** lived in blocks of flats known as *insulae*. These were built of brick, wood or wattle and daub. They were often owned by rich families who rented them out to tenants.

▲ *Roman* insulae, *or blocks of flats. People spent little time at home, preferring to meet friends and do business in the streets, cafes and taverns.*

- **On the ground floor** of an *insula* were shops, and on the first floor were flats and apartments for families. These had several rooms, including a kitchen and triclinium. On the top floors were single rooms for the poorest families.

- **The types of housing** found in Rome were copied throughout the empire. People in Britain, Spain and North Africa thought it was fashionable to live in a similar style to people in Rome.

365

Family life

- **The basis of Roman life** was the family. Most laws and customs were related to the family and to Roman concepts of family duties and privileges.

- **The oldest man** in a family was known as the *paterfamilias*. He was responsible for all members of his family. He was expected to arrange the education of children, the marriage of young adults and to ensure that everyone obeyed the law.

- **Under the kings** and early republic, the *paterfamilias* had to enforce the law on his family. If someone misbehaved it was the *paterfamilias* who beat, fined or even executed them. Later, the *paterfamilias* merely had to report crimes to the state.

▲ *A gold* bulla *acted as good luck charm to a newborn baby.*

- **People** with the same surname were linked into *gentes,* meaning the same family group. The members of a *gentes* were expected to help and support each other. Richer men gave jobs to poorer men or helped to pay off debts.

- **The most important** *gentes* were the patricians who lived in Rome during the time of the kings. These were the Aemilii, Cornelii, Julii, Fabii, Claudii and Valerii. Their members occupied top government posts throughout the Republic and early empire.

- **When a baby was born** it was shown to the father on its ninth day of life. The father presented the baby with a *bulla*, a good luck charm that was often made of silver or gold.

- **The child** had to carry the *bulla* at all times. When the child reached adulthood, he or she took the *bulla* to a temple and dedicated it to a god in thanks for having reached adulthood.

▶ *A rich family at home. The boy comes to greet his mother, but most of the time he would be cared for by a slave.*

- **Marriages** were usually arranged by the parents of the bride and groom, though the views of the couple were sometimes taken into account.

- **A wedding** began with a sacrifice to the gods, then a meal and a procession from the bride's house to the groom's. A dowry was paid by the bride's family to the groom.

  - **Funerals** took the form of a procession that carried the dead body to a site where it was burnt on a fire. Speeches were made then the ashes placed in a jar and buried.

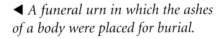

◀ *A funeral urn in which the ashes of a body were placed for burial.*

367

Women in society

- **Roman women** were expected to lead quite a different life from those of the men. Their main role was to work for the good of the family or the *gentes*.

- **Women were not allowed** to stand for election or hold government jobs. They were not even allowed to vote in elections.

- **Some temples**, such as that of Vesta, were reserved for women only. Priestesses of Vesta had ceremonial roles and wielded considerable political influence.

- **Before about 200** BC, women were expected to be under the control of their *paterfamilias*. They were not allowed to own property and could not enter into any business deals.

- **By the time** of the first emperors, women were allowed to own property and run shops and other businesses. Changes in laws had been introduced over a period of about 150 years.

- **Even under the emperors** it was thought to be a scandal if the wife of a rich man ran went to work. It was thought that women should work only if they needed to do so.

- **Poorer women** were able to work without disapproval. Wives and daughters of shopkeepers and craftsmen were expected to help with the business. Farmers' wives always helped on the farm.

◄ *Spinning wool into yarn, then weaving it into cloth, were skills that Roman women were expected to learn.*

- **By the time** of Tiberius, around AD 14, it was accepted that when a wealthy woman got married, she would retain control of any property or money that she had owned before the marriage. Before this date, her husband was given a share in her wealth.

- **One skill** that all women were supposed to have was that of making cloth. Women had to spin wool using a weighted spindle, then weave it into cloth on a small loom that was kept in the private part of a house.

- **A popular social activity** was for women to get together to spin and weave. Men were not allowed at such parties.

▶ *Slaves attending their mistress. Make-up, perfumes and other cosmetics were widely used in ancient Rome.*

Education and schools

- **From their birth** until the age of about seven, children stayed at home with their mothers. They were taught basic household skills and good manners, as well as how to count and how to behave in public.

- **At the age of seven**, children began their formal education. But until about 150 BC there were no schools or professional teachers in Rome at all. All children were educated by their own family.

- **Girls were taught** domestic skills such as cooking, spinning, weaving and how to recognize fresh fish and vegetables in shops. They were also taught how to run a household, giving orders to slaves or servants.

- **Boys were taken** to work by their fathers. Younger boys were expected simply to watch, but as they grew older they would be given simple jobs to do and later on, would be taught the more complex skills.

◀ *Only boys went to school. Boys from richer families were prepared for public life by educated slaves.*

▶ *Pens, ink and a writing tablet. Pupils practised writing on wax tablets before moving on to use more expensive papyrus.*

- **In this way** most Romans grew up to work at the same jobs as their fathers. The sons of farmers became farmers, the sons of blacksmiths became blacksmiths.

- **After the Roman** conquest of Greece, around 146 BC, many educated Greeks travelled to Rome, some as slaves and others looking for work. Many of them were employed as teachers.

- **By about 100** BC, there were many schools open to the public in Rome and other cities of the empire. Only the richest families had private tutors for their sons – most noblemen and businessmen sent their sons to school.

- **At school**, the boys were taught reading, writing and mathematics until they were about 12. After that, most boys left school to work for a living.

- **Older boys** who stayed on at school learnt history, science and rhetoric – the art of speaking in public. Those who intended to become lawyers also took lessons in law and studied famous court cases of the past.

- **All boys** were expected to keep fit and to take part in sports on a regular basis. Adult men were liable to be called up to serve in the army, so they had to be physically able to carry weapons on long marches.

371

Country life

- **During the time** of the kings and for most of the republic, the majority of Roman citizens were farmers living on small farms in the country.

- **Large estates** owned by the rich and worked by slave labour became more numerous after about 200 BC. Some estates were rented out to free men who each worked a small farm on the estate.

- **By 50 BC** there were few farmers who owned their own land. Most land was owned by the rich or the state. However, owner-occupier farmers were more numerous in the provinces.

- **The Romans** introduced many innovations to farming. They developed a plough tipped with iron that could cut heavy soils, and a cart with knives that could harvest grain. They moved crops and livestock around the empire, introducing new strains to many areas.

- **In some areas** of the empire, an agricultural system based on the villa became widespread. The villa was the home of a rich man who owned a large estate, but it was also the processing plant for the estate.

◀ *A country villa surrounded by the fields of the estate. Villas were working buildings as well as homes to the families that owned them.*

◄ Boar hunting was a popular sport in rural areas. Hunting dogs were used to help catch the boars.

- **Most of a villa** estate would be rented out to individual farmers, each of whom farmed a small area. Their crops were taken to the villa and bought by the landowner. The landowner then transported the goods to market to sell at a profit.

- **In the northern provinces**, rural people lived a different type of life due to the crops that would grow in the cooler climates. Barley and oats were grown more often than wheat, while apples and pears were more usual fruits than olives or grapes.

- **In Britain** and northern Gaul, livestock was more important than elsewhere. Large herds of cattle and sheep grazed on the lush grass of these lands, where rain fell in summer as well as winter.

- **Britain was famous** for its wool. Sheep were grazed on the hills and shorn of their wool once each year. The wool was baled up and exported to Gaul or Italy for processing into cloth.

- **In Greece and Egypt** local ways of farming continued almost unchanged. Egypt produced huge crops of wheat and that were exported to Rome.

373

Food and drink

- **The Romans** are famous for eating huge meals of luxurious food and drink. Some of them are quite bizarre, such as larks' tongues or bears' feet in honey.

- **Such meals** were consumed only by the richest families on special occasions. Most people ate simpler meals.

- **In Rome** and Italy, fish and seafood were very popular. Most fish was either grilled or stewed whole, then served at the table. The rare turbot, a kind of fish, was eaten only by patricians and later, by emperors.

- **Bread** made from wheat was eaten in large quantities. Most loaves were round and marked into eight portions by cuts made in the top before the loaf was baked.

- **Barley**, oats and other cereals were crushed and then stewed with water to produce porridges. These were often cooked with vegetables such as celery, leeks or cabbages.

- **Most cooking** was done over charcoal fires, which burnt at a higher, steadier temperature. Meat was cooked on a spit, other dishes were boiled in pots.

- **Meals were served** with several foods arriving on the table at once in a number of dishes. Spoons were used to serve food onto plates, but people used their fingers to eat.

- **Apicius Caelius** was a wealthy Roman famous for his love of good food and wine. He lived in about AD 30 and wrote a book of his famous recipes. Copies of this book, *Arti Coquinaria* have survived.

- **One recipe** from the cookbook of Apicius tells the cook to boil a bottle of red wine until it is reduced by one-third, then add 750 g of mushrooms together with salt, pepper and some chopped coriander leaves and simmer for five minutes. The mushrooms should be put into a small dish for each person and served with brown bread.

- **The Romans loved** to eat pork and ham. Large joints were served at dinner parties, then cut cold and eaten in the days that followed by the family. Sometimes a young pig would be cooked whole.

◀ *Slaves at work in a Roman kitchen. The oven was fired by a wood fire, which also provided heat for cooking pots placed above.*

375

The gladiators

- **Gladiators were men** who fought in the arena, sometimes to the death, to entertain the citizens and public. The word gladiator means 'a man who uses the sword', though some gladiators fought with other weapons.

- **The gladiatorial fights** began as a sacrifice at the funeral of a rich man. They were held to commemerate the dead man and keep his spirit alive. The first known contest was held in 264 BC as part of the funeral of the nobleman, Brutus.

- **Because all citizens** were allowed to attend a funeral, anyone could watch a gladiatorial fight. Some men realized that they could win popularity by putting on shows. They delayed this part of a funeral until they were standing in an election.

- **Most gladiators** were slaves, prisoners of war, condemned criminals or men who were in debt. They trained for months with their weapons before fighting in the arena.

- **At first gladiators** fought with army weapons, but later used specialized weapons of their own. Theses weapons were always impressive to look at. Most were decorated with paint or feathers and some were plated with gold or silver.

◀ *A Thracian gladiator with his curved dagger faces a Murmillo gladiator with an army shield.*

- **All fights** might end in death as the weapons were very sharp. However, an injured man could ask for mercy. If he had fought well, the man staging the show might spare his life.

- **A gladiator who won** a fight would be rewarded with a sum of money. Some gladiators saved up large sums of money in their careers. Successful gladiators might buy their freedom or become trainers of younger men.

- **Wild animals** were used in the arena. They were made to fight each other or to kill criminals condemned to death. Gladiators called *venatores* specialized in fighting lions, tigers and other dangerous animals.

- **Nobody was allowed** to stage gladiatorial fights without the emperor's permission, as he did not want any nobleman to become too popular.

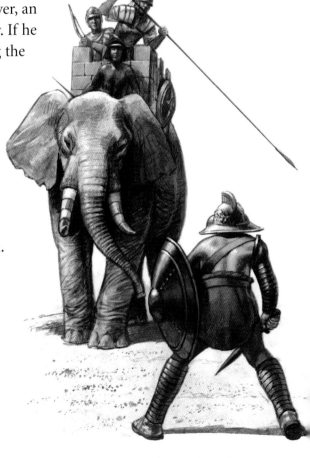

▲ *Some shows featured exotic combats to impress the audience. Here an elephant is shown fighting a gladiator, as actually happened in a show staged by Pompey.*

- **The last known** gladiatorial show was staged in about AD 430 by a Consul in Rome. After this date few men were rich enough to pay for the show, and increasingly large numbers of Christians opposed them.

Chariot racing

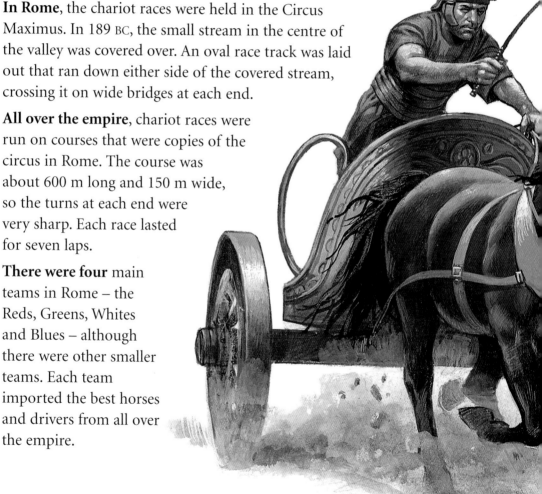

- **Even more popular** than gladiatorial shows were the chariot races. People followed the chariot race teams as keenly as they follow football teams today.

- **In Rome**, the chariot races were held in the Circus Maximus. In 189 BC, the small stream in the centre of the valley was covered over. An oval race track was laid out that ran down either side of the covered stream, crossing it on wide bridges at each end.

- **All over the empire**, chariot races were run on courses that were copies of the circus in Rome. The course was about 600 m long and 150 m wide, so the turns at each end were very sharp. Each race lasted for seven laps.

- **There were four** main teams in Rome – the Reds, Greens, Whites and Blues – although there were other smaller teams. Each team imported the best horses and drivers from all over the empire.

- **The chariots were** lightweight vehicles with two wheels and pulled by four horses. The horses could travel at a full gallop while pulling the chariot, so races were fast and furious.

- **The drivers wore** a helmet, but no other protective clothing. The reins were tied around the waist, so the driver steered by leaning from side to side.

- **Chariots often overturned** on the bends. So that the drivers were not dragged along by the horses, they carried a sharp knife to cut the reins. Horses sometimes tripped or stumbled.

- **If a chariot crashed** it was called a *naufragium*, or 'shipwreck'. Men and horses would be killed in these wrecks, but they did not seem to happen often.

- **Men riding horses** galloped alongside the chariots. They probably shouted advice to the drivers and tried to stop chariots of opposing teams from getting in the way.

- **Successful chariot drivers** could become extremely rich. One man earned so much money that he retired at the age of 35 to a country estate that was larger than those owned by most senators.

◀ *The most popular sport in Rome was chariot racing. Huge sums were bet on the results and vast crowds attended the races.*

379

The free food

- **Famine was a constant fear** in the ancient world. The onset of a plant disease or sudden bad weather could ruin a crop. If the failure was bad there would not be enough food for everyone.

- **It was a basic duty** of governments to ensure an adequate food supply. From earliest times, the Roman government stored vast quantities of grain in case of a poor crop. It also had the power to force merchants to bring food to Rome instead of other cargoes.

- **One of the reforms** of the Gracchi brothers was to sell grain from the government stores at cheap prices to Roman citizens. Once a month, each citizen was entitled to about 15 kg of half-price grain.

- **This grain dole** was popular with voters. In 58 BC, the radical politician, Publius Clodius, swept to office after promising in the election to make the grain dole free of charge.

- **Many poor Roman citizens** living outside the city moved to Rome so that they could get the free food. By 50 BC, no fewer than 320,000 men were getting the free grain every month.

▶ *Typical food for poorer people included fruit, vegetables, olives, honey and meat. Wine was drunk by most people nearly every day.*

- **Julius Caesar** reformed the dole by ordering a crackdown on men pretending to be citizens, or feigning poverty. In 44 BC, the number of citizens receiving the dole fell to 150,000.

- **Most citizens** took their grain to a baker. The baker exchanged it for a number of loaves of bread handed out over the weeks until the next grain dole. Bakers kept a percentage of the grain for themselves as payment.

- **The poorest citizens** swapped their wheat grain for rye grain. This was cheaper, so there would be more rye given in exchange for wheat. Rye grain produced a darker, less popular bread.

- **In AD 270**, the emperor Aurelian replaced the monthly grain dole with a daily dole of six loaves of baked bread. During festivals there was free wine and olive oil. About 1.2 million loaves of bread were baked every day.

- **Government records** of the late empire are poorly recorded due to the threats of invasions and wars. It is thought that the free bread dole in Rome ended about AD 440.

Money and markets

- **Trade was important** to the economy of the Roman Empire. Less than one-tenth of the population worked in manufacturing and trade, but about one-fifth of the wealth of the empire came from this source.

- **Most traders** were small businessmen who made goods that they sold locally. A smaller number of merchants transported goods by boat along rivers or by ship overseas.

- **When Rome was founded** nobody had yet invented coins. Goods were swapped at markets for other goods. In about 400 BC, bronze ingots stamped with a cow began to be used in central Italy.

  - **The first coins** issued in Rome were bronze coins stamped with the portrait of the god Janus. About the year 200 BC the silver coin known as the *denarius* was introduced.

  - **Rome became** a money economy, meaning that people tended to buy and sell things using money instead of swapping them. People could borrow money to finance business ventures.

◀ *A coin of the emperor Constantine has the figure Britannia on the reverse. Constantine was in Britain when his father died and he inherited power.*

. . . FASCINATING FACT . . .
There were very few merchants who shipped large quantities of goods around the empire. The largest single commodity, the bulk transport of grain, was organized by the state.

◀ *A Roman merchant ship sails into harbour. Trade between the colonies was carried out mainly by sea.*

- **During the republican period**, coins were stamped with a picture of the goddess Roma or of the wolf that saved the lives of Romulus and Remus.

- **The emperors** made sure that their portraits and names were stamped on coins issued during their reigns. The other side of the coins had either a picture of a deity or of a famous event.

- **Because the same coins** were used right across the empire, it was easy for merchants to buy and sell goods in different places. This helped increase trade and made the empire more prosperous.

- **After the year** AD **300**, the government began to devalue coins by reducing the amount of silver that they contained. This meant merchants no longer trusted the money of the empire. Trade and prosperity declined. By AD 400, a denarius contained one-tenth of the silver it had in AD 300.

Provincial life

- **The city of Rome** was the centre of the empire, the richest and most powerful city in the world. But most of the people lived not only outside Rome, but outside Italy. These were the provinces of the empire.

- **In many ways,** life in the provinces was like that in Rome. People liked to follow Roman fashions and Roman lifestyles. But in other ways, the provinces were very different.

- **The provinces** in the eastern Mediterranean had been part of the empire of Alexander the Great, king of Macedon and a brilliant military commander. Centuries before they became part of the Roman Empire, they had been ruled by the Greeks.

- **Greek culture** was kept by much of the eastern provinces. Many people spoke Greek, using Latin only when dealing with Roman government. They worshipped Greek gods and lived in Greek-style houses and cities.

- **The eastern provinces** did not absorb much Roman culture. Life in the east bore little resemblance to life in Rome.

- **The western provinces** of Europe, including Spain, Gaul and Britain, had been inhabited by Celts before they were conquered by Rome. The Celts preferred to live in the country rather than in towns.

◄ *A Celtic blacksmith shoes a horse. The Celts continued to live in their round houses and wear checked clothes after being conquered by Rome.*

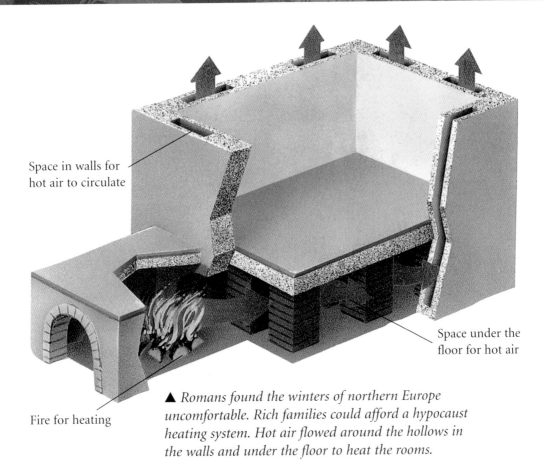

Space in walls for hot air to circulate

Space under the floor for hot air

Fire for heating

▲ *Romans found the winters of northern Europe uncomfortable. Rich families could afford a hypocaust heating system. Hot air flowed around the hollows in the walls and under the floor to heat the rooms.*

- **In these areas** the Romans founded new cities and towns. People who wanted to share Roman culture and be promoted in the Roman state moved to live in the cities. But most people stayed in the countryside.

- **Life in the western** provinces was more like life in Rome, but only in the cities. In the rural areas people continued to live in Celtic houses and worship Celtic gods.

- **However**, all the provinces were subject to rule by Rome. Governors were appointed by the Roman government, and most of them were Romans. Roman money was the only kind in circulation.

- **When the empire** was prosperous, all provinces benefited. But civil wars and decline affected all provinces badly.

Republican legions

● **After the defeat** of Rome by the Celts in 390 BC, the republican leaders reformed the army. The *phalanx* was abandoned in favour of a more flexible battlefield organization – the legion.

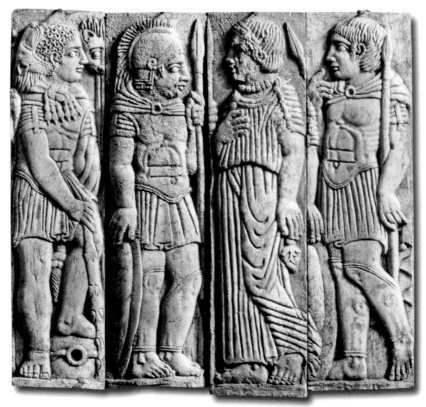

▲ *Roman soldiers from about 350 BC. The heavy infantry wore armour and helmets, while the lighter infantry might have wore animal skins.*

- **Each legion** consisted of 5000 men divided into four lines, each of which had 15 units. Each man had to bring his own equipment, but was given a small sum of money to pay for food while on campaign.

- **The front line** was made up of the *leves*, men armed with small shields and javelins. They began the battle by throwing javelins at the advancing enemy.

- **The second line** was the *hastati*. They had helmets, armour and shields. As the enemy closed, they threw javelins then charged to attack with swords.

- **The third line** was the *principes*, formed in three ranks. If the *hastati* were defeated, the *principes* threw javelins, then attacked with swords and shields. The *principes* were the experienced veterans of the legion.

- **Behind the *principes*** were the *triarii* – older men with spears and shields. If the *hastati* and *principes* were defeated, they retreated behind the *triarii*.

- **The *triarii*** were the final reserve. They retreated backwards, holding the enemy at bay with shields and spears.

- **By 170 BC**, Rome would usually field four legions of 5000 men, plus 1200 cavalry. The cavalry were the richest Roman men and could afford to buy a horse and armour. Rome's allies provided additional units.

- **During the republic**, the army was commanded by the consuls. Sometimes, one consul led the army on campaign while the other stayed in Rome. On other occasions, both consuls went to war and took turns to command.

. . . FASCINATING FACT . . .

Only Roman citizens could serve in the army. A man could be called to serve in 16 campaigns before he was 46 years old. If he had served 16 times, he was only expected to fight if Rome itself was attacked.

Reforms of Marius

- **By around 120 BC**, the army was experiencing problems. Longer and more extensive wars called for more soldiers, but fewer citizens could afford the cost of weapons and armour. Even fewer wanted to be away from Rome for years on end.

- **In 107 BC**, Gaius Marius, a general who had worked his way up from the ranks, stood for election as consul. He promised to reform the army so that men who did not want to serve would be forced to do so.

- **Marius was elected** to be consul six times. His reforms of the army were dramatic and wide ranging. They formed the basis for the Roman army until the collapse of the Roman Empire almost 600 years later.

- **Marius decided** that the government should pay for the military equipment of the soldiers. This meant that a man did not need to buy his weapons to serve in the army.

- **The pay given** to soldiers was increased dramatically. Instead of being just enough to pay for bread and water on campaign, the wages were increased to be the equivalent of an unskilled worker in Rome.

- **The length of service** was changed from just the length of the campaign to being a full year, renewable each year up to a total of 20 years. At the end of 20 years, retiring soldiers would be given a small farm to live on.

> **...FASCINATING FACT...**
> Finally, Marius made the legion a permanent formation,
> not a unit raised afresh for each campaign. He gave each legion a
> number and a sacred standard in the form of an eagle. Rome now
> had a permanent, professional army.

- **Service in the army** was no longer a costly duty, it was a good career choice for even the poorest citizen. Men could earn a good living and comfortable retirement. They might even become rich through plunder.

- **Tens of thousands** of poor citizens flocked to join the legions of Marius. They wanted to serve for years on end so that Rome could launch campaigns far from home.

- **In 89** BC, the various Italian allies were merged with Rome and all their citizens became Roman citizens. This meant even more men volunteered for service in the legions.

◀ *A legion* aquilifer, *or standard bearer. He wears heavy armour and carries the eagle standard of the legion. This has a laurel wreath around the wings, indicating that the legion has won a victory.*

The legion organization

- **The new legions** were given a new organization that would endure for centuries. There were now 5500 men in a full strength legion, although many legions had rather less men due to disease and battle.

- **Each legion** was divided into ten cohorts, each made up of six centuries of 80 men each. The century was commanded by a centurion, assisted by an *optio*.

- **The first cohort** was often twice the size of the others and might be divided into five centuries of 200 men each. Each century in the first cohort had two centurions and two *optios*.

- **Centurions were promoted** through the cohorts, with the centurions of the first cohort being senior to those of the second cohort, and so on to those in the tenth cohort who were the most junior.

- **Each cohort** had a standard bearer, the *aquilifer*, who carried the unit's standard into battle and who dealt with pay. He probably had some religious duties, such as setting up a small shrine in camp.

- **The *tesserarius*** was junior to the leading centurion. It was his duty to post guards and arrange sentry duty. The *cornicen* had a trumpet that he used to pass on orders to the cohort.

- **Each legion** had at least six tribunes who had to be either *equites* or the sons of senators. These officers dealt with the day-to-day running of the legion.

- **One of the tribunes**, the *tribunus laticlavius*, was a temporary appointment. He was a man about to join the senate, who had to serve with a legion on campaign to gain experience. He was given non-combat duties, such as arranging food supplies.

- **The *praefectus castrorum*** was second in command of the legion. His main duties were to ensure that the legion was always ready for action, well fed and properly equipped.

- **The commander** of the legion was the *legatus*. Like the *tribunus laticlavius*, this was a temporary appointment for one year, or one campaign at a time.

▶ *Roman forts were built and repaired by the troops themselves. The everyday work of a soldier involved carpentry, construction and engineering as much as fighting battles.*

391

Arms and armour

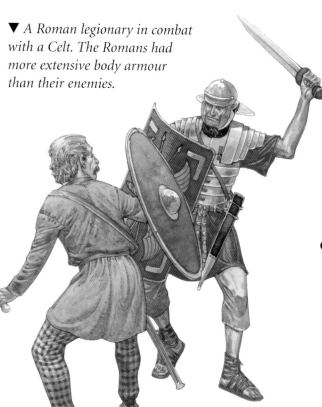

▼ *A Roman legionary in combat with a Celt. The Romans had more extensive body armour than their enemies.*

- **The government** was now paying for the arms and equipment of the soldiers, which meant that all men carried the same kit. Although details varied over time, the basic equipment of the legions remained the same from 100 BC to about AD 300.

- **Each man carried** a large shield called a *scutum*. This was rectangular, but until about AD 30 had rounded corners. It was 1.3 m tall, 60 cm wide and was curved to deflect enemy weapons.

- **Helmets were made** of bronze or iron. They had a rounded skull with a neck flap that projected about 10 cm from the rear. There were also cheek pieces that reached to the chin and flared out to protect the neck.

- **On top** of the helmet was a crest. Ordinary soldiers had long, flowing crests of horse hair that dangled down the back. Officers had shorter, upright crests of feathers. The shape and colour of the crest indicated rank.

- **Body armour** took the form of a short-sleeved shirt of iron mail. This was made by interlinking hundreds of rings made from iron wire. There were reinforcing strips of mail or bronze scales over the shoulders.

- **After about AD 50**, body armour became more sophisticated. Strips of iron or steel were shaped so that they could be strapped around the body and over the shoulders. This new armour was called *lorica segmentata*.

- **The *lorica segmentata*** was lighter and more effective than chain mail. It weighed about 9 kg, as opposed to 16 kg. It was expensive, so its use spread slowly through the army.

- **Each man** had two javelins, called *pilum*. These had a steel tip mounted on a soft iron shank, fitted into a wooden handle. They were designed to stick in an enemy shield and so make it clumsy in battle.

- **The soft iron shank** of the *pilum* would bend on impact so that it could not be thrown back at the Romans by the enemy.

- **The main weapon** was the *gladius*. This was a heavy stabbing sword that inflicted deadly wounds.

▲ *The* lorica segmentata *body armour of the 1st century AD. This complex design allowed the wearer to move easily while being protected from enemy weapons.*

393

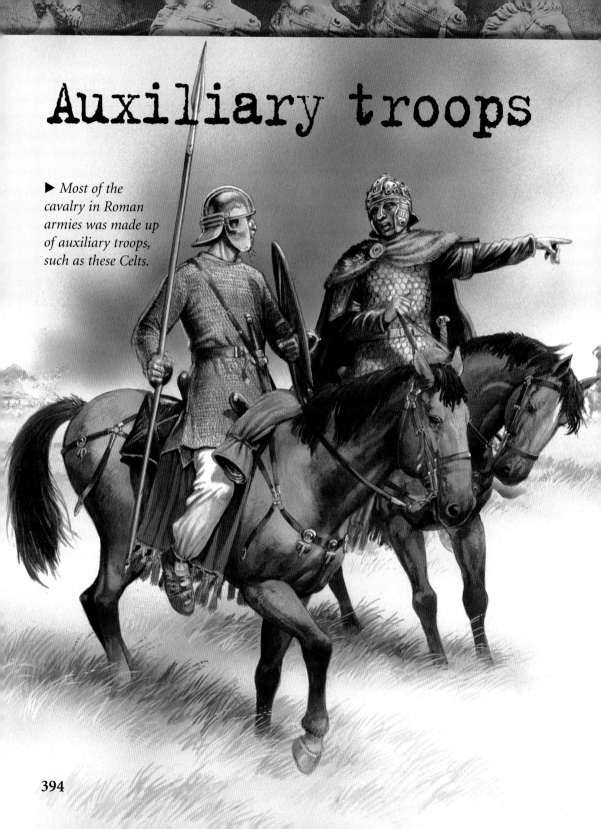

Auxiliary troops

▶ *Most of the cavalry in Roman armies was made up of auxiliary troops, such as these Celts.*

- **Roman citizens joined** the legions. Non-Romans joined the auxiliary units. Most of these were raised from within the empire.

- **Before about** AD **40**, most units supplied their own arms and armour. This meant men carried weapons they used before being conquered by Rome.

- **Auxiliary units** were of varying sizes and composition. Some were infantry, some were cavalry and some were mixed. They were recruited for various periods of time and paid about one-third of the pay of the legionaries.

- **Some German units** were made up of cavalry and infantry. Men on foot ran into battle beside the cavalry, holding onto the horses' bridles to keep up.

- **During Tiberius' rule**, auxiliary units were reformed. They were subject to the same discipline as the legions, and pay and service was standardized.

- **Each unit** was a cohort of 500 men divided into six centuries. The centurions were from the same tribe of people as the troops, but the cohort was commanded by a tribune who was a Roman citizen.

- **Auxiliary infantry** wore mail shirts and bronze helmets. They carried oval shields and were armed with a heavy, thrusting spear and a sword. They were trained to fight in a similar way to the legions.

- **Auxiliary soldiers** were required to sign up for 25 years service. At the end of his service, the auxiliary soldier was made a Roman citizen.

- **Some specialist units** kept their native equipment. For instance, a Batavian cohort, from what is now the Netherlands, was skilled in crossing rivers and fighting from boats.

- **Archers were recruited** from Syria and the eastern Mediterranean. They sometimes fought wearing armour, but might discard the armour if they had to move quickly in battle.

Into battle

- **By the time** of the later republic and early empire, the army had developed new battle tactics that had evolved from those of the early republic.

- **The key** to the new tactics was the organization of the legion into cohorts. Each century was formed ten men across and eight men deep. Each cohort was formed three centuries across and two deep.

- **When forming** a line, the legion assembled itself with the first five cohorts standing in a line, leaving a gap the same width as a cohort, between each of them. The second five cohorts stood behind the first, arranged so that they covered the spaces in the first line.

- **The legion** could fight in this chess-board formation. More usually, the second line of centuries within each of the first five legions would march up to form a solid line alongside the first line of centuries.

- **If the first line tired**, it retreated between the gaps in the second line. The second line then formed a solid line to continue the battle.

▼ *The* testudo, *or 'tortoise' formation, shielded the men from missile weapons as they advanced.*

▲ *The Romans could sell healthy prisoners as slaves,
but wounded enemies were usually killed after the battle.*

- **Meanwhile**, the original first line of cohorts would form a new second line ready to take over if necessary.

- **When faced by** a solid line of enemy troops, the legion adopted a formation known as a 'pig snout'. The first cohort formed at the front, with the second and third close behind. The fourth, fifth and sixth cohorts formed a third line. The other four cohorts were in a final line.

- **The legion would** then charge forward and use the wedge shape of the 'pig snout' to smash a hole in the enemy line.

- **After a battle**, the general would reward soldiers or units that had fought particularly well with cash payments.

- **The soldiers** could expect to share any loot or plunder that was stripped from the bodies of the enemy, or the proceeds of selling the enemy as slaves.

Fortresses

- **Romulus** fortified the top of the Palatine Hill with a wooden palisade, with a ditch at vulnerable places. By 400 BC, the Capitol Hill was topped by a stone wall about 2 m thick and 8 m tall.

- **The Servian Wall** that was built around Rome in 380 BC, was built with stone blocks. It was 3.6 m wide and over 10 m tall, and stood behind a ditch 30 m wide and 10 m deep.

- **From about 100** BC, the Romans did not build walls around Rome or the provincial cities. They relied on the army to protect the empire and did not want rebellious cities to have fortifications.

- **Most fortresses** were built by, and for, the army. Hundreds of fortified bases were built across the empire, and several remain standing in various degrees of ruin.

- **When marching** through enemy territory, a Roman unit always built a temporary fortification for the night. This consisted of a square enclosure surrounded by a ditch, and a wooden fence about 1.4 m tall.

- **On routes** through provinces where enemy raiders might appear, the army built marching camps about 20 km, one day's march, apart. These could hold an entire legion. They had deeper ditches and proper wooden walls.

- **Stone forts were** built to guard permanent legionary bases and supply depots. These had walls up to 3 m thick and 10 m tall. There were usually towers at intervals along the walls on which catapults or ballistas were placed.

- **In some areas**, the stone walls were reinforced with layers of brick. Some walls were built almost entirely of brick.

▼ *A permanent Roman fortress surrounded by stone walls and towers. The barracks and store rooms inside might be built of wood or brick.*

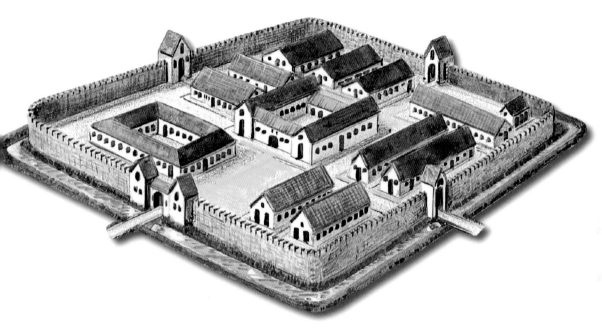

- **Gates were** protected by one or two towers and sometimes passed through a massive gatehouse. About the year 200 BC, the Romans invented the portcullis, which could be dropped down to block a gateway.

- **In AD 275**, the emperor Aurelian built a new wall around Rome as barbarian attacks on the empire became more serious. The new wall was 18 km long and had 381 towers. It remained the main defence around Rome until it was breached in a siege in 1870.

Frontier walls

- **The Roman Empire** reached its largest size around AD 116, during the rule of Emperor Trajan. After this, the government stopped looking for new conquests and began to exploit what it already had.

- **The army** was no longer needed to fight against powerful enemies, or to invade and conquer new lands. Instead, it defended the existing empire.

- **The best-known** and best-preserved frontier defence is Hadrian's Wall in northern Britain. It was built after Emperor Hadrian visited Britain in AD 122 and decided not to attempt to conquer the Picts to the north.

- **Hadrian's Wall** runs for 117 km from sea to sea. It was 2–3 m wide and stood about 5 m tall. A walkway along the top was protected by battlements facing north toward the barbarians.

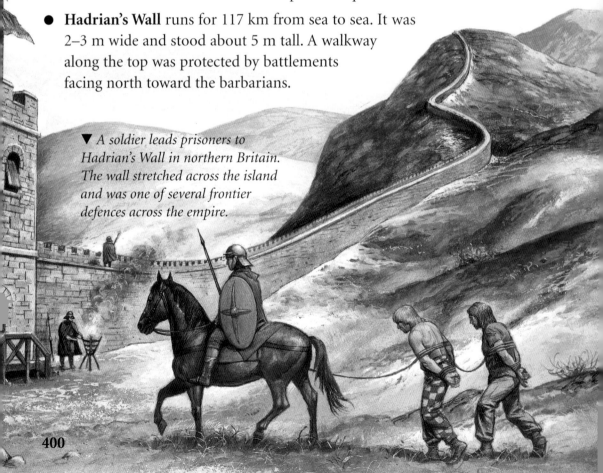

▼ A soldier leads prisoners to Hadrian's Wall in northern Britain. The wall stretched across the island and was one of several frontier defences across the empire.

▶ *The ruins of Hadrian's Wall. The square walled area in the foreground marks the site of a mile castle, where soldiers sheltered while on duty.*

- **At intervals** of 500 m, there were small turrets in which sentries could shelter from the weather and eat their food. Every 1.5 km were small forts where 20 men or so could live, cook and sleep.

- **In front of the wall** was a defensive ditch about 8 m wide and 3 m deep. Behind the wall was a second ditch that marked out the military zone in which only soldiers were allowed.

- **The garrisons** of Hadrian's Wall lived in 16 forts built on, or just south of, the wall itself. From there, they manned the wall and went out on patrol in the untamed lands beyond, to keep a lookout for trouble.

- **The rivers Rhine and Danube** were also fortified. Along the Roman bank was a string of small forts and watchtowers, each within sight of the next.

- **Big fortresses** were built close to the Rhine and Danube. These were bases from which the legions could march to man watchtowers and patrol rivers.

- **Only in Syria** and its surrounding areas, where the Romans faced the Parthian Empire, were cities and towns fortified. Here, the Romans relied on the cities holding out against attack, until an army could be marched up to fight a battle and drive off the attackers.

Early warships

- **During the time** of the kings and the early republic, Rome did not have a navy. All her wars were fought on land and the state had no merchant ships to protect.

- **After about 340 BC**, the Romans needed warships to protect their merchant ships and to transport armies. Rome used fleets belonging to her allies among the Greek cities of southern Italy.

- **It was not until** the First Punic War that Rome realized that it needed a fleet of its own. According to legend, the Romans copied a Carthaginian ship that ran ashore, but they probably also hired shipbuilders from their allies.

- **All warships** at this time were galleys. These were lightly built ships that were powered by oars in battle and on most journeys. They sat low in the water and had a ram at the front with which they could hole and sink enemy ships.

- **The first Roman fleet** had 100 *quinquereme* ships. These ships had two banks of oars on each side, making a total of 120 oars. The lower oars were pulled by two men, the upper by three men. The ships were about 35 m long and 5 m wide.

- **The Romans were not** such good mariners as the Carthaginians, and lost battles to the more nimble enemy ships and crews. The Romans countered this by inventing the *corvus*.

- **The *corvus*** was a gangway that had a long spike on one end and was lifted above the deck by a crane. When a Roman ship got close to a Carthaginian ship, the *corvus* was dropped so that the spike pierced the enemy deck. Then Roman soldiers poured across to capture the enemy ship.

- **The Romans defeated** the Carthaginian navy using the *corvus*. At the Battle of Ecnomus in 256 BC, the Romans lost 24 ships, while the Carthaginians lost 94 ships, most captured by Romans using the *corvus*.

- **By 100 BC**, the Romans had invented the *dekares* ship. This was 45 m long and 12 m wide, and was much more stable in the water than the earlier *quinquereme*. It had two banks of oars on each side, each oar pulled by five men.

- **The naval battles** of the civil wars were fought mostly between fleets of *dekares*. At the Battle of Actium in 31 BC, Mark Antony had 480 such ships and Octavius Caesar, 400. The battle was won by Octavius.

◄ *A Roman war galley. The ram at the prow was used to try to smash a hole in enemy ships.*

Ram

403

Later warships

- **After the end** of the civil wars of the 1st century BC, the Roman navy had no organized fleet left to fight. It no longer needed the large *dekares* or *quinquereme* warships.

- **The new naval** enemies of Rome were tribal fleets from Germany and the Black Sea, or pirates based in small harbours around the Mediterranean.

- **To face these** new enemies, the Roman navy needed plenty of small, fast warships that could patrol the seas, then move quickly to attack any pirates that came into sight.

- **The first** purpose-built pirate chaser was the *liburnian,* a ship developed in the 1st century AD. It was a slightly larger version of a ship used by pirates in the Adriatic Sea.

- **The *liburnian*** was about 35 m long and 3.8 m wide. It had 120 rowers, each pulling on a single oar. The oars were arranged with 60 on each side, on two banks.

- **Ships operating** in the North Sea formed the *Classis Britannica*, or 'British fleet', based in ports in southern Britain and northern Gaul. These ships often had a large wooden wolf's head carved on the stern.

- **One type of ship** that was present in large numbers in the *Classis Britannica* was the short *bireme*. This ship was 20 m long and 5 m wide. It was powered by 50 rowers, each pulling a single oar.

- **These short *biremes*** had oarports almost 2 m above the sea surface. They were fairly stubby in shape and had bows and sterns that were built up high. This allowed them to cope with larger waves than the Mediterranean ships.

- **The Romans developed** special craft to carry military supplies along the Rhine and Danube. These cargo ships were 20 m long and 6 m wide. They were powered by 20 oarsmen sitting in a single bank of ten oars each side.

- **The river ships** were protected against attack by special fast-rowing boats that carried a number of soldiers. These travelled with the cargo ships.

◀ *If the ram proved ineffective, Roman ships carried soldiers to hurl javelins at the enemy or even to board the opponent's ships.*

The later field army

- **In AD 260**, the Roman army in the east, led by Emperor Valerian in person, was defeated by an invading army of Persians under their ruler, Shapur. Valerian was captured and kept as a slave.

- **The new emperor** was Gallienus, son of Valerian. He began a thorough reform of the Roman army that was continued by his successors, Claudius II and Aurelian.

- **Gallienus realized** that the Romans could not hold the frontiers of the empire. The Persians and European barbarians could too easily mass a force at one point to cross the frontier and raid a section of the empire before retreating.

  - **Instead**, the lands close to the frontier were densely filled with fortified towns, river crossings and supply depots. These were garrisoned with detachments of the Roman legions.

    - **Meanwhile**, Gallienus created a mobile field army that was based at just a few key garrisons deep inside the empire. This was made up of the best troops, many of them cavalry, and had fast-moving supply columns.

      - **The new strategy** was to allow barbarians to cross the frontier, but to deny them the opportunity to pillage towns or to capture supplies, both of which were defended by walls and forts.

◀ *A cavalry officer from about AD 350. He has a small shield and long, slashing sword.*

- **Meanwhile**, the mobile field army would move at high speed to intercept the barbarians. Hopefully, the field army would arrive in time to meet and defeat the barbarian invaders.

- **The field army** would then march across the frontier into the lands of the invading barbarians. They would destroy farms, kill civilians and devastate the lands so thoroughly that other tribes would hesitate to attack the empire.

- **The field army** was kept under the personal control of the emperor, or of one of his most trusted supporters. This not only meant it would react quickly to barbarian attack, but was unlikely to be used as part of a rebellion.

- **The new system** was fully developed by AD 350. The barbarians were contained and the empire appeared to be safe.

▼ *Roman defensive walls were well built, and were often repaired and reused for centuries. They helped to fortify towns that were vulnerable to barbarian attacks.*

The kings of Rome

- **The system of government** under the kings of Rome is unclear. The Romans liked to claim that many features of government dated back to the time of the kings to make them appear older and more prestigious than they actually were.

- **The earliest kings** – Romulus and Numa Pompilius – ruled over a small state. They probably ruled directly, issuing orders and ensuring that they were carried out themselves.

▼ *The kings of Rome were in charge of religious ritual and ceremonies. The earliest Roman temples did not survive, but they probably had a sacred building in which rituals were carried out, as in this later example.*

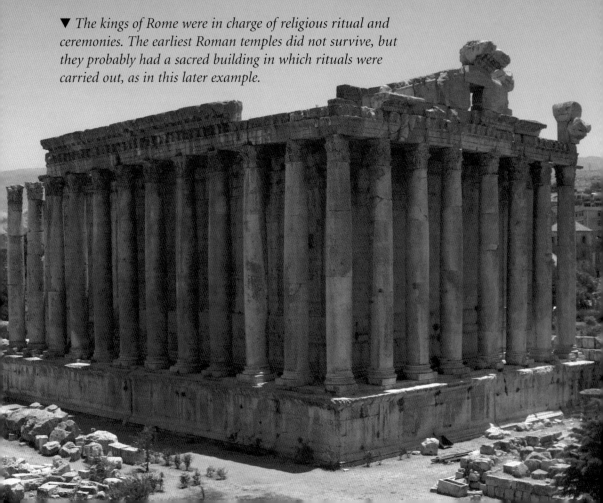

- **Each king** held the position of chief priest of Rome. He had to supervise the other priests to make sure that the correct rituals and sacrifices were carried out.

- **The kings** were also the commanders of the army. They had to supervise the mustering of the citizens, and the selection of those who would go on campaign and those who would stay in Rome.

- **On campaign**, the king was the general of the army. He decided what strategy would be followed, which tactics would be used and gave orders to the various units in battle.

- **When the citizens** of Rome gathered for the selection of men to join the army, they formed the *comitia*, or assembly. The king often used this event to make announcements about new laws or decisions he had taken.

- **The *comitia*** was sometimes asked its opinion by the king. He would ask a question that required a 'yes' or 'no' answer, and the men would shout out their reply. The king made his decision by which answer had been shouted the loudest.

- **At some point** the kings began to appoint rich, powerful or talented men to act as advisors. These advisors met together in a body called the Senate.

- **The king decided** who was in the Senate and what they were allowed to discuss. He would ask their advice, but did not necessarily take any notice of their opinions.

- **In theory**, the kings had almost unlimited power in early Rome. However, he would not ignore the wishes of the people, or his advisors, too often in case he became unpopular. An unpopular king was at risk of being killed or expelled.

The consuls

- **When Tarquin the Proud**, the last King of Rome, was expelled, the Romans needed to devise a new system of government to replace that of the kings.

- **The Romans** wanted to make the government more responsive to the wishes of the people. They decided to create a system of government based on the concept known as *imperium*. The word comes from the Latin *imperare*, which means to command.

- **The powers** that had been held by the king were divided between three people. It was hoped that this would stop any one person becoming too powerful and making themselves king.

- **The religious duties** of the king were given to the *Ponitfex Maximus*, or 'chief priest'. This man was elected for life, and a new *Pontifex Maximus* was only elected when the previous one died.

◄ *The* lictors *were officials who carried a bundle of rods and an axe in front of the consuls, as a symbol of their rank and authority.*

- **The military** and governmental duties of the king were given to two men, who had the title of consul. The two consuls had to decide between themselves how they would organize the division of duties.

- **Two consuls** were elected each year. A man could stand for election as many times as he wished and could serve as consul for as many times as he was elected.

- **At first**, only patricians were allowed to stand for election to be a consul. After 366 BC, any Roman citizen could stand for election, and one of the consuls had to be a plebeian.

- **To stand for election** as consul, a citizen had to be over 43 years of age, and to have already served as a *quaestor*, *aedile* and *praetor*. In an emergency, these restrictions could be ignored, but this rarely happened.

- **Each consul** had a guard of 12 men armed with axes. These men, called *lictors*, accompanied the consul wherever he went. The axes were carried wrapped in a bundle of twigs. This symbolized the power of Rome.

. . .FASCINATING FACT. . .
The Romans dated their history according to who was consul.
The year we call 435 BC, was the year of Marcus Cornelius Maluginensis and Lucius Papirius Crassus, and the year we call 58 BC was the year of Julius Caesar and Calpurnius Bibulus.

The Senate

- **The Senate** was the chief deliberative body. It was made up of men appointed by the king to be his advisors, and probably numbered 100 men.

- **Under the republic**, the number of men in the Senate rose to 300 by about 400 BC, and to 1000 by 50 BC. The emperor Augustus finally fixed the number of senators at 600.

- **To sit as a senator**, a man had to be a member of a patrician family, or he needed to have considerable wealth. By 100 BC, this was fixed at 800,000 *sesterces* – about £470,000 today.

- **If a senator died** or resigned, his place was taken by a former consul who was not already a senator. If there were no former consuls, then former *aediles*, *quaestors* and *praetors* would be appointed. If there were none of these, serving consuls would appoint a man to the Senate.

- **The Senate** had wide-ranging powers. It could appoint ambassadors to represent Rome, appoint governors to provinces and decided how much public money to spend on various projects.

- **Discussions could be held** on any matter the Senate liked. The Senate could discuss the actions of the consuls, provincial governors and other officials. If the Senate voted against an action it was difficult for the official concerned to continue.

● **Votes were taken** at the end of a debate. The senators had to walk to one side or the other of the meeting room, then they were counted. If the consul was asking for opinions, he would start with the man who had been a senator for longest and worked his way down to whoever had been most recently appointed.

● **The Senate met** three times a month, each sitting lasting one day from sunrise to sunset. Business not finished by sunset had to wait until the next meeting. Votes were valid only if at least one-third of the senators were present.

● **In the early years**, the Senate met inside the Temple of Jupiter on the Capitol Hill. Later, it might meet in the temples of Apollo, Castor and Pollux. After about 100 BC, the Senate met in a special building in the Forum.

● **Senators wore** a toga with a broad purple stripe around the edge to show their rank. They could also lodge free-of-charge at state-owned farms and properties when travelling outside Rome.

◀ The formal debates of the Senate took place in the Senate chamber, unofficial discussions and deals were struck in the hall outside.

413

Citizens and strangers

- **Under the rule** of the kings, a Roman citizen was any adult man living in Rome who was not a slave.

- **After the kings** were expelled, the citizens acquired new powers to decide who should rule Rome. This made it more important for the state to know who was, and who was not, a citizen.

- **The list of citizens** was called the census. At first, the consuls drew up the census each year, but after 443 BC two new officials, called censors, were elected to do this job. The census listed all citizens by name, address and wealth.

- **Roman citizens** were put into three classes, each of which had its duties and rights within the Roman state. Although only adult men could be citizens, other members of their families had similar status.

- **The patricians** were made up of two groups. The first group were the people who were descended from the six noble families who had lived in Rome during the time of the kings.

- **The other type** was men who were eligible to sit in the Senate, and who were the sons of Roman citizens. These men were usually very rich.

- **The *equites*** were citizens who had a wealth of 400,000 *sesterces*, about £240,000 in modern money. All citizens who were neither patricians nor *equites*, were plebeians.

- **Foreigners** were considered to be non-citizens. They could own property, do business and were free to travel as they wished. However, they did not vote and could not hold government office.

- **People** who had formerly been slaves but were now free were called freedmen. They had similar rights to non-citizens.

- **Slaves had few rights**. They had to obey all orders given to them by their owner. They were not allowed to own anything or make agreements with anybody, unless specifically given permission to do so by their owner.

◀ *A slave auction. Roman citizens wore a flowing white toga, while non-citizens wore tunics and cloaks.*

415

The tribunes

- **In 494 BC**, the consuls mustered the army and ordered it to march against the city of Aequi. However, the plebeians in the army marched to a hill three miles from Rome instead, and refused to move.

- **The dispute** that followed centred on the fact that only patricians were allowed to stand for election to office, at this date. The plebeians wanted to be able to stand for election as well.

- **A compromise** was suggested by the patrician, Menenius Agrippa. A new position was created called *tribunus plebes* – tribune of the people. Plebeians could stand for *tribunus plebes* and only plebeians could vote in the election to that office.

- **At first**, the tribunes of the people had no direct power themselves. Instead, they were allowed to inspect all government accounts and watch any official at his work.

▶ *A Roman tribune. He wears a toga over a tunic to show he is a citizen of Rome.*

...FASCINATING FACT...

The tribunes were considered to be sacred persons, or *sacrosancti*, like priests. Anyone who interrupted them while they were speaking committed a crime, and anyone who struck them faced execution.

- **If the tribunes** thought that any official was being dishonest, lazy or corrupt they could collect evidence against them. This was then presented to the Senate or the *comitia* for judgement to be passed.

- **As the years passed**, the tribunes gained greater powers. However, they could exercise those powers only within the city of Rome. Tribunes were not allowed to step outside the city walls while they held office.

- **By 250 BC**, the tribunes could imprison any government official and seize all of his official records. The man would remain in prison unless the Senate or *comitia* voted to free him.

- **Tribunes** were able to supervize the meetings of the Senate. If he thought that the rules of debate were not being followed or that a motion was improper, a tribune could shout out 'veto', and that meeting had to end immediately.

- **The great weakness** of the tribunes was that all their decisions had to be unanimous. As there were ten tribunes in office at any one time, it was often difficult for them all to agree.

Junior government officials

▲ *A surveyor checks the route of a road that is being built under army supervision. The* aediles *were elected to plan and carry out public building works.*

- **All the elected government officials** in ancient Rome served without pay. This meant that most of the men who held these posts were wealthy enough to be able to spare the time away from their business. In addition, most officials worked only part time.

- **Until about 200** BC, the junior officials of Rome – the *quaestors*, *aediles* and *praetors* – handed out private contracts to men to do work. The officials checked that the work was being done correctly and for the right price.

- **After about 200** BC, the officials had paid assistants. At first, each official hired his own, but by about 70 BC the staff were permanent and continued in place no matter who won the election.

- The *quaestors* were responsible for raising taxes, and keeping an account of how state money was spent. They also cared for ambassadors arriving in Rome, supplying them with a house and slaves.

- **The two most senior** *quaestors* supervised finances and kept guard over the state treasury. Two others were responsible for paying the army. After 150 BC, each provincial governor and most generals had a *quaestor*.

- The *aediles* were responsible for the public buildings. These included roads, aqueducts, city walls and temples.

- **The two plebeian** *aediles* looked after the roads and law and order within Rome. The *cerialis aediles* looked after the aqueducts and ensured that Rome had stocks of food. The major *aediles* were the most senior. They looked after all other public buildings.

- The *praetors* were the most senior of the junior elected officials. If neither consul was in Rome, the oldest *praetor* took over their duties.

- **The** *praetors* **judged** law cases. They decided if a crime had been committed and who was guilty. They also heard civil cases, such as disputes over who owned property, or if a business contract had been broken.

...FASCINATING FACT...
Until 250 BC, there was only one *praetor*, then two until 80 BC when two more were appointed. Under the emperors there were 16 *praetors*, one of which specialized in street crime, the other in legal disputes between foreigners.

The rule of Augustus

- **The system of government** established by Augustus lasted for over 200 years. Even then, it never collapsed completely, but its essentials continued to the end of the Roman Empire.

- **By the time** Augustus had won the civil wars against Mark Antony, there were few people left alive who remembered the time when the republican government worked smoothly.

- **Augustus decided** to pretend to restore the republican system, while in fact keeping most power to himself. Augustus called himself *princeps*, or 'first citizen', but others saw him as the first emperor.

- **The traditional elections** of men to government office began again in 27 BC. Citizens were free to vote as they wished, and the men who were elected were free to carry out their tasks as they saw fit.

- **The Senate** was allowed to meet as often as it had done before, and was free to debate and vote on anything that its members wished.

◀ *Augustus commissioned many portraits of himself in painting, sculpture and on coins – he wanted everyone in the empire to recognize him. Many of these survived so we know exactly what he looked like.*

▶ *A statue of Augustus. He is shown
in a traditional pose used by army
commanders when issuing an order.*

- **There was only one** formal change
  introduced by Augustus. He made
  himself the senior tribune of the people.
  He had all the traditional powers of the
  tribunes, but without being elected annually.

- **The vast wealth** of his position as king of
  Egypt, and his massive estates inherited from
  Julius Caesar, made Augustus the richest man
  in the empire. He sometimes used this wealth
  to influence elections.

- **Augustus divided** the provinces into those that
  were controlled by the Senate, and those that
  were controlled by officials. He made sure that the
  officials controlled provinces with army bases.

- **Because Augustus** had such influence over the
  government officials, he effectively controlled
  the army. Without the army, nobody could
  oust him.

Patronage of the emperors

- **The power of Augustus**, and other emperors who followed him, was based on informal powers. The most important of these was the power of patronage.

- **With his wealth**, Augustus lavished gifts on those whom he liked, or who did things that pleased him.

- **Augustus would personally** hand out patronage to the richest or poorest Romans. He would spend as much time granting a loaf of bread to a beggar, as installing a senator as a provincial governor. All Romans expected access to the emperor.

- **Augustus** could usually rely on getting his way when it came to votes because men were so eager to please him. He could even send letters to distant provinces asking the governor to do things – and they usually did as he wished.

▲ *When he was emperor, Caligula spent money to win friends, but was soon almost bankrupt.*

- **The giving and returning** of favours was very important. Augustus might arrange for a young man to be taken onto the staff of a successful general, then ask the man's father to vote for a particular measure in the Senate.

- **With his control** of the army, Augustus enforced law and order throughout the empire. This made him popular in the provinces, which had suffered during the civil wars.

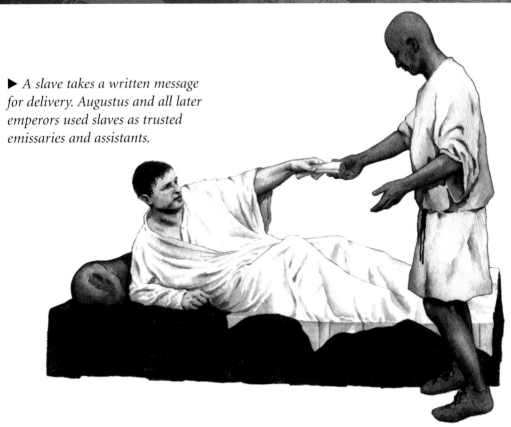

▶ *A slave takes a written message for delivery. Augustus and all later emperors used slaves as trusted emissaries and assistants.*

- **The convention** by which provincial governors had to be former consuls, or *praetors*, was important. It meant that governors had to be experienced, and it provided a reward for men who had worked hard for Rome.

- **Augustus stuck** to the convention, but got around it by having four consuls elected each year. The first pair were nominated by the Senate, the second pair were men suggested by Augustus.

- **Augustus** and all later emperors were the *Pontifex Maximus* of Rome. This put the emperor at the centre of public ceremonies and celebrations so that he was often seen by all the people. The title is now used by the Pope.

- **After the time** of Augustus, the emperor's personal household became increasingly important. Men working directly for the emperor gained great influence and wealth as they could bring things directly to the emperor's attention.

The imperial Senate

- **In the time** of the kings, the Senate had acted as advisor to the king. During the republic, it was the most powerful administrative and body in the state.

- **During the time** of the emperors' the role of the Senate changed again and again. The Senate was a prestigious and important organization.

- **Augustus saw** the Senate as being his partner in the business of governing the empire. He knew that the richest and most important men in the empire were all senators. He often asked their advice on matters, and allowed the Senate to make many decisions.

◀ *In an election, each man had to declare who he was voting for. Men loyal to the emperor checked how people were voting.*

- **The Senate** was a place where the leading men of the empire could debate and discuss matters of concern. This was a way to bring to the attention of the emperor that there was a problem that needed dealing with.

- **The criminal courts** increasingly looked to the Senate as a court of appeal. If a difficult point of law was involved, or a man was rich enough to seek a hearing, the case would go to the Senate.

- **The governors** and many other officials of the empire, had to be drawn from members of the Senate. These men travelled to and from their positions, spreading news and views among the top class of the empire.

- **By about AD 100**, the meetings of the Senate were becomingly increasingly concerned with the government of Rome and Italy, not the empire. The men who attended the Senate were increasingly local men.

- **By AD 150**, rich men living in the provinces were being made senators as a mark of respect by the emperors. This gave them prestige in their local areas and made them eligible for positions in the government.

- **These senators** from the provinces rarely went to Rome or attended meetings of the Senate. The position of being a senator and the Senate itself, soon had little to do with each other.

. . . **FASCINATING FACT** . . .

As the government of the late empire began to collapse, the Senate took upon itself the tasks of daily administration in Rome and nearby areas. It was one of the very few institutions of ancient Rome to survive. There is still an elected Senate running the local government of the city of Rome today.

Elections to office

- **When the last king** of Rome was expelled from the city, the Romans decided that the government officials, who were previously appointed by the king, should now be elected by the citizens instead.

- **Elections to office** were held at assemblies of all the citizens of Rome. These assemblies took place in the open air, often in the Forum. Any man who was a citizen could attend and vote, but nobody was forced to turn up.

- **The origins** of the assemblies relate back the musterings of the army by the kings of Rome. At these assemblies the men were divided into the units they would serve in, in the army.

- **This type of assembly** was called the *comitia centuriata*, and it was used when consuls and other officials were to be elected. All citizens were classified depending on whether they were rich enough to serve as cavalry, legionaries or *leves*. Then each section was divided into ten groups.

- **Votes were held** within each group. The group leader announced which way his group had voted, and this counted as one vote in the final election.

- **Because there were** always fewer men rich enough to serve as cavalry, those groups were smaller, but they still had one final vote per group. This meant that the rich had more say over the final result than the poor.

- **The second type** of assembly was the *comitia tributa*, which was used when voting on new laws. This assembly also voted by groups, but this time the groups were allocated according to tax-paying districts.

▲ *The Roman Forum seen from the south. The citizens of Rome gathered here to vote in elections once each year.*

- **The voting** in the *comitia tributa* still favoured the rich, but not so much as in the *comitia centuriata*. During the time of the emperors only the *comitia tributa* was called, and it elected officials as well as passing laws.

- **If a man was taken ill** during a meeting of either *comitia*, the meeting had to be halted immediately and called to meet again on a different day.

- **During the time** of the emperors, only motions, or candidates approved by the Senate, were put to a vote in the *comitia*. Since the emperor effectively controlled the Senate, citizens were powerless to pass laws he did not want.

427

The organization of empire

- **A key problem** facing the government of the Roman Empire was its sheer size. It measured about 4200 km from east to west, and 2400 km from north to south.

- **Government messages** and orders could travel only as quickly as the man carrying them. Even travelling virtually non-stop, it would take a man three months to travel from one end of the empire to another.

- **The central government** could not physically administer the more remote areas of the empire. Any instructions issued in response to events would be out of date before they arrived.

- **Instead**, the empire was divided into a number of provinces, each of which was administered by a governor appointed by the government. Under the republic governors were former consuls, or *praetors,* appointed for one year at a time.

- **The governors** were in control of all aspects of government in the province and commanded any troops stationed there. They acted as the head judge as well as the head of government, and had almost unlimited power.

- **After their year** in office, the governors had to return to Rome. There, they were questioned about their actions and finances. Any governor who was suspected of dishonesty or breaking the law would be put on trial.

- **Provinces** had governing systems based on that of Rome. There were *quaestors* to look after finances, and other junior officials.

- **During the time** of the emperors, the governors were usually formerly elected officials, but they might stay in post for years at a time. The emperor sent officials to keep an eye on governors while they were in office.

- **Provinces that were peaceful** and relatively easy to administer had governors appointed by the Senate. The emperor himself appointed governors to provinces that had armies stationed within them.

- **In the later years** of empire, the governors no longer had control over troops, who were by then commanded by generals responsible to the emperor. Most provinces were divided up into several smaller provinces.

▼ *In AD 43, Britannia became a province of Rome. In AD 60, Queen Boudicca led a revolt against Roman rule, but was eventually defeated.*

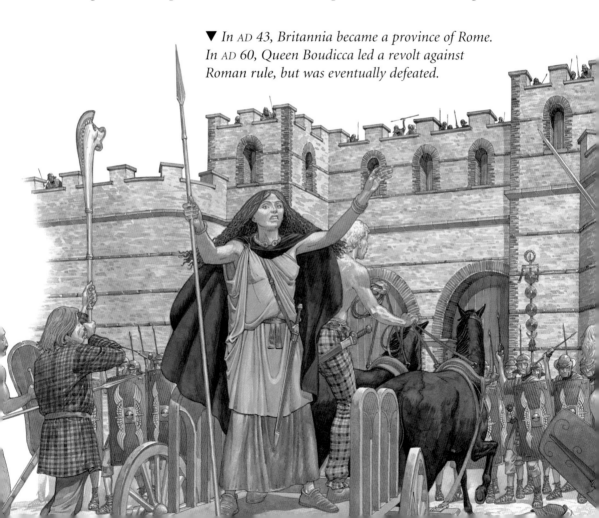

Governors and their staff

- **Much of the administration** and government of a province was in the hands of local government, not of the governor. The main job of the governor was to ensure that the province provided to Rome what it was supposed to.

- **The most important task** of a governor was to raise the taxes due to the Roman Empire and make sure that they reached Rome safely. The governor might also have to raise auxiliary troops and send them on campaign.

- **Taxes were usually** collected by private men. These men agreed an annual contract with the governor. They might be paid a percentage of the taxes collected, or be allowed to keep anything over a set amount that was paid to the governor.

▲ *A tax collector inspects his official list to see how much a farmer is expected to pay.*

- **A second duty** was to carry out the orders of the central government. Such orders usually related to keeping roads in good condition, and providing food and accommodation for officials or soldiers passing through.

- **A third duty** was to ensure that the inhabitants of the province obeyed the law and did not cause any trouble. Most governors spent most of their time on this task.

- **Some areas kept** their own legal systems, others adopted the Roman legal system. In both cases, the governor was expected to act as a court of appeal if there was a difficult case or if important men were involved in a dispute.

- **To help him** with these tasks a governor would have only a few men. The governor of Britain might have a full-time staff of only 20 or 30 men. Most work was contracted out so that the governor and his officials only had to check work done by others.

- **The written records** of the province were not kept for very long. Storing paper rolls was difficult and expensive, especially in damper countries, such as Britain or Gaul. As soon as the central government had approved accounts and records, they were thrown out.

- **In the later empire**, governors were expected to write to Rome regularly. They had to keep the central government informed of local events and often asked advice about what to do next.

...FASCINATING FACT...
Important decisions, such as the granting of Roman citizenship to a provincial, were usually engraved on bronze tablets so that they would be kept more easily.

Local government

- **Throughout the Roman Empire** most people lived their entire lives without coming into direct contact with the government at all. Instead, it was the local government organizations that regulated daily life.

- **The cities** that already existed before the area was conquered by the Romans were generally allowed to keep their own system of government. Athens, for instance, retained its democratic town council.

- **However**, the existing governments knew that their powers had been drastically reduced when it came to relations with other cities or states. Neither Athens, nor any other state within the empire, could declare war or make a treaty without permission from Rome.

- **Although such cities** were free to run themselves, they had to pay taxes or tribute to Rome.

- **Where cities did not exist** before the time of Roman rule, the Romans encouraged them to thrive. Rome had been a city state and Roman systems of government were based on those of the city.

- **Some new cities** were artificial creations of the Romans. The modern city of Cologne began as a Roman colony on the river Rhine. It was populated entirely by Roman citizens from elsewhere in the empire.

- **Other new cities** grew naturally. London was a small village before the Romans conquered Britain, but after the Romans built a bridge there, the village grew quickly to become a prosperous city filled with merchants and traders.

- **Local people** were encouraged to take a lead in local government. In Britain, the province was divided into areas called *civitas*, each of which was based on the territory of the pre-Roman Celtic tribes.

▲ *The city of Londinium (London) in about* AD *300. The city became a*
great centre of trade and was the biggest city in the province of Britannia.

- **Each *civitas*** was administered from a new city. The local landowners and
  nobles were granted Roman citizenship and expected to play a lead role in
  local government.

- **Whatever form** the local government took, it was always closely watched
  by the governor. Some independence was considered a good thing, but too
  much might encourage rebellion or withholding of taxes.

433

Roman architecture

- **The earliest buildings** in Rome were constructed of wood, roofed with thatch. By around 600 BC, brick was being used more widely. Stone was used only for defensive walls and other military purposes.

- **In about 520 BC**, the Romans began to build a new temple to the god Jupiter on the Capitol Hill. The new building was made of stone and followed Greek designs. Soon most public buildings in Rome followed Greek designs.

- **Temples were rectangular** and had roofs supported on rows of columns. Within the temple was a room in which stood a statue of the god. Like the Greeks, the Romans sometimes built small round temples.

- **The Romans copied** three styles of Greek architecture. The Doric was plain but had numerous carvings attached to the structure, the Ionic had more complex decoration while the Corinthian was lavishly embellished.

- **Two more styles** of architecture were developed by the Romans. The Tuscan was similar to the Doric, but lacked the carvings. The composite was an eclectic mix of styles that varied widely.

- **The Romans invented** a new type of building – the basilica. This style was most often used for law courts, but basilicas was also used for council chambers or markets.

- **Basilicas** had a long central nave with a lower-roofed aisle along either side. The style was copied by early Christians for their churches. Even today many churches have a nave and aisles.

- **The Romans developed** the arch, which they copied from the Etruscans. An arch spreads the weight of a building evenly over an empty space, pushing down on the supports on either side.

- **By extending** an arch into a long structure, the Romans invented the barrel vault, an entirely new way of roofing over a building. When two barrel vaults met at right angles, the Romans produced the groin vault.

- **The dome** was a Roman invention. It was made by producing an arch that was circular, rather than linear. The Romans produced gigantic domes so large that nobody was able to build anything like them until the 16th century.

▼ *Romans borrowed the use of upright pillars from the Greeks, but added their own invention of the round-topped arch.*

Public baths

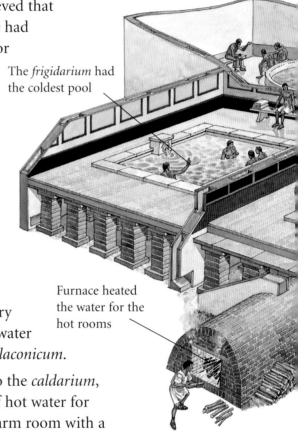

- **From the earliest times**, Romans believed that baths were a sign of civilization. Rome had dozens of public baths, and all towns or cities in the empire had at least one. Even army posts had baths for the soldiers.

The *frigidarium* had the coldest pool

- **A Roman bath** was a public building where people went to relax and enjoy themselves. Most were built by the emperor or a rich local man, as a gift to the public. They were either free or very cheap to enter.

- **The process of bathing** was complex and might take up to two hours. The first stage was to enter a very hot room, which had a pot of boiling water to fill the air with steam. This was the *laconicum*.

Furnace heated the water for the hot rooms

- **After the *laconicum*,** bathers moved to the *caldarium*, another hot room with a small pool of hot water for bathing. Next was the *tepidarium*, a warm room with a warm pool.

- **Attendants** in the *tepidarium* would massage the bathers. Olive oil was rubbed into the body to draw out any dirt and impurities. The oil was then scraped off with a curved bronze tool called a *strigil*.

The *tepidarium* had a tepid, or cool, pool

◀ *A small public bath in a provincial town provides a hot bath, warm bath and cold plunge pool for the use of male citizens.*

The *caldarium* was the hottest room

● **The next stage** was the *frigidarium*. This was an unheated room or an open courtyard, in which was a pool of cold water. People might spend hours relaxing around the pool.

● **The heat** for the hot rooms came from large furnaces located beside the baths. Hot air was piped under the floors and up cavities in the walls. Water was heated by the furnace in large copper pots.

● **Roman baths** were more than just places to get clean. There were also libraries, lounges, gardens and snack bars. Many men used the gardens and lounges as places to meet business contacts and discuss deals.

● **Women** went to the baths too but on different days to men.

● **Baths were often decorated** with marble panels and beautiful sculptures. The great baths built by the emperor Caracalla in AD 217, stood on the Celian Hill and remained in use until the aqueduct broke in AD 549. Today it is used as a venue for opera.

Roman roads

- **The most famous** of the Roman structures are the roads. Thousands of kilometres of road ran across the entire empire.

- **The construction** of Roman roads varied considerably depending on where they were, what materials could be found easily to hand and what its use would be.

- **In towns and cities**, roads were made of stone slabs laid over layers of sand that were packed down hard before the stones were put down. On either side of the road was an underground drain to carry away rainwater and dirt.

- **There was usually** a raised pavement on either side of city roads for pedestrians. Stepping stones allowed people to cross the road without treading in the horse dung and other mess that accumulated in the roadway.

- **In open country**, roads were surveyed by men who were trained to find the best route from one town to the next. Slaves were brought in to do the heavy labour. Army roads were built by soldiers.

- **Army roads** ran in long straight lines. This is because soldiers found it easier to march in a straight line, even up a steep hill, rather than to march along more level, windy roads.

◀ *Milestones were erected on roadsides to show distances between towns. Many showed which emperor was ruling at the time. This milestone bears the name Victorinus, who came to power in AD 269.*

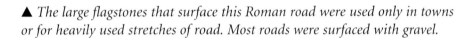

▲ *The large flagstones that surface this Roman road were used only in towns or for heavily used stretches of road. Most roads were surfaced with gravel.*

- **Roads for civilian use** were not so straight. They were used by merchants and farmers with pack animals, or carts pulled by oxen or horses. Animals pulling heavy loads prefer to move on level roads, even if they are longer.

- **Roads** that were expected to take a lot of traffic were started by digging a trench about 12 m wide and setting large kerbstones along its sides. The trench was then filled with sand and gravel, which was packed down hard.

- **If the road** was close to a city or was to be used by important people, the upper surface was covered by slabs of stone that were curved to throw rainwater off to the sides.

- **Roads in rural areas** were rarely well-built. For most of their length they were dirt paths. In damp areas the road surface might be improved to stop it becoming muddy, while river crossings were improved with bridges or fords.

439

Bridges and arches

- **The Romans knew** that crossing rivers was often the most difficult part of a journey by road. People might get wet or lose possessions when crossing, and if the river was particularly high, there might be a long delay.

- **Fords** could be built up where the river was wide and shallow. Large quantities of stone and rock would be dumped into the river to form a firm foundation. On top of this was laid a flagstone surface, like an underwater road.

- **Bridges** were more effective where rivers were deeper or narrower. A narrow stream could be crossed by a single stone arch, which supported a humped road surface above.

- **Wider rivers** had to be crossed by bridges with more than one arch. Each arch was supported midstream by an artificial tower built up from the riverbed.

- **First**, the engineers hammered a circle of wooden stakes into the riverbed to form a watertight compartment. The water was pumped out and workmen dug out the riverbed to remove loose mud and reveal a firm surface.

◄ *The Roman arch enabled the weight of a wall to be spread evenly across an opening, such as a doorway or window.*

- **A stone tower** called a pier, was then built up to stand about 3 m above the river surface. The tower was usually wider and stronger at, and below, the water surface so that it could withstand floods.

- **On important roads** the bridge was completed by building a stone arch between each pier. On less important roads, wooden beams connected the piers. The road surface was then built on top.

▲ *The Ponte St Angelo, over the river Tiber in Rome, is carried on a succession of rounded arches.*

- **The Romans sometimes** built large arches over roads. These had no practical purpose, but were ornamental structures built to mark boundaries or commemorate famous events.

- **At Richborough** in Kent, there was a vast arch over the road that led up from the docks to the fort. This was the main military port for Britain. All soldiers entering or leaving Britain had to march through this arch.

- **In Rome**, a series of triumphal arches were built over the sacred road. These stone arches were decorated with carvings of battles and campaigns won by the general who was being honoured in the triumph.

441

Mosaics

▲ *A mosaic of a dolphin made up of hundreds of pieces of coloured stone.*

● **One artform** the Romans perfected was the mosaic. Several other ancient cultures made mosaics, but it was the Romans that used them most often and developed new an exciting styles.

● **A mosaic is a picture** made up of large numbers of small coloured stones, pieces of pottery or fragments of glass. Mosaics were often placed on floors as they are decorative and very hard wearing, but they may also be used on walls and ceilings.

● **Before creating a mosaic** the artist first draws a design that will fit the space of the right shape and size. He then collects enough pieces of stone, pottery or glass of the right size and colour for the design.

● **The floor is divided** into a number of smaller sections according to the artist's design. A section of floor is then covered with a smooth layer of wet plaster. The *tesserae*, as the small pieces of stone are known, are pushed into the plaster and rolled level.

● **Work on a mosaic** must be completed quickly before the plaster dries and hardens. Once the plaster has set, the design cannot be altered. Many mosaics have small errors in them that were not noticed until it was too late.

● **Especially complex** sections of design might be prefabricated. They were glued face down onto a roll of cloth using water-soluble glue. The cloth was then unrolled over the wet plaster. When the plaster had set, the cloth was soaked in water to loosen the glue, and then removed.

...FASCINATING FACT...

One house at Pompeii, south of Rome, had a mosaic in the doorway that was a picture of a dog with the words *cave canum* or 'beware of the dog' written beside it.

- **Master craftsmen** were hired to produce central panels showing animals, gods or men. Less skilled workers completed areas of plain colour, or geometric patterns around the edges.

- **Prestigious buildings** in Rome and other cities had mosaics made from chips of marble stone. These were the most durable and expensive types of mosaic.

- **Even houses** belonging to poor families would have a mosaic floor in rooms where visitors might enter in order to make a good impression.

▼ *An elaborate mosaic showing gods and goddesses in a ruined house. Mosaics such as this were extremely expensive and could be afforded by only the richest families.*

Poems and histories

- **One of the earliest Roman poets** was Quintus Ennius, who is often referred to as the founder of Roman literature. There were poets before Ennius, but their work has not survived. This early work seems to have been dominated by short poems composed to honour a famous man, or an event.

- **Ennius began** by writing similar poems to those of earlier writers. Around 200 BC, he adopted Greek styles of rhythm and rhyme to Latin. Later poets copied him, and he became known as 'the father of Roman poetry'

▲ *The Roman writer Virgil wrote several books of poems as well as a history of Rome.*

- **In 180** BC, Ennius began composing a poetic history of Rome that ran for 20,000 lines and took him over 15 years to complete. Only 550 lines have survived.

- **Titus Lucretius Carus**, known as Lucretrius, was a nobleman who began writing poetry about 75 BC. He compiled allusions to the gods and myths into works about nature and famous events.

- **The rich young politician**, Gaius Valerius Catullus (84–54 BC) , turned to writing poetry after an unhappy love affair. The works of Catullus are lyrical and have a steady rhythm. He wrote about everyday events, such as when the man next to him at dinner stole his napkin.

- **Quintus Horatius Flaccus** (65–27 BC), known as Horace, was the favourite poet of Emperor Augustus. Horace included lots of jokes and humour in his work – which was mostly in the form of short poems about life in Rome.

- **Publius Ovidius Naso** (AD 43–17), better known as Ovid, wrote beautiful love poems as well as more earthy works that poked fun at famous men and government officials. Because of this, he was exiled to a Greek city on the Black Sea by Augustus.

- **Sallust,** Gaius Sallustius Crispus (86–35 BC), was a politician who retired after the murder of Julius Caesar. He wrote histories of the civil wars and the careers of Marius and Sulla. He established a style of historic writing followed by all later historians.

- **Titus Livius,** better known as Livy, lived during the rule of Augustus. He wrote a history of Rome in 142 books, of which 35 survive. The Romans thought that he had produced the finest history of Rome ever written. Later historians concentrated on producing accounts of their own times.

> ...FASCINATING FACT...
> The most famous work by Lucretius is *De Rerum Natura*, a poem running to six books in length. It shows a passionate concern for nature and all living things and includes vivid descriptions of forest fires, earthquakes and other natural events.

445

Oratory

- **Oratory**, the art of public speaking, was highly regarded in ancient Rome. It was taught to boys in secondary schools. Some scholars thought that oratory was the most important of all the arts.

- **Most Roman citizens** would be expected to speak in public at some stage of their lives. They would give their opinions during meetings of the *comitia*, speak out at meetings of local government and take part in court cases.

- **Even when a citizen** hired a lawyer for a court case, he was still expected to make a speech putting forward his point of view. Being able to speak with skill and confidence was vital.

- **Oratory** was a wide-ranging subject. The basics include the ability to speak clearly and loudly so that an entire audience could hear what was being said. A speaker had to be able to make points powerfully, be able to debate effectively and have a good knowledge of politics and philosophy.

- **Vocabulary** was a prized skill. This did not men knowing lots of different words, but knowing the precise meanings of words, and how to vary the intensity of meaning by putting different words together in a sentence.

- **History** was also included in the subject of oratory. It was thought to be useful to compare the subject of the speech with the actions of famous men from Rome's past.

> **. . . FASCINATING FACT . . .**
> Cicero rose to be consul in 62 BC, and made some of his most famous speeches in defence of the republican constitution in the face of attack by Julius Caesar. Cicero was executed in 43 BC after trying to oust Mark Antony from power.

▲ *Cicero was a famous orator who was famous as the best speech-writer in Rome during the time of Julius Caesar.*

● **A knowledge of the gods** and religion was considered vital. An orator who could include references to the gods and their actions in his speech in an appropriate way was highly regarded.

● **Philosophy** was also considered to be important as it allowed an orator to produce underlying reasons why the subject of his speech was important, to persuade people to agree with him.

● **The Romans believed** that their greatest orator was Marcus Tullius Cicero (106–43 BC), a politician and lawyer who lived during the time of the civil wars. Many of Cicero's speeches were written down and used in schools.

On the stage

- **The Romans enjoyed** going to the theatre, which was enormously popular for many years. The first theatres were built around the year 200 BC, when the idea of staging plays was brought to Italy by the Greeks.

- **Roman theatres** were built in the open air and plays were performed during daylight. The theatres had a semi-circular stage with banks of seats rising up to enclose the rounded front edge of the stage.

- **Behind the stage** was a wooden or stone façade, built to resemble a town house. Many plays were written with characters going in and out of doors, or appearing on balconies to make the most of this backdrop.

- **When a different backdrop** was needed a painted curtain was hung up from the balconies of the house.

- **Actors dressed up** to appear like their characters. They also wore masks to help the audience recognize them whenever they appeared on stage.

- **One popular form** of comedy play was based around the legends of the gods. The plays showed deities and humans getting involved in ridiculous situations that were loosely based on well-known myths.

- **The very first plays** staged in Rome took place in 240 BC. They were Greek plays translated into Latin by a Greek playwright named Livius Andronicus.

◀ *Actors on stage wore masks to show which characters they were playing.*

▶ *A Roman theatre had seating in a semi-circle around the stage.*

- **The first** popular plays in Rome were by Titus Maccius Plautus (*c.* 250–184 BC). Plautus translated Greek plays, then added new jokes and references to Roman figures. These comedies included slapstick, puns and crude jokes.

- **The works of Terence**, Publius Terentius Afer (*c.* 193 or 183–159 BC), are more sophisticated and cultured. Later Roman playwrights tended to write broad comedies like Plautus, or artistic works like Terence.

. . . **FASCINATING FACT** . . .
Most plays featured a limited number of characters. Among the most popular were the cunning slave, the strict father, the drunken son, the foolish wife, the angry neighbour, the dishonest cousin and the lovesick daughter.

449

Statues and sculptures

▲ *Marble was used by most Roman sculptors as it can be carved in tiny detail.*

- **Until about 250 BC**, the Romans did not produce much sculpture. There were some wooden carvings in the temples, but none have survived. It was only when Greek-style architecture became fashionable that sculpture became common.

- **At first**, wealthy Romans bought statues and reliefs from Greece. Then, around 170 BC, they began commissioning new works. At first, these were copies of famous statues, but later, entirely new works began to be produced.

- **The most important** Roman invention in sculpture was the portrait bust. This was a statue of a person from the shoulders up that attempted to reproduce the features and appearance of the person.

- **From about 100 BC**, the Romans produced large numbers of portrait busts. Most were of famous men, but there were also busts of ordinary people.

- **Relief carvings** were produced to commemorate a specific event. A famous early example is the *Ara Pacis*, produced in 13 BC to celebrate a religious sacrifice held by Augustus to commemorate the end of the civil wars.

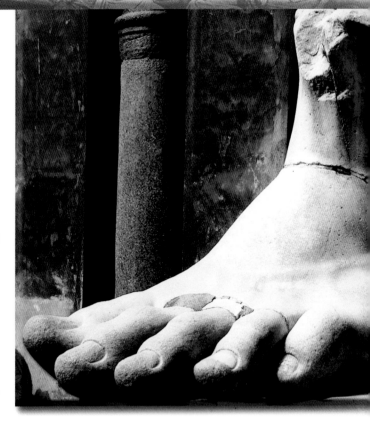

▶ *A gigantic marble foot that stands in a street in Rome is all that remains of a large statue.*

● **Commemorative** reliefs often featured on triumphal arches. By AD 50, copies were sent to province cities so that people living there could see them.

● **After the death** of Augustus, the emperors commissioned large numbers of statues of themselves to impress the public. Most show the emperor in formal dress and pouring a drink as an offering to the gods.

● **Trajan's column** is a 40-m-tall marble column in Rome that has a continuous frieze spiralling up it, showing scenes from Trajan's conquest of Dacia (modern-day Romania) in AD 106. The carvings reproduce military equipment in highly realistic detail.

● **A new style** of sculpture became common after about AD 175. This favoured movement and emotion rather than realism. Figures are shown in less detail, but they are running, jumping and walking with more vigour.

● **Nearly all Roman** sculpture that has survived is in stone. However, the Romans produced large numbers of bronze statues and sculptures as well. Most were melted down after the fall of the empire.

451

The Capitoline Triad

- **The three greatest gods** of ancient
  Rome were Jupiter, Juno and Minerva.
  They were honoured by a temple on
  top of the Capitoline Hill, and are
  known as the Capitoline Triad.

- **Jupiter** was the chief god of Rome.
  In his earliest appearances, Jupiter
  controlled all weather. He had a
  thunderbolt that he threw down
  to Earth to destroy anybody who
  offended the gods.

- **Jupiter symbolized** the virtues of justice
  and honour and kept promises. He was
  invoked when treaties were made, or war
  declared. He was sometimes called Jupiter
  Optimus Maximus, meaning 'the greatest
  and best' of the gods.

▶ *Jupiter was the most important of the Roman
gods. This is a copy of the statue of him that
stood on the Capitoline Hill.*

- **Juno** was the wife of Jupiter. She presided over family life and the private aspects of the Romans. Juno was invoked at weddings, births and around the time when children became adults.

- **Juno gave advice** to the Romans. In 390 BC, her sacred geese began to cackle when the Gauls tried to attack the Capitoline Hill. Consuls and emperors would pray to her when they needed advice about affairs of state.

- **Minerva** was originally an Etruscan goddess. Her worship was brought to Rome by King Tarquin Priscus. She was considered to be the goddess of wisdom and skill.

- **The first great temple** on the Capitoline Hill was built by Tarquin Priscus to honour the native Roman deities, Jupiter and Juno, as well as his new goddess, Minerva. The building was Greek in style, but was accidentally burnt down in 83 BC.

- **A new temple** to the Capitoline Triad was built. This temple covered two hectares of ground and was built on a rectangular platform of cut stones. A flight of 100 marble steps linked the temple to the Forum.

- **The temple** had three rows of columns across its front and two rows down either side. The floor was covered with sheets of bronze and the roof was covered with gold. The interior was decorated with numerous sculptures and trophies.

> ...FASCINATING FACT...
> The worship of Minerva was strongest among workers such as potters, blacksmiths or musicians. She was also worshipped by warriors who wanted to gain greater skill in using weapons.

Gods of Rome

- **The Romans believed** in many gods and goddesses. Some of these were worshipped throughout the ancient world, others were only worshipped in Rome.

- **Janus** was a god found only in Rome. He had two faces, one at the front of his head, the other at the back so that he could look in opposite directions at the same time. He was the god of gates and doorways.

- **People prayed** to Janus when they passed through the gates of Rome on a journey. He became linked to the start of any journey or venture. The first month of the year was sacred to Janus and is still called January.

- **The temple of Janus** stood in the Forum over a natural spring of warm water. The main gates of the temple were kept shut during times of peace, but open in times of war.

- **Mars** was the father of Romulus and Remus. He had power over livestock, and each spring a bull, a ram and a boar were sacrificed to him.

◄ *The god Vulcan at work in his forge. He was believed to make weapons and tools for the gods.*

- **Mars is better known** as the god of war. Before a general left Rome to lead an army he went to the Temple of Mars to make a sacrifice, and pray to be given the power to instil terror in the enemy.

- **Inside the Temple of Mars** was an ancient shield that was said to have been left there by Mars himself. It was believed that as long as the shield was kept inside the temple, Rome would not be captured by an enemy.

- **Vulcan** was the god of fire. He was especially revered by smiths who needed a hot forge to work with, and by the disabled, as the god walked with a limp. An altar sacred to Vulcan stood in the Forum.

- **Egeria** was a goddess linked to springs and fresh water. She was the favourite goddess of King Numa. She was thought to be able to foretell the fate of newborn babies.

...FASCINATING FACT...
The goddess Roma was the personification of the city of Rome.
She was usually shown sitting on a rock, holding a spear and
wearing a helmet on her head.

The Vestal Virgins

- **Vesta** was considered to be the most beautiful of all the goddesses of Rome. She was so lovely that when she came to the mortal world, she had to wear a veil to stop humans being blinded by her beauty. Statues of her always show a veiled woman.

- **Vesta was the goddess of the hearth**, and of fires used in homes for domestic purposes. Whenever a stove or grill was used for the first time, a portion of the meal had to be thrown into the flames as an offering to Vesta.

- **The temple of Vesta** was a round building that stood in the Forum. Only women were allowed to enter, and for most of the year the temple was closed to all except the six priestesses who were known as the Vestal Virgins.

- **Every five years**, a new Vestal Virgin was chosen at the age of six, by the *Pontifex Maximus*. He then shaved her head to symbolize her new birth as a priestess. The girl had to be free of any handicap or scar.

- **For the first ten years** of their service, the virgins were taught the secret rites of Vesta. For the next ten years, they carried out the rituals. For the third ten years, they taught new priestesses their tasks.

- **At the age of 36**, a Vestal Virgin was given the choice to leave the worship of Vesta to marry a Roman citizen, or to stay in the temple for the rest of her life.

- **The secret rituals** are long forgotten, but the public rituals involved keeping the sacred fire burning on the hearth of the temple and each day collecting a pot of water to put beside the fire.

- **The Vestal Virgins** were the only female priests in Rome. They were given a guard carrying an axe, and he escorted them whenever they went outside the temple of Vesta. Everyone had to step out of their way or risk being whipped in the Forum.

▼ *The priestesses of the goddess Vesta, who were traditionally known as the Vestal Virgins, leave their temple in procession. The chief festival of Vesta began on 7 June, when people came to offer food to the goddess.*

● **Whenever a festival** was held the best seats were reserved for the Vestal Virgins. A chariot was maintained at public expense for their sole use.

● **One power** of a Vestal Virgin was the ability to pardon any criminal of any crime, but only if she met him as he was led from his trial to his punishment.

457

Gods of the country

- **People who lived in rural areas** had their own gods. Most of these were connected to agriculture in some way, but some were deities of the wild and untamed lands that had not yet been been farmed.

- **Faunus** was the most important Roman agricultural god. He ensured that crops grew and ripened, and that animals produced plenty of young. He had a temple on the slopes of the Palatine Hill.

- **Consus** was the god of granaries (harvested or stored crops). He had no temple, only an altar that stood on the slopes of the Palatine Hill overlooking the Circus Maximus. For most of the year the altar was buried underground, but the earth was stripped off in December while crops were sown.

- **Pales** was a goddess who was thought to live beneath the Palatine Hill, to which she gave her name. She looked after the welfare of flocks of sheep and goats that roamed the hills and wilder areas of countryside.

- **Liber, and his wife Libera**, were the gods of the soil in farmland. At first, they were honoured by all farmers, but after about 100 BC, they became increasingly linked to the vine and so to winemaking.

- **Silvanus** was the god of forests and woodlands. He looked after the trees and was worshipped by the men who worked in forests, whether they were growing the trees or cutting timber.

- **Flora** was the goddess of flowers and of the spring. She had a temple on the Quirinal Hill that was guarded by a family called the Hirpini, who also supplied priests to the temple.

- **Vertumnus** was the god of fruit trees. He was deeply in love with Pomona, the goddess of apples, who lived in a sacred grove of apple trees a few kilometres west of Rome.

- **Ceres** was the goddess of growing corn and other grain crops. She had a small temple in Rome that was served by a single priest, who had to be a freed slave.

- **Venus** was a goddess who symbolized fertility among domestic animals, such as cattle and sheep. She was later linked to the Greek goddess, Aphrodite.

▲ *The goddess Venus was thought to have been born from the sea, and to have first reached dry land on the island of Cyprus riding on a giant shell.*

459

The Underworld

- **The Romans believed** that a dead person's soul was grabbed by two spirits, one pulling from the front, the other pushing from behind. The spirits led the soul deep underground to the land of Hades to meet the god Dis, who would decide its fate.

- **Dis** met the soul and read out from a scroll the deeds that the person had performed while alive. If there were more deeds that pleased the gods than displeased them, the soul was allowed to enter Hades.

- **If a person had committed** more acts that displeased the gods, the soul would be handed over to the goddess Tuchulcha, and her husband, Charon. Tuchulcha had eyes of fire, pointed ears and snakes wrapped around her body.

- **Februus** was the god who caused death. He walked across the Earth searching for those whose lives were coming to an end. The second month of the year was sacred to him, and is still called February.

- **Lara** was a terrifying goddess who hated naughty children. She stalked around searching for the naughtiest children to drag them off to Hades. She could not talk, and moved silently.

- **The Manes**, or the good ones, were the servants of Dis who were thought to visit the Earth for several days each year. During this time, all temples were closed and business deals could not be concluded.

- **When a person died**, the body was dressed in the finest clothes available and laid out in their house overnight. Friends and relatives gathered to pay their respects.

- **A procession** carried the body from the house, out of the city gates to a special place set aside for funerals. People who had known the deceased made speeches to honour his or her memory.

- **The body was burned** on a fire. The ashes were gathered up after the fire had died down and placed in a special jar called an urn.

- **Rich families** had large tombs placed alongside a main road leading out of the city into which urns were placed. Poorer families put their urns into underground communal tombs called *catacombs*, or simply buried them in the ground.

▼ *When people died, their souls were thought to be carried by the ferryman, Charon, across a sacred river to the Underworld.*

Family gods

- **Each Roman family** had a number of deities that were sacred to them, and to nobody else. It was believed that these gods took care of the members of the family.

  - **The most important** family gods were the *lares*. The *lares* may have been a deified ancestor of the family. Each family had a small wooden statue of their *lares* placed in a small shrine somewhere in the house.

    - **Whenever a person** joined or left the family, a sacrifice had to be made to the *lares*. If a woman joined the family by marriage, or a man was adopted, incense and wine had to be offered to the *lares*.

      - **After a funeral**, another sacrifice had to be made to the *lares*. Rich families offered two sheep, but poorer families probably offered just some bones and fat from a sheep.

        - **Viriplaca** was a goddess who had the task of soothing quarrels within a family. A small statuette of Viriplaca might be placed alongside that of the *lares* if the head of the family wanted to see a dispute ended.

◀ *A gladiator prays to a shrine sacred to the god Mars. Small places of worship were commonplace.*

▶ *A household shrine with small statuettes of the gods revered by the family.*

- **Each household** had two *Penates*. Small figures of these two gods were placed near the entrance to a house. Their main task was to care for the food of the family, making sure that stored food did not go bad.

- **When a meal was served**, a small sample of the food was put before the statuettes of the *Penates*. This was so that the gods could bless the food and make sure that it was nutritious.

- **When a baby was born**, the gods were believed to send a 'genius' to care for it. This genius stayed with the person all through life, returning to the gods only when that person died.

- **The genius** was thought to summon other spirits to help it. Vaticanus helped the baby to speak, Educa taught it to eat and Ossipago made sure that its bones grew properly. Adeona helped the child learn to walk while Sentinus helped it become intelligent.

- **Each person** was expected to honour his or her genius on their birthday. A small amount of wine, or some flowers were offered at a shrine to the genius. There was a short ritual dance that was supposed to be performed.

Festivals

- **The greatest** festival was *Saturnalia*, held in honour of the god, Saturn. It lasted seven days. *Saturnalia* began on 17 December, when the priests of Saturn entered the temple that stood at the foot of the Capitoline Hill.

- **At dawn**, the priests of Saturn untied ropes of wool that held Saturn inside his temple for most of the year. The god was then free to wander the Earth. Everyone washed themselves so that they were clean if they met the god.

- **While the priests** of Saturn carried out rituals inside their temple, all public buildings were closed and locked. Schools were closed down, no law cases could proceed and the Forum was closed to business.

- **When the rituals ended**, the feasting began. People wore simple tunics with no sign of their status in society. In particular, the toga that marked a man as a citizen of Rome was taken off.

- **The god Vulcan** was honoured in the festival of *Volcanalia*, which was held on 23 August, the hottest part of the year. Priests carried out rituals at the god's altar, then marched to the Tiber, where live fish were thrown onto a fire in the hope that Vulcan would spare citizens from heat of summer.

- *Lupercalia* was held on 15 February in honour of the god, Faunus. This was considered to be a very important festival and all the inhabitants of Rome were expected to be out on the streets to celebrate it.

> ...FASCINATING FACT...
> Slaves were freed for *Saturnalia*. They could say or do what they liked, but had to return home at the end of the festival. *Saturnalia* lasted seven days, ending on 24 December.

▲ *A Triumph parade marches through Rome. Triumphs were held to welcome commanders back to Rome who had won a military victory.*

- **The festival began** when the priests of Faunus sacrificed goats on the altar outside the temple. The goat skins were then used to make cloaks for the priests and whips for them to carry. Two young men were smeared with goat's blood and had to laugh out loud.

- **The priests of Faunus** ran through the streets of Rome. They were naked except for the goat skins, and they used the whips to lash out at women they met. To be struck by the whips was considered to be good luck.

- **Triumphs** were military or political clebrations. A Triumph was held when a successful general and his army returned from a successful battle. The general rode in a chariot, leading his army to the Temple of Jupiter where sacrifices were made.

The rise of Christianity

- **In about the year** AD **40**, Christianity began to spread across the Roman Empire. The religion began with the life and teachings of a Jew named Jesus and, at first, spread among the Jewish communities.

- **Christianity** spread gradually outside the Jewish communities to other provinces of the Roman Empire. Christianity was, for many centuries, the faith of a minority of the population of the empire.

- **In about the year** AD **50**, a Christian leader named Peter came to Rome. He organized the small Christian community in Rome, and was later regarded as having been the first Bishop, or Pope, of Rome.

- **In** AD **64**, a large area of Rome burnt down. The emperor Nero blamed this on the Christians, which resulted in many Christians being executed.

- **Meanwhile**, a Christian leader named Paul was spreading the religion through the eastern part of the empire. By AD 100, small Christian communities existed in most provinces of the empire.

▲ *An early Christian prays in a secret, underground church. Some emperors persecuted the Christians.*

- **Christianity** had many followers by around AD 200. However, Christian communities were split by disputes about the nature of Jesus, mainly over the issue of whether he was human, divine or both.

- **By this date**, most Romans saw Christianity as a successful religion, and did not see it as a threat to their own gods. However, the Christians believed that all other gods were evil and that their worship should be stopped.

▲ *A mosaic showing the head of Christ. By the time this mosaic was made, about AD 350, many Romans were Christians.*

- **In AD 303**, Emperor Diocletian ordered a persecution of the Christians. All Christian books were destroyed, churches closed, and no Christians were allowed to hold government jobs. He thought Christian opposition to traditional gods opposed the rule of Rome.

- **Emperor Constantine** made Christianity legal again in AD 313, when he became a Christian himself. Constantine then confiscated the wealth of the pagan temples, some of which was used to build Christian churches.

- **In AD 360**, the pagan, Julian, became emperor. He did not persecute the Christians, but promoted his own religion. He failed. In AD 391, Emperor Theodosius I closed pagan temples and made pagan worship illegal.

The eternal city

- **The city of Rome** fell to the barbarian king, Alaric of the Visigoths, in the year AD 410. The news shocked people throughout the entire empire.

- **After the sacking** of Rome by the Goths in AD 410 and the Vandals in AD 455, urban life continued in the city. The population fell dramatically, but the people who remained were part of the empire.

- **The last emperor** in the west abdicated in AD 476. At first, few people noticed as the move was thought to be only temporary.

- **In the east**, an emperor continued to rule from Constantinople. The culture of the eastern empire changed, becoming more Greek than Roman. The eastern empire did not fall until 1453.

- **In the west**, a succession of barbarian kings ruled the areas that had formerly been the Roman Empire. They led a military elite, but most people were the descendents of the population of the Roman Empire.

468

- **People in Spain**, Gaul (France), Italy and elsewhere continued to speak Latin. The languages of those countries today is based on Latin. They lived according to Roman laws, and the legal codes of those countries are derived from those of Rome.

- **In Britain**, the country was invaded by Germanic tribes. Roman law was forgotten, and Latin was replaced by English. Only in remote areas was Christianity retained.

- **The Christian church** preserved much of the Roman culture. Latin remained the language of the Church until the 20th century. Special robes worn by bishops and cardinals today, are based on those of ancient Rome.

- **The bishops of Rome**, the popes, were able to combine the authority handed down by Peter and the prestige of the city of Rome to become the most important bishops in Christendom.

- **There is a saying** in Rome, 'While the Colosseum stands, Rome will stand. When the Colosseum falls, Rome will fall.' The Colosseum is still standing.

▲ *Castel St Angelo was originally built as a tomb for Emperor Hadrian around AD 135. During the Middle Ages it was converted into a fortress. It shows how modern Rome has adapted and used its ancient heritage.*

469

Early American cultures

- **The Americas were cut off** from Asia by rising sea levels at the end of the last Ice Age, about 12,000 years ago. By this time, people had moved into America from Asia.

- **Settlements spread slowly southward** until humans were living in every area of the Americas. People lived by hunting wild animals and gathering wild plants.

- **Most Native Americans** lived nomadic or semi-nomadic lifestyles, moving about in search of food. A tribe might occupy a certain territory, but move from one area to another as different sources of food became available.

▲ Farming peoples lived in many areas of the Americas, but only in the shaded areas were population densities high enough to lead to the building of cities.

- **In some areas** people settled in villages. On the coast of Peru, people who fished off the coast lived in small villages because they did not need to travel to find their source of food.

- **By around 3000** BC, some groups of peoples were beginning to plant and harvest crops. At first several different types of plant were used, but later only a few were grown as crops.

- **In North and Central America** the most important crop was a cereal plant called maize. By around 2000 BC, farmers in this region had developed a type of maize that grew easily and gave a good crop.

- **The peoples of South America** preferred to grow the potato plant. This was originally a mountain plant from the Andes, but by around 2500 BC a type of potato was being grown at lower altitudes and even on the coast.

- **Other plants grown as crops** included the avocado, beans and squash. The chilli pepper was popular in South and Central America, as was the maguey cactus.

- **Llamas were also used** to carry heavy loads, while both llamas and alpacas produced wool that could be spun and woven to make fabric.

. . .FASCINATING FACT. . .
Guinea pigs and ducks were kept as domestic animals for meat,
as were llamas and alpacas in South America.

The northern farmers

- **By about 200** BC the cultivation of maize had spread from Central America into North America. Not all land was suitable for this crop, and each region that grew maize developed its own culture.

- **The Anasazi** lived in what is now Arizona and New Mexico. They farmed maize and squash on small patches of watered land amid the deserts. They built houses made of sun-dried mud bricks.

- **The Hohokum tribes** lived east of the Anasazi. They constructed small canals that carried water from wells and springs to gardens where crops were grown.

- **In the woodlands of the east**, peoples such as the Iroquois established a village-based culture. Each village was surrounded by fields where farmers grew maize, beans and squash.

- **The woodland peoples** did not keep domestic animals, but relied upon hunting and fishing to get meat.

- **The wigwam** was a type of hut used by the woodland peoples. Wigwams were made from frameworks of thin saplings over which coverings of bark, leather or grass were stretched. Wigwams tended to have domed or curved roofs.

- **In the Ohio Valley**, the Hopewell culture dominated between AD 100 and AD 750. The Hopewell peoples farmed in a similar fashion to the woodland peoples, but culturally they were very different. They built enormous earth mounds on which to hold religious rituals.

▲ *In the drier areas of North America small villages were built by farmers who relied on irrigation to produce crops.*

- **The Hopewell peoples** knew how to mine and work copper. They produced beautiful pieces of decorative copper by hammering the metal carefully, but continued to use stone for tools.

- **The Mississippi culture** replaced the Hopewell culture after around AD 800. These peoples farmed maize intensively and lived in villages, but did not build mounds.

- **Cotton farming** spread to most of the farming peoples of North America by about AD 600, though leather obtained from wild animals remained in common use.

473

The Olmec culture

- **The peoples of Central America** told many legends and stories about the Olmec civilization.

- **The first Olmec sites** were established around 1300 BC in the swampy areas along the coast of what is now southeastern Mexico. Within three centuries the culture had spread to include a wide area along the coast.

▼ *One of the stone heads that has been found throughout Olmec lands. Each head was carved from a single block of volcanic basalt.*

- **The Olmecs lived** in small villages. Villages were grouped together around central ritual centres, which had large stone temples and other buildings.

- **Olmec temples** took the form of pyramids built of stone, with small temples built on top of them. Large open spaces in front of the pyramids may indicate where people gathered to worship.

- **Carvings of animals** including eagles, jaguars and snakes were placed on the Olmec temples.

- **The Olmec culture is best known** for the massive stone heads they carved, some of which were up to 3 m in height. Most of the heads are depicted wearing tight-fitting helmets, and it is thought that the heads may represent famous ball players.

- **The Olmec ball game** was played on a court shaped like an I, with sloping walls and stone hoops set high up on either side. The game was played with a rubber ball that was propelled by elbows, knees and torsos only.

- **All later peoples** in Central America copied the ball game, which almost certainly had a religious meaning as well as being a popular sport. Ball courts were erected at the heart of all cities.

- **Olmec farmers** cleared areas of land to plant crops. When the crops had exhausted the land's natural fertility, a new area of land was cleared and the old one left for a few years to recover.

- **Around 400 BC**, the Olmec culture began to decline. The temples were abandoned and populations fell in the villages. By 300 BC the Olmecs were gone.

Teotihuacan

- **The peoples of Central America** seem to have abandoned the idea of ritual centres uniting several villages after the fall of the Olmec culture. Instead it appears that villages began to organize their own rituals.

- **Around AD 100**, some villages began to expand in size and importance. Stone temples were rebuilt, but this time inside the villages.

- **The new temples** were constructed by building a series of square platforms, one on top of the other to form a rising pyramid structure with a staircase up one side. Sometimes a small pyramid was built in front of a larger one to form an entrance platform.

- **Cuicuilco was one of the first villages** to become a town with a population of around 10,000 people. The populations of nearby villages moved to Cuicuilco, walking out each day to work the fields.

- **By around AD 500**, the village of Teotihuacan had become a vast city of about 50,000 inhabitants. At this time it was probably one of the four largest cities in the world.

- **The large population of Teotihuacan** could no longer survive by relying on food grown in nearby fields. Instead the people of the city produced goods that were traded for food from other areas.

- **The main export of Teotihuacan** was obsidian, and tools made from it. This natural volcanic glass could be made into strong, sharp tools.

- **The huge temples** of Teotihuacan were built in the form of pyramids with sloping sides and flat tops. At the time they were built, they were among the largest structures in the world.

● **By AD 650**, Teotihuacan had a population of over 100,000 people. Smaller cities built in identical styles were founded in other areas of Central America as the influence of the city grew.

● **Around AD 750**, the great city of Teotihuacan was abandoned for reasons that are not fully understood. A warrior people called the Toltecs then overran the area, but whether they caused the end of the city or not is uncertain.

▼ *One of the largest pyramids at Teotihuacan is the Pyramid of the Moon. It contains the remains of six smaller buildings.*

477

The Maya

◀ *The Maya tried to capture enemy noblemen and rulers to use as sacrifices to the gods.*

● **While the great city** of Teotihuacan was dominating the uplands of central Mexico, the areas of lowland rainforest further south saw the rise of a new civilization, the Maya.

478

- **The Mayan civilization** depended on intensive farming of forested areas and swampy riverside meadows to produce large crops of maize and other plants. The agricultural wealth was used to support cities and craftsmen.

- **There were dozens of cities** in the Mayan area, each of which ruled over many villages and extensive farmlands. Smaller cities were often under the control of larger cities nearby.

- **Each city had its own ruling dynasty** of kings who were also the religious leaders.

- **At the centre** of each city was a complex of stone temples, palaces and ball courts. The temples were stepped rectangular pyramids with a flight of steps to the entrance climbing one of the longer sides.

- **In the square** in front of the temples the Maya erected stone pillars, known as stelae, on which they carved details of events in the life of their rulers. Historians have deciphered some of the Mayan script, allowing us to know the history of several cities.

- **The Maya had a sophisticated calendar** known today as the Long Count Calendar. The information carved on the stelae allow us to give precise dates to events in Mayan history.

- **The Maya believed in many gods**. They thought that all gods demanded sacrifice from their worshippers. Sacrifices ranged from offerings of food to blood, which was dripped onto the god's statues from cuts made on worshippers' tongues or arms. Human sacrifice was the most important form of worship.

- **The Mayan priests spent** much time working out when eclipses of the Moon would take place and how the planets moved through the skies.

- **Around AD 900**, the Mayan civilization went into a decline. Populations fell, perhaps because the climate changed and crops failed. The cities were abandoned and people went back to living in villages.

People of the Andes

- **The western areas** of South America combine tropical sunshine with the coolness of high altitude in the Andes Mountains. Even along the coast the climate is cooler than elsewhere in the tropics due to a cold ocean current.

- **The combination of bright sunlight**, plentiful rain and cool air is ideal for crops such as potatoes and chillies. By about 2500 BC, villages of people had begun farming in the area.

▼ *A stone building at Pisac, where the earliest forms of terracing spread rapidly to support numerous villages.*

- **People began to construct** irrigation ditches and canals around 1800 BC in the flood plains of the rivers that flowed out of the Andes on the west coast. Towns began to appear as food production boomed.

- **Farmers created terraced hillsides** (a series of raised level banks of earth, like large steps), which enabled them to grow crops on steep slopes, making farming possible in the high valleys of the Andes.

- **Around AD 500**, people living on the shores of Lake Titicaca began to worship a new type of sky god. Within 250 years the cult had spread to all the farming peoples of South America.

- **At Chanchan in the Moche Valley**, a civilization based on the irrigation of the coastal plain using the waters of rivers and streams from the Andes developed. It was ruled by priest-kings who organized human sacrifices.

- **The Moche peoples** developed great skill in working gold and silver into ornaments and knew how to make tools from bronze. These skills later spread to all the peoples of the Andes.

- **Vast platforms were constructed** from sun-dried mud bricks by the Moche peoples to serve as temples. The peoples around Nazca constructed huge pictures on the desert floor using stones.

- **A catastrophe struck** the cultures of South America around the year AD 950 that may have been triggered by drought. Populations fell, cities were abandoned and people ceased to worship the sky god.

- **After the collapse of the Moche culture**, the peoples of South America returned to living in small villages, and worshipped their own local gods and cultures. Gradually the population began to rise again.

The Incas

- **The Incas were one of the many peoples** that established an independent state after the collapse of the Moche. They were ruled by kings who claimed to be descendents of the sun god.

- **In 1438**, the Incas defeated the Chanca at the Battle of Cuzco. The Inca ruler Pachacuti then began a campaign of conquest.

- **Most of the central Andes** had been conquered by the Incas by about 1450. In 1470 the Incas defeated the Chimu Empire of the northern Andes. By 1500, the Incas ruled an empire that ran for 3200 km along the Andes.

- **The Incas blended the cultures** of the peoples they conquered with their own to produce a new civilization.

- **Children were sacrificed** to the gods. The Incas hoped that in return the gods would provide rain for crops, good health and prosperity. The children's bodies were left at the top of freezing mountains, where they slowly turned into natural mummies.

▶ *Inca children stand in front of a priest as they prepare to be sacrificed to the gods in a religious ceremony.*

- **The language of the Incas**, Quechua, was spoken throughout the empire. It is still used today in the Andes.

- **The wealth of the Incas** was vast, and its basis was in agriculture. This was organized and controlled by the government, which took taxes from the peasants. As a result of these funds, the Inca were able to build temples covered with thick sheets of gold, nobles wore heavy gold and silver jewellery, and even jugs and cups were made of solid gold.

- **Houses were built of stone** with thatched roofs. Each family had three houses arranged around a courtyard in which they lived with their domestic animals.

- **Most Inca cities** were built on hillsides. Streams were channelled so that they flowed down the streets. A gutter on one side was for drinking water, and the other side was to wash away waste.

- **The city of Cuzco** was the capital of the Inca Empire. It was built high in the Andes. The emperor and nobles lived there, and the main temples were in the city centre.

483

The Aztec Empire

- **After the collapse** of Teotihuacan and the fall of the Mayan culture, the peoples of Central America had divided into a number of small tribal states. Warfare was almost constant between them.

- **A wave of invaders** came down from the north around 1100. One of these tribes was the Aztec. They settled on the island of Tenochtitlan in the middle of the swampy Lake Texcoco.

- **The Aztecs learned** to build fertile fields in the swamps by piling up wild vegetation and covering it with mud. These 'chinampas' proved to be very fertile, producing good crops of maize and other foods.

- **Few domestic animals** were kept by the Aztecs. They relied on fishing and catching wild birds to provide meat. Birds were caught by being driven towards large nets spread between trees.

◄ *The Aztecs often created masks using mosaic pieces of precious stones. This Teotihuacan mask has been made from coral and turquoise pieces.*

- **An alliance was formed between** the Aztecs and two nearby states in 1426. Together they attacked their neighbours. The war proved successful and the Aztec alliance took tribute from the conquered areas.

- **In 1440 the Aztec ruler** Montezuma I launched a campaign against tribes to the east. Again the Aztec army proved successful and the areas were conquered, then forced to pay tribute.

- **The allied cities** merged in about 1455 under the rule of the Aztec king. A massive rebuilding programme began in Tenochtitlan that saw a huge temple constructed to honour the Aztec war god Huizilopochtli.

- **The Aztecs allowed conquered peoples** to retain their own laws and rulers, but on strict conditions. All conquered peoples had to pay tributes of food and wealth to the Aztecs, and they had to send hundreds of people to be sacrificed to the Aztec gods.

- **The Aztec army** was well organized and very disciplined. The men were armed with spears, axes and clubs. Elite warriors wore costumes designed to make them look like eagles, jaguars or serpents.

...FASCINATING FACT...
The most usual form of human sacrifice was to stretch the victim across an altar and then cut out their heart. Parts of the body were then eaten. In some ceremonies hundreds of people were killed.

The fall of the Americas

- **The peoples of the Americas** were experiencing a period of growth and prosperity by 1500. The climate was good for growing crops and no major upheavals were affecting society.

- **In South America** the Incas had conquered nearly all the farming peoples. In Central America the Maya were living in a village society while the Aztec civilization was at the height of its power.

- **In 1492**, Christopher Columbus sailed from Europe to the Caribbean. He was trying to find a route to China, but instead discovered the Americas. Europeans began arriving in the islands in search of trade, farmland and wealth.

- **Spaniard Hernan Cortes** invaded the Aztec Empire with 500 men in 1519. They were helped by tribes eager to break free of Aztec control. The Aztec ruler Montezuma II mistook Cortes for a god.

- **By 1521**, Cortes had conquered the Aztec Empire and killed Montezuma. The Spanish were horrified by the human sacrifices, and deliberately stamped out Aztec religion and culture.

- **Encouraged by the vast quantities** of gold captured by Cortes, other Spanish adventurers set out to conquer the peoples of the Americas.

- **In 1528**, disease, probably smallpox, killed one-third of the Inca population.

- **The soldier Francisco Pizarro** invaded the Inca Empire in 1532. The empire was weak because the ruling family was engaged in civil war over the succession to the throne.

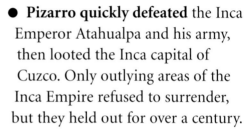

- **Pizarro quickly defeated** the Inca Emperor Atahualpa and his army, then looted the Inca capital of Cuzco. Only outlying areas of the Inca Empire refused to surrender, but they held out for over a century.

- **The cultures of North America** had little gold to tempt European soldiers. However their fertile farmland was gradually taken over by settlers while a series of wars, as well as outbreaks of disease, destroyed their power.

◀ *The Aztecs had a well organized army, but their warriors were no match for the guns, swords and metal armour of the invading Europeans.*

487

Index

Entries in **bold** refer to main subject entries. Entries in *italics* refer to illustrations.

Acknowledgements

All artworks are from the Miles Kelly Artwork Bank

The publishers would like to thank the following
sources for the use of their photographs:

Page 180 Stéphanie Marassoglou/Fotolia.com; 188 TopFoto.co.uk; 190 TAOLMOR/Fotolia.com;
198 Araldo de Luca/Corbis; 202 Gianni Dagli Orti/CORBIS; 205 Araldo de Luca/Corbis;
207 TopFoto.co.uk; 209 TAOLMOR/Fotolia.com; 210 Isselée/Fotolia.com;
212 Eugene Bochkarev/Fotolia.com; 213 Stephen Orsillo/Fotolia.com;
218 The British Museum/HIP/TopFoto.co.uk; 222 Topham Picturepoint/TopFoto.co.uk;
232 Topham/AP/TopFoto.co.uk; 238 alfiofer/Fotolia.com; 240 TopFoto.co.uk;
259 Francis G. Mayer/Corbis; 262 TopFoto.co.uk; 268 tzam66/Fotolia.com;
282 Topham Picturepoint/TopFoto.co.uk; 305 © yousaf FAYYAZ/Fotolia.com;
330 2006 Alinari/Topfoto.co.uk; 332 The British Museum/HIP/Topfoto.co.uk;
337 Albo/Fotolia.com; 338 Art Media/HIP/Topfoto.co.uk;
342 Charles Walker/Topfoto.co.uk; 355 Roger-Viollet/Topfoto.co.uk;
386 Topham Picturepoint/Topfoto.co.uk; 408 javarman/Fotolia.com;
410 Stapleton Collection/Corbis; 426 Andrea Seemann.Fotolia.com;
441 NYPhotoboy/Fotolia.com; 454 Topfoto.co.uk;
456 Christie's Images/Corbis; 461 Charles Walker/Topfoto.co.uk

All other photographs from:

Castrol; CMCD; Corbis; Corel; digitalSTOCK; digitalvision;
Flat Earth; Hemera; ILN; John Foxx; PhotoAlto; PhotoDisc;
PhotoEssentials; PhotoPro; Stockbyte